STRATEGY
FOR
ACTION

STRATEGY FOR ACTION

USING FORCE WISELY IN THE 21st CENTURY

COMMODORE STEVEN JERMY RN

FOREWORD BY MAJOR-GENERAL JULIAN THOMPSON RM

KNIGHTSTONE PUBLISHING

KNIGHTSTONE
PUBLISHING

Unit 36,
88-90 Hatton Garden,
London
EC1N 8PN

Published in the United Kingdom by
Knightstone Publishing Ltd
First Published 2011

Cataloguing in Publication Data available

ISBN 978-1-908134-00-4

Printed and bound in Great Britain by
CPI Cox and Wyman, Reading, Berkshire

This book is dedicated to Lieutenant Tom Adams USN, Lieutenant Philip Green RN, Lieutenant Antony King RN, Lieutenant Marc Lawrence RN, Lieutenant Philip West RN, Lieutenant James Williams RN and Lieutenant Andrew Wilson RN, all Fleet Air Arm officers, killed in action off the Al Faw Peninsular, Iraq, 22 March 2003.

Contents

About the Author   ix

Acknowledgements   xi

Foreword   xiii

Introduction   1

PART I:
WAR & STRATEGY

The Nature of War & the Role of Strategy   13

PART II:
INSIGHTS

The Classical Epoch: 1750-1850   29

The Industrial Transformation: 1850-1914   48

The Modern Epoch: 1914-1991   67

Modern Theory: Contemporary Thinkers, Military Doctrine
         & Corporate Theory   100

PART III:
THEORY

Strategy's Context: The Information Transformation: 1991-Future   133

Making Strategy: Thinking about Thinking   151

Making Strategy: Thinking about War   167

Strategy for Action: Frameworks for Thinking   192

PART IV:
PRACTICE

Strategy Making & Institutions: A Politico-Military School   223

Strategy Making in Coalition: Internal & International   239
Strategy Making in Time: Contests & Culminations   256

PART V:
REFLECTIONS

Strategy Making Improved: Philosophy, Policy, Process & People   277
Conclusion   294

Further Reading   *301*
Endnotes   *305*
Index   *319*

About the Author

Commodore Steven Jermy RN retired from the Royal Navy in 2010 after a successful and varied military career that encompassed carrier aviation, sea command and high level staff appointments. His commands included HM Ships Tiger Bay, Upton, Arrow, Cardiff, the 5th Destroyer Squadron and the Fleet Air Arm. His staff appointments were in the Ministry of Defence Directorate of Policy Planning and as Principal Staff Officer to the Chief of Defence Staff. He saw active service flying from HMS Invincible during the Falklands War and his final operational tour was as Strategy Director in the British Embassy in Kabul in 2007. He gained an MPhil in International Relations from Pembroke College, Cambridge in 1993, graduated from the Royal College of Defence Studies in 2008 and now writes, lectures and consults on modern strategy, including strategy in Afghanistan.

Acknowledgements

A number of people have assisted me either directly or indirectly during the writing of this book.

On the ideas, the manuscript was produced over five years and, during that time, a number of academics and military officers, serving and retired, helped me to refine my thinking. Professor Hew Strachan at Oxford was an attentive ear and challenging voice for my early musings in 2005 and 2006. Work interactions in and around Kabul in 2007, particularly with the staff of the British Embassy, the International Security Assistance Force HQ and the United Nations Assistance Mission Office, exposed me to the practical problems of strategy making in the multi-national complexity of a live contemporary operation. The invitation, from Vice Admiral Charles Style and Rear Admiral Simon Lister, to lecture on strategy at the Royal College of Defence Studies in 2008 was the catalyst that caused me to sit down and 'crash out' the main draft. The positive feedback from my fellow students after the lectures, particularly from Colonel Lauren Kolodzicj, French Army, encouraged me to keep moving. Dr Jonathan Githens-Meyer of Exeter University, Dr John Stone of King's College London, Brigadier Tim Bevis Royal Marines, Major General Julian Thompson Royal Marines and Brigadier General H.R. McMaster US Army all read and provided important feedback on early drafts in 2008-2010. On specific chapters: discussions with Professor Joe Lampel at Cass Business School helped with my analysis of corporate strategy in Chapter 5; Professor James Lovelock was particularly generous with his time and reassured me that my climate change analysis in Chapter 6 was accurate. And throughout the whole period, my good friend Major

General Andy Salmon Royal Marines has always been an excellent foil for my ideas.

On the writing, three individuals played key roles. My daughter, Charlotte, pointed me toward some important books on the art of written English and thus ensured that what I'd first set down was translated from service and academic English into something a touch more digestible. Beth Torvell, my copy editor, proved to be the word zealot she promised, whilst also providing inspired feedback on the content. And finally, there is a nothing like having an editor who is an Oxford-educated ex-Intelligence Corps officer to 'red-team' your writing and thinking — Rob Johnstone was first class in both respects.

Others have helped in other ways. My mother and family have been an encouragement throughout. Penny Hawkins supported in the early years. Alison Baverstock's advice on the publication business was particularly helpful, especially for a book that doesn't fit into a natural genre. Sophy Robinson helped me keep my feet to the fire during the final manuscript preparation. Katrina Aitken's friendship in Kabul and subsequently (including on the salsa floor) has always helped my inspiration. And finally my son, Alex, an English graduate, has provided me, throughout, with a steady stream of modern English literature to broaden my reading and rest my mind.

But, ultimately, responsibility for errors herein are mine and mine alone.

Foreword

Steven Jermy opens his book with a quote from Clausewitz:

> No one starts a war — or rather, no one in his senses ought to do so — without first being clear in his mind *what* he intends to achieve by that war and *how* he intends to conduct it.

I believe that the wars in Iraq and Afghanistan were not subjected to the Clausewitz test. When the relevant papers are opened to the public, I may be proved wrong.

Nevertheless, I am convinced that at the highest levels of decision making in the UK, both civil and military, there is an insufficient grasp of how to formulate strategy. The Army is the least proficient in the art. It took until the late 1980s and a former Chief of the General Staff, Field Marshal Sir Nigel Bagnall, to drag the Army's corporate brain up from the tactical to the operational level. This is not sufficient. Competence at the operational level is not enough to win wars as the Germans, the leading operational practitioners, discovered, having lost two world wars through flawed strategic decisions.

In my day, 1980, the Royal College of Defence Studies never taught strategy. To be fair, we were straitjacketed by the Cold War which, I contend, dulled the strategic senses of many serving soldiers, sailors and airmen — soldiers especially, exercising on tactical 'tramlines' on the North German Plain. The outcome of the UK's 2010 Strategic Defence and Security Review will demonstrate whether or not the Army, immersed tactically in Afghanistan, is able to raise its sights and think strategically about the defence of the UK.

The Air Force's strategy has always been aimed, above all, at its continuing survival; a prime example, in the inter-war years, being its advocacy of strategic bombing. To support his theory Trenchard deployed Liddell-Hart's views on the indirect approach, including the dubious unique selling point that strategic bombing, by shortening war, would make it more humane. Steven Budiansky has commented, 'Behind the dogma was the consideration that if Trenchard's theory was correct, it was an unassailable case for the continuing independence of the RAF — and for a hefty chunk of the defence budget.'* I am glad that Steven Jermy has little time for Liddell-Hart as a strategist.

The Navy's strategy of distant blockade in the First World War played a key part in the defeat of Germany. However, Fisher's attempt at deterrence by building a huge battlefleet failed to prevent the war in the first place.

Too often the prospective strategy makers did not meet Steven Jermy's precept:

> If we want to make superior strategy, we need to start our strategy making by answering two key questions. What is the political issue at contest? And what is the desired political object? In other words, before we make a decision to fight, we must know what we will be fighting about and we must know what we want to achieve by fighting.

To formulate strategy demands an organization. The old Defence and Overseas Policy Committee went some way to meet this. Perhaps the National Security Council (NSC) will fill the bill. The NSC could start by reading Steven Jermy's excellent book.

Julian Thompson, 2010

* Stephen Budiansky, *Air Power: The Men, Machines and Ideas that Revolutionized War, From Kitty Hawk to Gulf War II*, (New York, 2003) p.133.

Introduction

Preparation for war is an expensive, burdensome business, yet there is one part of it that costs little — study.

Bill Slim

Flying into Kandahar Airfield on 7 May 2007 to join the West's deployment in Afghanistan, it was almost 25 years to the day after I had entered the Total Exclusion Zone in HMS Invincible off the Falkland Islands. Picking up my sidearm and backpack and cadging a lift on a Special Forces C130 Hercules to Kabul, I felt the same sense of privilege as I had in 1982; the opportunity to be part of history. And yet this time round, there was also a sense of uncertainty, strategic uncertainty to be precise.

This time there would be few of the risks of the front line. I would be operating at the strategic level, in and around Kabul and the main NATO HQs. Although Kabul would have its odd 'moment', they would be as nothing compared to our operations on and around the Falklands or, for that matter, those for NATO soldiers and marines operating out in Afghanistan's Pashtun provinces. My uncertainty was not due to the relatively small risks of Kabul, but rather a lack of clarity about where the campaign was heading. It was an uncertainty borne on what I sensed to be a lack of strategy.

But what do I mean by strategy? As he laid out the logic for a decision to wage war, General Carl von Clausewitz, war's greatest philosopher, exposed the essence of the answer:

> No one starts a war — or rather, no one in his senses ought to
> do so — without first being clear in his mind *what* he intends
> to achieve by that war and *how* he intends to conduct it.[1]

Strategy should answer the '*how?*' question: 'How are we going
to do this?' At its starkest, strategy should explain how a state or
coalition will fight a war, then guide the actions of its forces once
operations begin.

Sometimes there may be little time to consider the '*how?*' question.
This was classically the case for defensive parties to conflicts in the
20th century. After Pearl Harbour, did Roosevelt have any other
realistic political alternative than to respond militarily to Japan's
attack? In such circumstances, unless you have contingency plans
that match the situation, your strategy will have to be made on the
hoof, at least to start off with.

But times change and the experience of the post-Cold War years
suggests that events such as the great wars of national survival of the
20th century are less likely in the early 21st century. Complex armed
conflicts, including those where one or more of the belligerents is not
a state, appear more likely. Afghanistan and Iraq are obvious examples.
Such conflicts are motivated less by threats to national survival, more
by intricate political issues, such as national security. If this view is
correct then, by deduction, the future will see proportionately fewer
wars of necessity and proportionately more wars of choice. And in
these wars of choice, there will be less excuse to begin operations
without having first done the thinking.

Yet post-Cold War history suggests the West has not always done
the thinking. Operations have followed paths different from those
envisaged by political and military leaders. At times, our strategies
have seemed unclear or faulty or both. Why has this been so?

I had started to consider this question in 2005 as a possible subject for a part-time fellowship at Oxford. I had been prompted by no more than an intuition, borne of experience of operations and war, that Western thinkers — including Western military thinkers — had lost sight of the importance of strategy. Yet in the great endeavours of our time it seemed to me that strategy mattered. Superior strategy would not of itself guarantee success in an operation, but without it the prospects of success would surely be reduced.

My extended operational tour in Kabul did little to change my mind. Indeed once I had had the chance to get around the campaign, I found the problem in Afghanistan was worse than I had originally sensed. Visiting the various Regional Headquarters of NATO's International Security Assistance Force (ISAF) in mid-2007, I asked the military planners in the Regional Command (West) and Regional Command (East) HQs the same question: 'What strategy are you using for guidance and to help you shape your operational designs?' The response from the uniformly impressive, well motivated and highly intelligent young Majors — US in the East, Italian and Spanish in the West — was essentially the same. Paraphrased: 'There's nothing, Sir. We're just getting on with it. We're just doing what we think is best.' In short, notwithstanding that we were over five years into a mission that had, since October 2006, been under unified NATO command with, first, a British commander and then an American, there was no sense in these regional HQs of a strategy to guide the campaign.

Worse still, in Kabul there seemed to be little recognition that this lack of strategy was a problem. Senior military officers had some instinctive feel for the need for strategy — but this was much less so amongst politicians, diplomats and officials, not surprisingly because they had had no formal training in the subject. Yet in a counter-insurgency operation, such as in Afghanistan, military acts should support a broader politico-military strategy. In these cases, strategy is not just military business, but rather the guiding force which brings coherence to all actions, civil and military. Consequently, an understanding of the need for strategy matters as much, if not more, to the non-military actors who must help create and execute the strategy.

This lack of practical understanding added weight to my theoretical intuition that we in the West had lost sight of the importance of strategy. It also made me ponder on the cause of the blindness. There are a number of plausible reasons. First, although derived from the Greek word *stratëgia* meaning 'generalship', the word strategy is now chronically overused in the public and private sectors and its original meaning has become obfuscated. Second, even for those who understand the meaning, the creation and execution of strategy is hard work, particularly in coalitions. It is often easier to revert to more enticing issues, with operations, tactics, finance and media the most magnetic. In the modern political milieu, this is understandable, indeed forgivable for those not trained in strategy. But, with lives at stake, it is not right.

Sitting alongside these practical reasons is an equally important theoretical one. Modern academic literature and military doctrine offer surprisingly little thinking to support the men and women who must make strategy. In the eyes of most practitioners, the best book on strategy is Clausewitz's *On War* — it was published by his widow after his death in 1831. The best 20th century book on strategy making is *An Introduction to Strategy* written by a French soldier, General André Beaufre — it was translated into English in 1963 but is now out of print. Thereafter the strategy cupboard is all but bare. Important texts exist on strategic theory, but there is no substantive body of modern knowledge on the art of strategy making, that is the intellectual act of creating strategy and the practical act of executing strategy. Indeed, with the sole exception of Professor Yarger's recent book, *Strategy and the National Security Professional*, there is nothing.[2]

Of course, getting strategy right will not of itself guarantee success. But getting it wrong may be the first key step down a road to failure. This may be a shared failure because we all potentially have a role to play in strategy making. An American sailor, Admiral Wylie, said of strategy and those who might contribute:

> Essentially all strategic comment or strategic criticism is an *ad hoc* sort of business, having not much more than personal judgement or hunch or emotion or bias or sometimes even self interest behind it. The only advantage the professional seems to have over the amateur is a little personal experience and it is seldom that anyone questions whether or not the personal experience is actually relevant. I do not criticize the amateur strategist. On the contrary, I believe deeply that strategy is everyone's business. Too many lives are at stake for us not to recognize strategy as a legitimate and important public concern. But what I do decry is that strategy, which so clearly affects the course of society, is such a disorganized, undisciplined intellectual activity. And I believe that this state of affairs might be improved.[3]

I agree that strategy is a 'legitimate and important public concern.' And I agree that, even forty years on, strategy making still feels a 'disorganized, undisciplined, intellectual activity.' Most importantly, I agree that 'this state of affairs might be improved' — this book seeks to do just that.

The book's purpose is twofold. Firstly, I want to provide a theory for those who must create and execute strategy; the strategic leaders and strategists — politicians, military officers, diplomats or officials — who shoulder the strategy making responsibility now or in our imminent future.

Secondly, I want to provide insights to all those with a general interest in strategy and the use of armed force in operations and war. Strategy is, as Wylie says, 'everyone's business' but if public debate on the use of armed force by a modern democracy is to be intelligent and productive, then citizens need a sound grounding in the subject.

My position on the moral questions concerning the use of armed force is neutral and by writing I am not suggesting that the use of armed force is a good or a bad thing. Rather, in the absence of a *volte-face* in international society, it seems likely that armed conflict and war will be with us for some time yet. If so, it seems best that, first, political decisions that lead to the use of armed force are properly thought through and that, second, once a decision to use force is made, the actions that follow are reasoned and rational.

That said, I do not pretend that strategy making is an easy subject. It is not. Rather, my experience is that it is difficult, sometimes excruciatingly so. This may help explain why post-Cold War military operations have not always followed the paths first envisaged by political and military leaders. Strategy making is problem solving of the most complex order, because it deals with three of life's great imponderables: people, war and the future. But this does not mean that it is not susceptible to hard thinking. And if we can introduce more rigour into our hard thinking, I believe we can move forward.

A metaphor may help explain how I have structured the book. I have found that the idea of the jigsaw is a useful way to explain the strategy maker's *modus operandi*. Strategy is, if you like, an organic but coherent framework of ideas, judgements and decisions. When creating a new strategy, the strategic leader or strategist might be fortunate and begin with a blinding glimpse of the big idea, the underpinning strategic concept. But a more common experience is akin to patiently gathering pieces of a strategic jigsaw and then working out how to form them into a coherent picture, which in turn becomes the basis for analysis, decision and action. And the jigsaw metaphor seems to work as well for the analysis of strategy making in theory, as it does for the experience of strategy making in practice.

In Part I, *The Nature of War and Strategy*, I set the scene for our quest for insights by discussing the nature of war and the role of strategy in guiding operations. The best ideas on strategy making are lodged in the past and in Part II, *Insights*, we begin the search for jigsaw pieces. The great US strategic theorist, Bernard Brodie, explains the importance of historical study:

> We are not here interested in the history of strategic thought for its own sake. On the contrary, we are concerned with a body of ideas or axioms to which *in our own time* millions of lives have been sacrificed ... More to the point, we are concerned with a heritage of thought that even today dominates the great decisions of our national defense.[4]

Just so. Brodie may have been writing in 1959 and I half a century later, but on this thought we are as one. Taking the last 250 years as the primary historical reference, I examine the periods 1750–1850, 1850–1914, 1914–1991 for convenience entitled *The Classical Epoch, The Industrial Transformation* and *The Modern Epoch*. I conclude Part II by examining the contemporary sources of insight in modern strategy making theory. The examination is not, though, a detailed history of strategy and war nor a lengthy examination of modern theory; quite the reverse. It is a focused analysis, selected by a practitioner on the lookout for insights that could be of use to contemporary strategy makers. It is a search for doers, not an in-depth analysis for political scientists nor a detailed reflection for historians.

In Part III, *Theory*, I set out the political and military context for modern strategy making, the *Information Transformation* in which we now find ourselves and then propose an intellectual basis for analysing strategic problems and developing strategic solutions to deal with them. There is no recipe here for strategic success, but rather a framework for thinking when devising strategy, if you like, a doctrine for strategy making. But even the term doctrine may be too prescriptive. This is because an important theme throughout is that, paradoxical though it may seem for an activity that guides destructive forces, strategy making is inherently creative. As such, it requires teams of clever, well-informed and operationally-experienced people — the brightest and the best — with sufficient time and space to think. Teams that must not be rigidly constrained by decision making doctrine, processes or structures. That said, in operations and war, creative people often need to organize their thinking with discipline and urgency and Part III provides structure for this.

In Part IV, *Practice*, I focus on the issues that bear on strategy as we execute it including, for example, how strategy making approaches may vary in different stages of a campaign and in coalitions. Finally, in Part V, *Reflections*, I look at priority areas for nations and institutions that seek to improve their strategy making. And I conclude the book by highlighting the key themes of Parts I, II, III, IV and V and reiterating the caution that there is nothing within this — or any other — book which can substitute for hard-headed thinking about the specific strategic problem at hand.

Finally, although I draw from time to time on my own military experiences, the book is not a tale of 'derring-do' from the Falklands, Kosovo, Afghanistan or anywhere else for that matter. There are many excellent books by individuals with tales far more courageous and exciting than mine. Nor is the book a detailed academic analysis of the history of strategy or of contemporary strategic theory, such as it is. This is not necessary for our purposes. Rather, I have used the thinking of others and my own insights selectively, not to floodlight strategy in the round, but to spotlight the ideas I seek to develop. My focus is practical strategy, that is strategy for the real — rather than the academic — world: strategy for action. As such, I am inspired by Theodore Roosevelt's words:

> It is not the critic who counts: not the man who points out how the strong man stumbles or where the doer of deeds could have done better. The credit belongs to the man who is actually in the arena, whose face is marred by dust and sweat and blood, who strives valiantly, who errs and comes up short again and again, because there is no effort without error or shortcoming, but who knows the great enthusiasms, the great devotions, who spends himself for a worthy cause; who, at the best, knows, in the end, the triumph of high achievement and who, at the worst, if he fails, at least he fails while daring greatly, so that his place shall never be with those cold and timid souls who knew neither victory nor defeat.[5]

I want, most of all, to help those standing in today's strategic arena — or those who may one day stand in tomorrow's — faced with issues of international gravity, be they in Afghanistan or somewhere else in our future. These are people with whom I have a familial empathy, not least because lives and history will depend on the adequacy or otherwise of their strategic decisions. Like those before them, most will be trying simply to do the right thing. And if this book helps them in this I will have achieved my primary objective.

PART I:

WAR &

STRATEGY

Chapter 1

The Nature of War & the Role of Strategy

War is nothing but a duel on a larger scale. Countless duels go to make up war, but a picture of it as a whole can be formed by imagining a pair of wrestlers. Each tries through physical force to compel the other to do his will; his immediate aim is to throw his opponent in order to make him incapable of further resistance. War is thus an act of force to compel our enemy to do our will.

Carl von Clausewitz

Introduction

Although at its heart war is political, no individual has managed to develop a unified theory of strategy and war. Indeed, with the complexity of the factors involved, it is doubtful that this will ever be possible, even if it were politically (or morally) useful. But as we shall see, there are, scattered throughout the practice of the great strategic leaders and the writings of the great strategic thinkers, enduring insights for our conceptual jigsaw. If we can identify these, piece them together and add others from first principles and experience, then we may have the basis for something less ambitious but more immediately useful, a theory for rational strategy making.

As we start to think about armed conflict and war, our first challenge is the unpredictable nature of it all. Notwithstanding war's capricious personality, if we are to bring rigour to our strategic calculations on how to use armed force to pursue political objectives in a rational way, we need a means of organizing our thinking.

As a first step, we need to explore the strategy makers' world. We need to consider more deeply the elemental nature of armed conflict and war, this complex environment in which leaders and strategists operate. In particular, we need to clarify what we mean by the term 'war'. We need also to clarify what we mean by 'policy', a term that is all too often conflated with strategy. This done, we can then examine the need for and the role of strategy in armed conflict and war. This, in turn, will allow us to deduce a contemporary definition of strategy. Taken together, these analyses will provide a starting point for our historical examination and help build the basic foundations of a theory of modern strategy making.

Armed Conflict and War

During the 19th century, international politics had a polar character: peace reigned or you were at war and there was not much in between. Whereas now, at any modern moment, a spectrum of conflicts of differing intensities exists. Some of these conflicts may be popularly characterized as war and others not.

This leads us to an important observation. The term 'war' is popularly used as shorthand for three interrelated, but nevertheless distinct, ideas:

- First, war is an *instrumental act* which uses armed force for the violent settlement of international disputes.

- Second, war is a *political condition* that is caused by the use of armed force but that has an elementally different nature to the political condition of peace.

- Third, war is a *legal institution* or international regime of agreed norms, values and rules, that sets legal boundaries on armed conflict.[1]

These ideas overlap but are nevertheless distinct and the distinctions matter. It is important to understand the idea of war as a framing legal institution as, although there have been no recent formal declarations of war, the laws of armed conflict apply in circumstances where war has not been declared. And war crimes fall within the jurisdiction of the newly established International Criminal Court But for strategy, the key distinction is between war as an instrumental act and war as a political condition.

In earlier times, there was no need to distinguish between the instrumental use of armed force on the one hand and the resultant political condition of war on the other. The two were synonymous, the latter very much a shorthand for the former and the distinction unimportant.

Now though, armed forces include a broad spectrum of *means*, ranging from lightly armed infantry to strategic nuclear forces. Furthermore these armed forces can be used in a broad spectrum of *ways*, ranging from low-level peace-keeping to general war-fighting. And, if armed force is used instrumentally in particular ways with particular means, then its use can result in a political condition that we recognize and term as war.

Put another way, the use of armed force can lead to an armed conflict of such military intensity and political temperature that a subjective threshold is crossed and a political condition that can be rationally described as war comes into existence, whether or not war has been formally declared. The current operation in Afghanistan is a case in point.

The distinction is important because war as a political condition can also arise when force is used irrationally, for example in circumstances now described in strategic jargon as 'instability'. In other words, these days, it is not solely states using armed force instrumentally for political purposes that gives rise to the political condition of war.

The Balkan wars during the 1990s illustrate the case. The parties to the various Balkans conflicts were motivated by political imperatives, but the absence of recognisable and effective state apparatus meant that the resulting conflicts had an emotional and irrational nature. This, incidentally, is why they were always likely to be more difficult to defuse. However, the political conditions that arose in the Balkans were clearly those of armed conflict and war where — and this is the key point — different political rules of the game were in action.

So although many still use the term 'war' for 'instrumental act', when making strategy we are better to think of 'war' as a 'political condition'. And we are better to think of armed force, not war, as the instrument of policy. But critically, we must recognize that, when we use armed forces in certain ways, the political condition of war may result — intentionally or unintentionally. And for strategy makers, the characterization of war as a political condition matters because of the different rules of the political game that apply.

When political contests evolve into war, the philosophical, psychological and practical rules of the political game change. Rational thinking is more difficult. Strategic problems are not always solved by cause-and-effect logic. The existence of a sentient opponent who does not always do what you expect gives war a paradoxical logic.[2] Your enemy gets a vote and if he or she takes an unexpected route then the whole basis of your campaign design may be upset.

But the paradox in modern war is doubly complex. The subtle point is that, because the use of armed force is inherently political, then through its very use the original nature of the political issue at contest may evolve. In exactly the same way that the enemy gets a vote, so too do the political events that result from your use of force.

An example is the Vietnam War. Initially, the US political objective was to prevent the fall of the South Vietnamese government. But as the US used more military force, the military prestige of the US became a political issue and a new factor in the political calculation, thus changing the fundamental nature of the political contest.

So the political condition of war has its own peculiar logic. As Khrushchev observed to Kennedy, at the height of the Cuban Missile Crisis, 'if indeed war should break out [between the US and USSR] then it would not be in our power to stop it, for such is the logic of war.'[3] It is because of this peculiar logic that, on occasion, an intended military solution can contribute to and then become an integral part of, an unanticipated political problem. Strategy makers must be constantly alert to the enduring risk that, through this peculiar logic, the underlying rationale for the instrumental use of armed force can itself be undermined.

By logical deduction and borne out in historical experience, when the instrumental use of force leads to war, the strategic trajectories that result are often unanticipated and can lead to unforeseen political results — as Hitler and Mussolini would no doubt have testified, had they survived. War is where the law of unintended consequences has its freest reign and it is for this reason that the definition of war as a special and peculiar political condition matters to the strategic leader. He or she knows that in these circumstances strategic calculations will be more difficult and strategic predictions made with much less confidence.

All this said, for as long as we judge that we might use armed forces for political purposes — with the risk that this might lead to war even if not intended — we must find a way of getting to grips with it. History seems to show and first principles seem to suggest, that superior strategy, intelligently created and decisively executed, is a useful step in imposing some degree of rationality on the matter. But before we turn our microscope onto strategy, we need first to say something of its master, policy.

Policy

If policy is the foundation for the use of armed force, for the strategy that directs that use and for the armed conflicts or wars that may result then we need first to be clear about what we mean by 'policy'. A prominent UK diplomat has defined policy as:

> A course of action (or sometimes a statement of attitude) to deal with a situation or problem.[4]

This simplicity is attractive, as is the idea of 'statement of attitude'. But the definition is too vague for our purposes, not least because it risks conflating the terms 'policy' and 'strategy'. We need a tighter definition, encompassing policy and strategy yet distinguishing between the two.[5] Policy is thus defined here as:

> A government's (or an organization's) formed position on an issue, situation or problem, including what political objective the government seeks to achieve, what resources it is prepared to commit to the pursuit of that objective and what course of action it intends to follow.

Put simply, under this definition, policy is how a government approaches an issue in terms of *ways*, *ends* and *means*. And, as we shall see, strategy is the *ways* component of that policy. Strategy examines our possible courses of action and decides which will best deliver the objective. What *ways* should we employ to deliver the *ends* that our policy seeks within the *means* that our policy has allocated?

The roles of strategy

Why do we need strategy and what practical role does it have in armed conflict and war? We need strategy for a number of reasons, both conceptual and practical. Some are obvious, others less so, but they are generally based around the simple ideas of calculation, decision, execution and direction, together with the need to exert some limited control over the irrationality of war. Indeed, without the possibility of direction and control, the instrumental use of armed force would surely be impossible, as would its rational employment to deliver policy objectives.

If the use of armed force to deliver a political objective is to be rational, we must decide on the best course of action, calculate how the armed forces should be employed and then provide high level direction and guidance, first to the planners and then, as operations begin, to subordinates so as to manage the campaign. Indeed, it is difficult to conceive of any other way of operating that would satisfy the criteria of rationality.

This is an important starting point. But let us delve a little further and see whether, within this general explanation, we can further isolate the roles strategy might fulfil. It is useful to start by suggesting that strategy must face in at least three different directions: upwards toward policy, for whom it is servant; sideways towards other actors, for whom it may be opponent; and downwards toward the instruments of state power, civil and military, for whom it should be overseer. These faces are closely interrelated, but it is helpful to look at things from their three different perspectives.

Starting with the first (upwards-looking) face, we can begin to hone down what we mean by strategy. A first definition of strategy from the British military thinker, B.H. Liddell Hart, is a useful catalyst:

> The art of distributing and applying military means to fulfil the ends of policy.[6]

This has attractions, but weaknesses too. Describing strategy as art rather than science has an enduring resonance. But the weakness is to restrict strategy to just 'military means': to hard power alone. Contemporary experience is that strategy must do more than just direct the use of force. It must surely direct all the elements of state power, be they hard or soft.

There are few Western diplomats, soldiers, sailors, marines or airmen with field experience in Afghanistan or Iraq who would see military force as strategy's sole lever. Rather, the modern position — encapsulated in the British phrase 'the Comprehensive Approach'[7] — is that we must be prepared to draw on a range of state instruments, of which military force is just one. Our definitions should thus reflect that modern strategy may need to employ some or all of these instruments, depending on the circumstances of the case. This allows us to deduce a policy facing definition of strategy as 'a selected course of action to deliver a political objective using agreed state resources.'

However, we are interested in strategy for armed conflict and war, politico-military strategy as we will term it. And as we look from the perspective of strategy's second (sideways-looking) face, we see we have an opponent to think about. Politico-military strategy is thus strategy with a unique dialectical component, in that it has the prospect of a deliberate clash of wills, in both a political and physical sense.

And it is not only the existence of an opponent that makes politico-military strategy different. It is also the very nature of the environment in which politico-military strategy operates: armed conflict and war, governed by different rules of the political game; and beset with greater strategic uncertainties and higher political risks. For these reasons, politico-military strategy forms a highly distinctive sub-class of strategy in general.

Finally there is our third (downward-looking) face of strategy, its command face. This third face is rarely discussed in professional and academic literature. And yet, in my experience, it is as important as the other two faces. The plain fact is that strategy is — or should be — a key means of commanding and directing the instruments of power in operations and war.

The logic goes like this. Modern operations of any reasonable scale are complex endeavours. They may involve thousands of people, large quantities of equipment and stores and have a geographic scope that spans regions. And a key means of achieving unity of purpose in these great endeavours is through an effectively communicated strategy.

Such a strategy provides the concept around which to develop a plan, but is also a key source of reference to show others why the plan is shaped as it is. After reading a well thought-through strategy, commanders and civil leaders should be able to say, 'OK. I understand what we are trying to do and how we are seeking to do it. And I see how my team and I fit in. From this I can work out how to shape my own operational posture and tactical activities so as to best contribute to the higher design.' As such, from its downward-looking perspective, strategy must fulfil at least five component functions:

- It provides an essential basis for strategic planning and campaign design. The absence of strategy will not stop strategic planners getting on with their work. But, working in a conceptual vacuum, it is they as junior and middle seniority staffers, rather than political and military leaders, who will by default decide the general campaign direction. Similarly, the absence of strategy will not stop subordinate commanders and civil leaders forming their own operational plans. These people are not chosen because they are wilting flowers. Without a sense of higher intent, they will probably get on and do something, but it will necessarily be their own thing, working as best they can in what they believe to be the overall intent and spirit of the campaign. In other words, without an agreed strategy for reference, it will be those on the front line, civil and military, who will make strategy through their own actions, based on what they think is best.

- As operations begin, strategy provides the basis for decisions on priorities and helps people understand the reasoning. For example, during the Second World War, it would have been obvious to General Slim in Burma that, because the Allies had agreed on a 'Germany-first' strategy, he would not get all the resources he might otherwise have hoped for. He thus shaped his operational plans accordingly and engendered a culture of self help in his 'forgotten' 14th Army.

- As events unfold, strategy provides a key source of reference for operational decisions, particularly when responding to unexpected events and the actions of our opponents. You are less likely to be thrown off course and better able to make decisions under pressure, if you have the higher intent and design lodged in your mind for reference.

- Strategy and the deduced strategic plan, deduced campaign objectives and so on, provide key benchmarks for any framework, process or method for measuring campaign progress.

- Finally and perhaps most importantly, strategy combined with leadership is a key means of maintaining your unity of purpose and your people's morale. It is generally easier to fight on in difficult circumstances when you know in broad terms what the higher objective is, how it is to be achieved and where you fit in.

These five component roles for strategy's (downward-looking) command face are certainly not difficult or revolutionary, but the ideas are not well exposed. Nor are they necessarily as well understood as we might expect.

The point should, though, be clear. If, at the higher level, we forget these five command roles of strategy, then the risk is that we will also lose sight of the importance of ensuring that our strategy is properly thought through and well articulated. Without a coherent and well communicated campaign strategy, our people will be rudderless.

Strategy Defined

From our discussion of both armed conflict and war and of the perspectives of strategy's three faces, we can now deduce a working definition of politico-military strategy:

> Politico-military strategy is a rational course of action that uses state power to achieve political objectives in the face of violent opposition.

Note though that, whilst this definition sets out the general logic of strategy, a specific strategy for a specific campaign is something that lives and is inherently adaptable. It is, to use my earlier description, the ideas, judgments and decisions of men and women, set out in a coherent and in a communicable form that, in broad terms, answers the critical question, 'How are we going to do this?'

Terminology

How does this definition relate to those commonly used definitions of strategy, in particular of 'grand strategy' and 'military strategy'? In what is essentially an organizing concept, military doctrine of most Western militaries divides warfare into four levels: grand strategic, military strategic, operational and tactical. And these divisions are used to classify strategy. 'Grand strategy is the application of national resources to achieve national policy objectives. ... Military strategy is the application of military resources to achieve the military aspects of grand strategic objectives. ... The Operational Level is concerned with the direction of military resources to achieve military strategic objectives. The Tactical Level involves the direction of military resources to achieve operational objectives.'[8]

Although useful in general conflicts such as World War II, attempting to distinguish between these levels in modern — and highly political — wars such as those of Afghanistan and Iraq is often problematic. As we have shown above, in modern military conflicts, strategy needs to direct more than just military means — and the term 'military strategy' is thus increasingly irrelevant. So, for simplicity, we will confine ourselves here to three terms. We will use the phrase 'politico-military strategy' as a generic term to describe strategy that directs the use of state power to achieve policy objectives in the face of violent opposition. I prefer 'politico-military strategy' to 'military strategy' because, fundamentally, armed forces are political instruments. And my experience is that to separate the political and military components in strategy confuses rather than clarifies.

On a case-by-case basis, we will occasionally subdivide politico-military strategy into two levels, 'campaign' and 'grand'. We will use the term 'campaign strategy' to describe a course of action chosen to prosecute a specific national or multi-national operation, such as one of the modern interventions in Afghanistan and Iraq. And we will use the term 'grand strategy' to describe a long-term course of action designed to tie a number of campaigns together, such as the overall Allied strategy in World War II or the US containment strategy in the Cold War. Both seek to answer the critical question, 'How are we going to do this?' but in grand strategy the question is likely to be truly international in nature and potentially generational in timescale.

Three final points need to be made on setting and terminology. First, generally I will talk about strategy making within the context of a modern democratic state or alliance of democracies, Second, in the coming chapters, I draw in part on strategy making theory from other disciplines, particularly corporate theory. When I do so, I will qualify the term 'strategy' accordingly, for example 'corporate strategy'. Third, although strategy has a central role to play in building armed forces for future conflicts and wars — 'force development' in the jargon — my focus is on strategy that guides the use of armed forces in the field today, not strategy that builds armed forces for tomorrow.

Conclusion

We have, in this opening chapter, brought important precision to our language and also grasped two difficult nettles. The first is the idea of war as a special political condition with different political rules of the game, increased uncertainties and higher risks of unintended political consequences. The second is that, notwithstanding these different political rules of the game, if we wish to use armed force and other state levers as rational policy instruments, we need to be able to calculate how to do this and we need then to deploy and direct the levers. From a practitioner's perspective, strategy must fulfil these needs and the definition of strategy should reflect this purpose.

We have seen that, to do this, strategy must face in at least three directions. For strategy in general, there is an upward-looking subordinate face, turned towards and continuously interacting with, policy. For politico-military strategy in particular, there is a second sideways-looking face, turned towards opponent or opponents. Finally, there is a third downward-looking guiding face that commands and directs instruments of power, coordinating their efforts and ensuring unity of purpose.

Ultimately, the fundamental point may be that strategy enables the *rational* application of state power, including armed force, for instrumental purposes.[9] This is not to say that the armed conflicts or wars that may result will fit a rational description. Rather it is to say that the analysis and calculations that underpin the creation and execution of strategy should be rational.

As we shall see in Part II, the theories of the great strategic thinkers can be broadly divided into two groupings, loosely described as the political science and historical schools; the former more prescriptive, the latter more reflective. And as we shall also see, we can link these schools through the idea of rationality. When *creating* strategy, we can use the prescriptive thinking of those in the political science school to shape a rational course of action to deliver the political objective we seek. And then, when *executing* strategy, we can draw on the reflective insights of those in the historical school to deal rationally with the irrational results that war so often delivers. Armed with these founding thoughts, we are now ready to begin our historical search for strategy's jigsaw pieces.

PART II:

INSIGHTS

Chapter 2

The Classical Epoch: 1750-1850

It is characteristic of our convictions, in strategy as in all affairs
of life, that we tend to regard them as natural and inevitable.
However, if we examine the history of ideas contained in these
convictions, we usually find they have evolved in a definitely
traceable way, often as the result of the contributions of gifted
persons who addressed themselves to the needs of their own times
on the basis of the experience available to them. Our own needs
and experience being different, we are enabled by our study to
glimpse the arbitrariness of views which we previously regarded
as laws of nature and our freedom to alter our thinking is thereby
expanded. Where new circumstances require fundamental
adjustments to our thinking, such aids to adjustment may be
useful.

Bernard Brodie

Introduction

Why study the history of strategy in the first place? The answer, as
this chapter will show, is that many of the ideas in strategy that we
take for granted now have their origins in the past. And if we are to
use them intelligently, we need to understand their origins and the
historical context of their birth.

There are different ways to organize this analysis. What ought to be the time frame? Should we reach back 100 years? Or 500 years? Or 2,500 years to include Sun Tzu, the great Chinese military philosopher? How should we consider strategy's interaction with parallel developments in politics and armed force? How have the reasons — the political *ends* — for which wars were fought changed over time? And how have armed forces — the military *means* — evolved? And what are the implications of these developments for strategy? The choice of structure is, however, largely arbitrary, because our sole purpose is to expose and extract key ideas and insights. So we will keep things simple.

First, I will limit the analysis to the period from 1750 AD to the present day. 1750 works well as a starting point. By this time, many of the early characteristics of modern war were visible. The German military historian, Hans Delbrück, observes:

> Between the Renaissance and Frederick the Great, the tactics of all arms underwent changes that gave them a completely new face from period to period. The close, deep squares of infantry became long thin lines; the heavy knights on powerful horses who sought to fight in tournament fashion became closely formed cavalry squadrons attacking at the gallop; and the artillery increased a hundredfold in numbers and effectiveness.[1]

By 1750, these new tactics had been widely adopted. Frederick the Great, one of strategy's master practitioners, was consolidating his thinking, through his writing and in his practice. Soon after this came the births of two soldiers-to-be — the Prussian Clausewitz and Swiss Jomini — whose writings would become seminal sources for modern strategic thinking.

Second, I will subdivide the 250 or so years into four periods. I base this subdivision on changes in the pace with which armed forces — the strategist's *means* — developed. There were two periods where the pace of development was evolutionary; and two periods where change was so rapid as to have a revolutionary impact on the nature of war and on the art of strategy making.

The first period, the *Classical Epoch*, lasted until 1850 and was one of incremental change. This was followed by a period of rapid change, the *Industrial Transformation*, lasting until the First World War. The impetus for this change was primarily technological, driven by the Industrial Revolution's developments, including mass production, locomotive power and electronic communications. The third period, the *Modern Epoch*, lasted until around 1991 and was one of incremental change. This, in turn, was followed by a second period of rapid change, the *Information Transformation*, that is still in progress. The impetus for this second period of rapid change has again been primarily technological, based on the Information Revolution's developments, particularly modern computers, electronic information management, global positioning systems (GPS) and miniaturization. The dates of the three boundaries — 1850, 1914 and 1991 — are not meant to be precise, but rather to give a broad indication of when the changes in pace occurred.

Although these boundaries are technology derived, they also work well in a political sense. Despite the Napoleonic experience, the political continuity in the 100 years of the *Classical Epoch* was the enduring view that war was a perfectly legitimate act in the conduct of international affairs. But then, as the *Industrial Transformation* started and modern warfare's more ominous character emerged, there were signs of a divergence in thinking about war's moral efficacy. At the start of the *Modern Epoch*, World War I changed, probably forever, international views on war's political utility. The political continuity of the *Modern Epoch* was the backdrop of two great political contests. The first, between Western liberal democracy and Fascist totalitarianism, finished in 1945. The second, the Cold War between Western liberal democracy and Socialist totalitarianism, played out in the shadow of thermonuclear weapons, ending with the fall of the Berlin Wall. Thereafter the *Information Transformation* encompassed and encompasses, the new security context of the late 20th and early 21st century, a period in which political leaders are trying to make sense of a new multipolar world. These four periods thus work as well for our political analysis as they do for our military analysis.

So to begin with the *Classical Epoch*, we will start by considering the technical development of armed forces, the *means*. We will then examine the political contexts in which war occurred and the political objects for which wars were fought, the *ends*. Finally we will focus on strategy, the *ways* and examine it in theory and practice, considering key strategic events, the practice and reflections of the great practitioners and the writings of the great theorists. And, for simplicity, we will use the same structure for the two chapters that follow.

But to be clear, we are not embarking on an in-depth analysis of the military developments and political history of war in the *Classical Epoch* — space precludes this, nor is it necessary for our purposes. Rather, we are setting out on a simple fishing trip, guided by the eye of a practitioner on the lookout for jigsaw pieces to fit into a theory of modern strategy making. We are in search of insights for leaders, strategists and the well-informed; not data for political scientists nor meaning for military historians.

Military Means in the Classical Epoch

The most advanced armed forces of the 1750s were European and comprised armies and navies that, from a strategist's perspective, had similar characteristics. And as we shall see, these shared characteristics endured through and thus delineate, the *Classical Epoch*.

First, warfare was slow. Armies and fleets moved slowly, at speeds limited by foot and hoof or wind and tide. The speed of strategic communications between capitals and armies and navies was dictated by the speed of despatch rider or naval picket and not much faster than the armies and fleets. Thus the strategic direction of war from national capitals was also slow.

Second, weapons were short ranged and battle was fought at close quarters, hundreds of yards at the most, a grim attritional affair usually including bloody hand-to-hand fighting. These short engagement ranges changed little between 1750 and 1850. Indeed, there is a strong case to say that they had changed little over the two millennia before 1750 — rifle and cannon were more lethal than longbow and catapult, but still of similar range to their forebears.

Third, because of their slow speed, their short range weapons and their (generally) limited sizes, armies and navies occupied small, well-defined, geographic areas. This too changed little over the Epoch. The size of armies increased as the French Revolution nationalized war and this in turn necessitated improvements in their organization, including sub-division into smaller self-sufficient divisions and *corps d'armies* to allow commanders to exercise command more easily. But, whilst the larger size of Napoleonic armies increased their geographic footprint before battle, once joined, the area of battle remained small, usually contained within the line of sight of the commander.

For these reasons, warfare at sea and on land shared common characteristics. Navies and armies moved slowly between theatres of operations. Because they occupied such small areas and because the reach of the reconnaissance forces was limited by the human eye, commanders were strategically semi-blind. Often groping to find one another, they relied heavily on their instincts and ability to predict the intentions of their opponents.

Battle, once joined, also moved slowly. These were stately affairs, often preceded by lengthy periods with the forces in full sight of one another and commanders generally commanded on the basis of what they could see. Indeed, not only could commanders see their own force and the enemy's, but they could usually sight their opposite number. Battle thus had a very personal feel. For these reasons and because they were so closely defined in time and space, we might term these collisions 'point battles.' They were the main currency of strategic exchange in the *Classical Epoch*.

Not only did battles move slowly, but so too did wars. The speed of march and the vagaries of the wind and current dictated the strategic tempo as much as the tactical tempo. The origins of the battle of Trafalgar, for example, can be traced to 18 months before the event. During the lead up to Trafalgar as with so many other battles of the Epoch, simple questions dominated strategic decision making. Where was the opponent? Where was he heading? What was his object? What was his most likely course of action? And ultimately, once battle was joined, the issue was decided largely on tactics.

Political Ends in the Classical Epoch

Turning from the military to the political developments of the *Classical Epoch*, what was the broad political context for strategy makers? What were the prevailing political attitudes in Europe to the use of armed force? And what were the political objectives for which wars were fought? The defining events of the 100 years were contained in the 26 years starting with the French Revolution in 1789 and ending with Waterloo in 1815 and we can thus loosely subdivide answers into a narrative comprising three periods, 1750-1789, 1789-1815 and 1815-1850.

In 1750, the lessons of the Thirty Years War, although over 100 years earlier, still conditioned political and popular attitudes to war. Warfare in the period 1750-1789 was strategically restrained — professional armies and navies were costly assets to be preserved — and wars were 'limited' and fought for incremental gain. Nevertheless, although restrained, wars were regular events in the years before the French Revolution. Although most often borne of disputes concerning territory, commerce and navigation, there were signs of new political causes emerging, notably state creation and ideological liberation. And the relative frequency of wars fought over territory increased with the predatory inclinations of the larger European states.

Although military forces were expensive, the low relative political and societal costs of war help explain its high relative frequency. Rulers saw the use of their armed forces to pursue political goals as perfectly normal; an important instrument of diplomacy not an international aberration or, worse, something evil that required reform of international custom and practice. Decisions to make war were routinely the result of careful planning, often years in advance and not a short notice response to an unforeseen crisis. In short, the accepted view of European leaders and polities was that war was as an entirely legitimate means for advancing the nation-state's interests, that is its political interests. These leaders thus demonstrated in the prior practice of the late 18th century, the validity of a central plank in the theory of the early 19th century, General Clausewitz's idea of war as a rational instrument of state policy — of which more shortly.

If anything could shake these utilitarian political views, it would surely be the seismic strategic shocks of the French Revolution and the Napoleonic Wars.

For the strategist, the crucial political development of the French Revolution and Napoleonic Wars was the 'nationalisation' of war — drawing the citizen into war and creating citizen armies — and for two reasons. First, in a popular sense, war became more political.

Second, by conscripting citizens, states could form larger armies and thus gain strategic advantage. These developments brought the connection between a state's desired political *ends* and its usable military *means* into intriguing relief. During the French Revolutionary and Napoleonic Wars, the French state fought for political objects (such as liberation, territorial annexation and empire-building) in pursuit of its national interests and to secure its ideology. But it also acted on the basis of what its larger armies now made possible. In other words, with these new military *means* French leaders could seek more ambitious political *ends*.[2]

These developments and Napoleon's military results stunned Europe and had the potential to change political views on the utility of war. The Emperor's assault was on the fundamental values and workings of the system that nations had been fighting for centuries to build. The threat to the very existence of Europe's prevailing order and ideology helps explain the strength of the Great Powers' coalition that defeated Napoleon at Waterloo in June 1815. With Europe's order thus secured, a new balance of power was established leading to a period of European stability that lasted until the end of the *Classical Epoch*.

But what is surprising is that, notwithstanding these seismic political and military shocks, attitudes to the utility of war remained broadly unchanged after Waterloo — as Holsti notes:

> After the Napoleonic Wars, political leaders and diplomats continued to see the military in instrumental terms. Armed forces had a distinct diplomatic purpose: to coerce, warn or deter opponents for specific military ends. ... Although the nature of war had changed considerably during the Napoleonic period, its functions in international relations had not.[3]

There may be a chicken-and-egg issue here. The wars between

Napoleon's defeat and 1850 had clearly defined political objects, broadly akin to those before 1815. However, with the new European order secure, they were fought on Europe's geographic periphery or further afield. Therefore, with no major war in Europe from 1815, there was no reason for European attitudes to war to change.

In summary, notwithstanding the Napoleonic experience, throughout the *Classical Epoch* political leaders, diplomats and military officers viewed war as an entirely legitimate instrument of state policy. This was perhaps the most important feature of the political context in which the great strategic theorists wrote and the great strategic practitioners acted.

Strategy in the Classical Epoch

To help us understand strategy in the *Classical Epoch*, we will blend into a single narrative our discussion of strategic leaders and their practice, strategic theorists and their theory and the key events that tested them. Of the leaders, Frederick the Great and Napoleon stand out. The actions of Napoleon have fascinated — and still fascinate — strategic theorists, but on the objective measure of historical success Frederick was the master practitioner. Of the theorists, it is late in the Epoch that two of strategy's greatest theorists, Clausewitz and Jomini, emerge.

We alight first on the practice and theory of Frederick the Great. Artistic, intelligent and a thinker by inclination, on succession he seemed a likely philosopher-king son to his soldier-king father — but Frederick's strategic successes in Silesia (1740-2, 1744-45), in the Seven Years War (1756-1763) and in the War of Bavarian Succession (1778-9) mark him out also as a great soldier and commander. His writings, set out in four major treatises, are evidence of a unusual mastery of the subject of war.[4] Many of his key tenets — improving tactical mobility, the skill of shifting from marching to battle order, the utility of horse-drawn artillery and steadiness under fire — sought to refine tactics but more interesting to us is Frederick's perpetual desire to turn his army into an instrument of a single will with all the thinking centralized in the mind of the king.[5] The corollary is that, for Frederick, strategy making was the preserve of the leader and occurred within the confines of the leader's mind.

From my strategic perspective, the historical evidence shows Frederick as an unusually gifted strategic leader and strategist, using war offensively to win territory and make Prussia more politically coherent and then switching to the defensive to secure his gains. Indeed, with Frederick's strategic performance as backdrop, I propose three simple objective tests that may help us identify superior strategic performance and distinguish good strategy from bad. First, did the strategy deliver the intended political object? By this measure, did the strategic leader win? Second, did the strategy deliver the object economically, using the resources originally envisaged? Third, were the results enduring? In short, was the strategy effective and efficient and were the results durable? On these tests, Frederick was successful. In broad historical terms, his strategies delivered the political objects he sought with the military means available and the results endured.

Some may question the efficacy of these simple tests. They are too hard on the strategy makers. War is complex. No one, no matter how talented, can foresee all. Unexpected events, bad luck, changing political situations and so on, all combine to deliver setbacks and defeats that could not have been anticipated. Perhaps. But ultimately political and military leaders make strategy in a hard Darwinistic school where there are no prizes for second best, no matter what the explanation. And these unforgiving tests may thus help us identify the fittest of the politico-military species and help us to focus our search for insights.

The prominent theorists in the pre-Napoleonic era were soldiers such as the Frenchman Guibert and the Prussian Bülow, but their influence faded quickly and so it is to Napoleon that we now turn. His influence was profound and it remains so. The events of the Napoleonic Wars have no earlier parallel. The raising of large citizen armies was unusual but the tempo and scope of French operations was unprecedented, as was the Emperor's violent combination of diplomacy with force to achieve his aims.[6]

Important military-technical developments were underway before Napoleon's rise to power: universal conscription; artillery reform; the system of living off the country; the breaking down of armies into 'all arms' corps and divisions, capable of quicker movement and better mutual support; and the expansion of staffs, to improve the command of dispersed forces.[7] Many have argued that Napoleon ushered in a fundamentally new style of warfare, but from a practitioner's perspective, his was the ultimate evolution of *Classical Epoch* warfare, not something revolutionary. However, it took a Napoleon to exploit the potential and a Napoleon to wage war with unmatched vigour — at least until the Allies responded in kind in 1814-15.

What lessons for strategy can we take from the Emperor? According to a fellow Frenchman, Napoleon 'never used the word "strategy", preferring "grand tactics" or, his particular favourite, "the higher parts of war."[8] For him, two tenets were key: strength in battle was to be maximized, with acceptance of risk elsewhere; execution was everything. These, combined with his ability to read battle instinctively and exploit weakness and opportunity more rapidly than his opponents, were the key to his genius. The aim of Napoleonic strategy was to maximize the opportunity for battle or the threat of it and his plans sought an overwhelming tactical decision that would eliminate the opposing army.[9]

But there were two crucial flaws in his approach. First, the combination of Napoleon's nature and the devastating style of Napoleonic warfare all but precluded the option of *limited* war, that is war fought for limited political objects. As the increasingly powerful coalition of states gathered against the Emperor, it threw the relationship between political *ends* and military *ways* and *means* out of balance. Lacking the strength to match the coalition and the inclination to accept more limited political objects, his grand strategic design collapsed, an unflattering politico-military failure that contrasts sharply with Frederick's successes.

But ironically, Napoleon's second flaw rests in an attribute that he shared with Frederick, the idea of unity of command in one person. Strategy was created in the Emperor's mind — Napoleonic strategy was Napoleon's strategy. His general staff was, essentially, an organization for gathering and providing him with the intelligence and information he needed and, once he had made his mind up, for transmitting his intentions and executing his orders. As a result, the French Army's institutional capacity for independent decision making was muted. This was fine as long as the Emperor was in close touch with his corps and divisions. But as the size of armies increased and their scope extended to different theatres of war, then Napoleon's 'strategic control broke down.'[10]

With the increased scale of Napoleonic war, what was a strength for Frederick had become a weakness for Napoleon and, as we shall see in the next chapter, the idea of strategy making being the sole preserve of the supreme commander finally failed as the scope and complexity of war grew further during the *Industrial Transformation*.

Napoleon's views on strategy died with him in St Helena. But despite his grand-strategic failure, his actions and campaigns have had a pervasive and enduring impact on strategic thinking, one that lingers today. Indeed, the early popular interest in the work of Clausewitz and Jomini, by far the most important theorists of the *Classical Epoch*, was in large part due to their insights into Napoleon's success. Both theorists remain influential, Clausewitz predominantly so and Jomini in more subtle ways.

The contrasts between the two men's thinking are important. It is an oversimplification but nevertheless a useful starting point to suggest that Clausewitz's thinking tends toward an 'historical school'. Theory helps expand your knowledge and understanding and thus improves your judgement. In contrast, Jomini's thinking tends toward a 'political science school'. Theory detects, frames and then sets out enduring principles that, if followed intelligently, lead to success. Perhaps for this reason, initially Jomini was the more influential, but Clausewitz has stood better the test of time, at least with soldiers and scholars. However, although Clausewitz is the name most often quoted in strategic discourse, in military doctrine the legacy of Jomini lives on. For example, terms used in modern strategic planning can be traced back to Jomini, reflecting our enduring appetite for principles for success. And although we view Clausewitz as the greatest theorist of war, it is Jomini who has been described as the father of modern strategy.[11] So we need to understand both men's ideas.

Born in Prussia in 1780, Clausewitz served the majority of his career with the Prussian Army. By the end of the Napoleonic Wars, he was richly experienced in war, in all its shades. He had fought in key battles, such as Jena and Borodino, been a prisoner-of-war of the French and assisted Scharnhorst with his reforms of the Prussian Army. He had also shown himself to be a gifted military thinker, reflected in his appointment in 1818 as Director of the *Kriegsakademie*, the Prussian War Academy.

A sensitive man with a 'richly endowed mind', Clausewitz's masterpiece, *On War*, was published by his widow, Marie, after his untimely death in the cholera epidemic of 1831.[12] A complex book, with inevitable flaws in its unfinished nature, *On War* nevertheless remains, in my view, the most important book ever written on war and its philosophy.

We now see Clausewitz's key tenets as self-evident, but this was not so in his time. A number of constants run through his theory. Key is the political nature of war — war is a political instrument that must be servant to politics and policy. Theoretically, war has an ideal form (in a conceptual sense) but also a more messy real-world form, whose inelegant nature results from the interplay of violence, chance and rationality.

Achieving progress in real war is difficult, because war's inherent 'friction' opposes your movement. Friction results from a combination of war's complex, irrational and unpredictable nature and the actions of your opponent. 'Genius' — not solely in the leader but more broadly in the body politic of your force — is the key to overcoming 'friction.'

Clausewitz's admirers comprise the glitterati of strategic theorists. Sir Julian Corbett, the brilliant British maritime thinker, said that 'today his work is more firmly established as the necessary basis of all strategic thought.'[13] And Bernard Brodie, the celebrated American political scientist, said 'Clausewitz stands almost alone in his eminence.'[14] Praise indeed from some of the greatest modern strategic thinkers.

But what of the tangible impact of Clausewitz's ideas? This is difficult to discern, but this is no surprise because Clausewitz sought to help leaders by improving their understanding of war. His influence on their minds would thus always be difficult to detect in historical events although, as we shall see later, there are numerous examples where strategic leaders ignored his thinking — and paid a high price. Ultimately, he wanted to improve judgement and had little time for prescriptive principles — which is the greatest contrast between his thinking and Jomini's.

Born in Switzerland in 1779, Jomini (in a career switch that has some contemporary resonance) gave up a career in banking at age 17 to pursue his interest in war. Bright but also arrogant and troublesome, his big chance came when General Ney took him under his wing in Napoleon's 6th Corps. Thereafter, Jomini served with Ney and later with Napoleon at the Battles of Ulm and Jena and in the Spanish and Russian campaigns. He switched allegiance to the Russians in 1813 and remained with them in various advisory capacities until his death in 1869.

Jomini's seminal work is his *Summary of the Art of War* but his key tenets run throughout his writing and were set down in 1803. Superior strategy was the key to success in war. This superior strategy could be created by applying invariable scientific principles. The key principles centred on the use of *massed forces* in *offensive action* against weaker enemy forces at a *decisive point*.[15]

Using these tenets, Jomini interpreted, explained and helped in the popular understanding of Napoleon's victories. The ideas are of interest to us still, for three reasons. First, Jomini's emphasis on offensive action would become a dominant feature in military thinking thereafter and was in contrast to Clausewitz's view that the defensive was the inherently stronger form of warfare. Second, Jomini is arguably the father of the notion of the 'Principles of War', still in use in most modern Western forces. Third, his idea that offensive action to mass forces against a decisive point was the key to success is an early example of a feature that we see in some of our later theorists. This is the offer, somewhere within their writing, of a timeless key to success. I will argue later that these are better thought of as strategic axioms whose appropriateness must be judged on the circumstances of the case.

More significantly, although the importance of strategic calculation in war preparations and conduct seems obvious now, it was Jomini who crystallized the idea. The crucial difficulty, in war after war, was strategic decision making. Key to success was to be able to correctly weigh the costs and benefits of the options and then to make and implement the correct strategic decision.[16]

The reason for the immediate popularity of Jomini's writing was his persuasive explanation of the shocking and perplexing phenomenon of French-Napoleonic Warfare. Indeed so successful was his explanation that Napoleon, in exile, praised the writing and 'offered information only on a few matters of fact for a new edition.'[17]

Some of Jomini's ideas may now seem dated but other elements of his thinking subtly pervade our military doctrine and, thus, modern military minds and mindsets. For strategy makers, Jomini's primary legacy comprises two interlinked ideas. First is the pivotal role that strategy plays in military success. Second is the related need for rigorous and balanced calculation to support strategy making. As with Clausewitz's insight into the political nature of war, these simple ideas have an enduring quality. And, as with Clausewitz, those who have ignored the ideas have paid a high price.

Finally, although these two soldiers tended to different philosophical schools — Jominian prescriptive and Clausewitzian reflective — they were similar in as much as both wrote on war, not strategy. Note the titles *Summary of the Art of War* and *On War*. But although war was the title subject in their two masterpieces, Clausewitz's key insights were on *war* in a *political* sense and understanding the political nature of war; whereas Jomini's were to do with *strategy* in an *instrumental* sense and the art of successfully conducting war for instrumental purposes. As we shall see later, these distinctions matter.

But what seems ultimately to link their thinking is the idea of rationality. If Clausewitzian war is the continuation of politics by other means, then it must surely involve the rational use of armed force for political ends. And it is difficult to see how armed force can be used rationally other than through the intelligent creation and execution of strategy — which, when all else is stripped away, is Jomini's key contribution.

Conclusion

Warfare with the military *means* of the Classical Epoch had a binary or Newtonian feel, with short-sighted behemoths — armies or fleets — lumbering through two dimensional battle fields, at sea or ashore, usually out of contact with each other except for their occasional bloody collisions. In the early 1800s, Napoleon shaped these pre-industrial armed forces into their most advanced state. Yet the speed, scope and destructive capacities of Napoleon's armies were broadly akin to their pre-Napoleonic predecessors. It would not be until the late 1800s that industrial technology would transform warfare.

Leaders' views on war as a political instrument changed little over the Epoch. The use of armed force through the institution of war was accepted, morally and in political practice, as a perfectly legitimate way of pursuing foreign policy goals. The events of the Napoleonic period gave rise to a much more politically charged international atmosphere, at least until Napoleon's defeat. But thereafter the historical evidence shows no significant change in leaders' perceptions on war's moral legitimacy and instrumental utility.

The quality of strategic performance varied but, for our two great practitioners, ultimately Napoleon failed and Frederick succeeded. Unlike Napoleon, Frederick delivered the political objects he sought with the military means at his disposal. Indeed, on our three Darwinistic tests of strategic success — effectiveness, efficiency and durability of result — Frederick's performance was close to faultless, whereas Napoleon's was reasonably disastrous.

Clausewitz and Jomini emerge as the two great commentators and theorists, thinkers whose influence echoes in our own times. Writing in 1982 about Vietnam, Colonel Summers, a veteran of that war, said:

> It might seem incongruous that much of [my] analysis ... will be drawn from a 150 year old source — Clausewitz's *On War*. But the fact is that this is the most modern source available.[18]

On War is a gold mine of insights for strategy makers, but we must not underestimate Jomini's influence as even now modern military doctrine is dusted with grains of Jominian thinking.

To conclude, let me summarize the insights that we have encountered in this canter through the *Classical Epoch*, re-ordering them to suit our purpose:

- The use of armed force through the institution of war is political and war is thus political in nature.

- Making progress in war is difficult because of: its complex, irrational and unpredictable nature; 'friction'; and the actions of your opponent.

- Strategy is key to success in war. Strategy makers must correctly weigh risks, benefits and probabilities and their strategy must intelligently balance *ways*, *means* and *ends*.

- The correct strategy will depend on the circumstances of the campaign.

- Three objective tests of strategy and strategic performance are:

    * Effectiveness — did we gain the intended political object?

* Efficiency — did we gain the object with the means first envisaged?

* Endurability — was the longer term political result durable?

- Because of the limited scope of battle, in time and space, strategy in the *Classical Epoch* could be created in the commander's mind and executed first hand through his orders.

- In war and strategy, execution is everything.

Herewith the first tranche of pieces for our strategy Jigsaw box. Some insights may seem obvious to us now, but this was not the case in their day. And it is Clausewitz and Jomini's two major ideas that are central: Jomini's key contribution is his recognition of the importance of strategy for success in war; Clausewitz's is on the political nature of war. Taken together, these two ideas are the fundamental building blocks in a theory of modern strategy making. So although Jomini has been cited as the father of modern strategy, for me these two soldier-scholars share the honour.

Chapter 3

The Industrial Transformation: 1850-1914

*No plan of operations can look with any certainty beyond the first
meeting with the major forces of the enemy ... The commander
is compelled during the whole campaign to reach decisions on
the basis of situations that cannot be predicted. All consequential
acts of war are, therefore, not executions of a premeditated plan,
but spontaneous actions, directed by military tact. The problem
is to grasp in innumerable special cases the actual situation that
is covered by the mist of uncertainty, to appraise the facts correctly
and to guess the unknown elements, to reach a decision quickly
and then to carry it out forcefully and relentlessly.*

Moltke the Elder

Introduction

Historians may differ over its starting date, but most would agree
that by 1850 the Industrial Revolution was in full flow. However, its
impact on warfare was fragmentary. Key technologies had emerged,
but they had not been coherently applied to war. Europe's relative
peace and the consequent lack of opportunity to experiment may
help explain this incoherence. But this peaceful backdrop was also a
canvas for significant developments in political thought, including

diverging views on both the legitimacy of war and the utility of armed force as an instrument of policy.

For simplicity, we will use the same approach as Chapter 2 and start with overviews on developments of military *means* and political *ends*, then follow these with a more detailed discussion of strategy in theory and practice. The significant difference is that, with the emergence of the United States as a great power early in the period, our geographical scope broadens to include North America. The slight complication for the narrative is that World War I sits on the boundary between the *Industrial Transformation* and the *Modern Epoch* — we will deal with this by considering the military developments of that war in this chapter, but then the political consequences and lessons for strategy in the next.

Although the *Industrial Transformation* lacks a defining war to rival the Napoleonic Wars of the *Classical Epoch*, there are significant insights in the wars that did occur — particularly in the US Civil War and the Prussian Wars of the 1870s — and in the writings of the great strategic theorists, albeit no one emerges to challenge Clausewitz.

Military Means in the Industrial Transformation

Early in the second half of the 19th century, *Industrial Transformation* technologies began to transform the slow speeds, short weapon ranges, constrained areas and slow communications that strategically characterized the armies and navies of the *Classical Epoch*. But the pace of change was not uniform. Instead, transformation generally began at sea, then moved to the land and, with the arrival of aeroplanes, into the air.

Steam power increased the speed of ships. Furthermore, ships could maintain these higher speeds consistently and strategic fleet movements could thus be planned with confidence. With the change from oak to ironclad then iron ships, bigger hulls could be launched and heavier guns shipped. But ironically, heavier rifled guns were also essential to penetrate ships' armour which had now defeated the round shot of cannons of the *Classical Epoch*. Rifled guns led in turn to a quantum — albeit unplanned — increase in the range of engagement, from the tens of yards of the Battle of Trafalgar, to the tens of thousands of yards of the Battle of Jutland. And in parallel, the area occupied by fleets increased, due to longer weapon ranges and the higher number of ships in fleets, the latter in part a consequence of mass production. Thus, whereas at Trafalgar 74 ships were contained in an area of less than 50 or so square miles, at Jutland in the daylight action alone some 259 ships were scattered over 300 square miles of the North Sea.

The impact of industrial technologies on armies was equally significant. Although armies still moved by horse and foot on the battlefield, rail accelerated their movement into and between theatres of war — or in the military jargon, although 'tactical mobility' was unchanged, rail improved 'strategic mobility' by an order of magnitude. Logistical mobility was also improved, albeit once armies moved from their railheads, it was still the horse that would supply the customer. Rail also reduced the impact of weather and season and, in a clear parallel with naval developments, meant that the movement of armies could be planned with confidence.

Rifled weapons and their shells and cartridges had a seminal impact on field tactics. The range of rifles, their accuracy and their increased rate of fire turned densely grouped infantry in the open into vulnerable targets and this vulnerability was exacerbated by the machine gun. Increased artillery ranges soon allowed targets to be engaged beyond the horizon. When combined with improved communications, this extended the zone of fire from hundreds of yards to depths measured in miles. Staying out of sight of the enemy artillery no longer guaranteed your safety, nor did trenches or fortifications.

Presaged in the American Civil, Prussian and Russo-Japanese Wars, the resulting changes in warfare were profound. The colourful military dress of the *Classical Epoch* did not survive the *Industrial Transformation*. Ornamental military tactics also perished. With the increased range and lethality of infantry and artillery weapons, well dug in troops could resist frontal assaults of much greater weight. And commanders became much more alert to the nuances of terrain. With all this, the advantage shifted decisively to the defender.

Longer weapon ranges also meant that troops were able to dominate larger areas. And when longer weapon ranges were combined with larger armies — mass mobilized troops armed with mass produced weapons — the area of the battlefield quickly grew. On land the 'point battles' of the *Classical Epoch* transformed into the 'area campaigns' of the First World War. And, as Admiral Castex observed, because of mass production and mass mobilized troops: 'Combat [was] extended in time, as well as in space.'[1] At sea, naval officers hankered after decisive sea battle, but the dogged reality was different. New weapons, such as mines, reduced the freedom of action of large fleets, particularly in shallow water. Additionally, submarines and aircraft enabled weaker maritime powers to threaten sea lanes and take offensive action deep into enemy waters. Thus, whereas on land, the 'front line' became well defined and a mark of territory gained, at sea the reverse was the case.

Together these changes altered the role of strategy and the strategy makers, largely because war's broader scope — in time, space and method — increased its complexity. With this increasing complexity came a requirement for strategy to become explicit.

With the limited scope of war in the *Classical Epoch*, explicit strategy was unnecessary. As we have seen with Frederick and Napoleon, strategy was implicit and lodged in the Commander's mind, unless and until discussed with his subordinates. But as the battlefield grew in time and space, strategy had to become explicit. It had to written down and communicated to direct these large forces spread across large areas and to thus ensure that their individual actions contributed to the overall aim — but this explicit role for strategy emerged only when the complexity of war grew beyond the controlling capacity of a single mind.[2]

In a similar way, the birth of military planning staffs in the late 19th century is usually viewed as an organisational advance of the *Industrial Transformation*, but in reality this was an essential response to war's new scale and complexity. For strategy and plans to be executed, fleets and armies had to be well organized, so their hierarchies evolved in parallel. But when interleaved with the scientific philosophy of the *Industrial Transformation*, these improvements changed commanders' attitudes.[3] The popular view in naval Victoriana was that science and technology could master the growing complexity of war and harness the new systems of armed forces. Commanders would direct the ballet of naval battle centrally, using modern signals and radio. But as the Battle of Jutland showed, war was a recalcitrant suitor for science. The centralising philosophy also had an unintended consequence. It neutered the initiative of subordinates, thus limiting their ability to exploit tactical opportunities in battle at sea.

Meanwhile, ashore armies had a different problem, not over-centralized control, but rather lack of portable communications. Without man-portable battlefield radios, commanders lost control of their dispersed forces from the minute troops crossed the start line. As World War I would show, there were numerous examples of initiative at local level, but the problem was the commander on the ground could not relay this to his boss and thus exploitation of success or opportunities was almost invariably too late. This problem was never really solved during World War I.[4]

So, in a curious way, whereas the destructive capability of armies and navies increased during the *Industrial Transformation*, the capacity to exploit this power, by seizing the operational and strategic initiative, ashore and afloat, failed to keep pace. The result would be an attritional stalemate, but we would be three years into the Great War before political leaders regained control of military events.

Political Ends in the Industrial Transformation

Early in the second half of the 19th century, we see the first signs of divergence in political and popular attitudes to war; both to war's moral legitimacy and to the utility of armed force as an instrument to deliver political objects. The new industrial working classes were beginning to define war as a problem, something that needed to be constrained by political action. Pacifist views were also flourishing in Great Britain and on the continent. But in parallel, other opinion formers were coming to regard war not as a problem but instead as desirable, good for societal health, something to be welcomed as a philosophical and moral good.[5]

At their extremes, both camps implicitly dismissed the notion of war as a rational instrument of policy. The idealist camp saw war as increasingly irrational. For them, the war calculation would always be lopsided because the costs — moral and financial — would outweigh the benefits in any conceivable scenario. Whereas the Darwinist camp saw war not as an instrument of policy, but rather as a policy in its own right. To them, war was a political philosophy for delivering national cohesion and social growth.

The British position was slightly different from the Continent's, but attempts to reconcile similar diverging views can be traced back to 1865. The 'idealists' of the British left grew to dislike overseas wars.

War slowed social reform and propped up the capitalist system. Whereas the 'realists' of the British right came to see the world as non-utopian. Government should not flinch from using armed force to defend national honour and pursue national interests.[6] These views did not correspond precisely to those on the continent: British realists did not view war through a Darwinistic lens and as a desirable end in itself. However, it is nevertheless informative that these divergent trends were evident in a mature democracy such as Britain's.

But many in the centre ground held to the Clausewitzian view. Karl Marx was but one of a number of heavyweight thinkers who saw the use of war as an instrument of policy as legitimate and rational in certain circumstances. It is instructive for us to see how this view played out in practice in the pattern of war in the *Industrial Transformation*.

The number of wars involving European powers in the second half of the 19th century (20) was broadly the same as in the first half (18). But, with the exception of Prussia's wars with Denmark, Austria and France, there were no wars between the Great Powers. There was instead a shift from wars of the European centre to wars of the Balkan and Eastern European periphery. Wars were not only fought to acquire or defend territory but also to liberate nations and to create and consolidate states. The new and smaller states of Southern and Eastern Europe were frequent participants.

But whilst wars between the Great Powers were rare, the sense of political foreboding in Europe was increasing, in part because of the changing nature of warfare and the diverging views on war's utility. By the 1870s and 1880s, the character of war preparation was changing fast. Military thinking was increasingly dominated by strategic rather than political issues. Short wars were envisaged, in which strategic surprise would offer great advantage. Railway timetables and logistic schedules had to be considered before war commenced. The use of conscript armies and with them the need to mobilize, further constrained plans. So, as Holsti notes:

> By the 1870s military establishments were perpetually posed for combat ... In the [*Classical Epoch*], cabinets and courts could carefully attune military responses to the unique nature of threats and challenges. [But by] the end of the century, the options had been reduced primarily to doing nothing and mobilizing fully.[7]

A sobering analysis, given what would transpire

Strategy in the Industrial Transformation

Setting to one side the Great War's irrational prelude, there are important prior insights for strategy in the *Industrial Transformation*. In the US Civil War, the first strategic leadership team combining politician and general, Lincoln and Grant, emerges and was repeated soon afterwards in the Prussian Wars with Bismarck and Moltke. Three influential theorists stand out. The first is a German soldier-scholar, Moltke the Elder. But for the other two we must move from land to sea and to the writings of the American sailor-scholar, Admiral Thomas Mahan and the British maritime strategist, Sir Julian Corbett.

Although notable for the introduction of the rifle, railroad and telegraph into the game of war, the US Civil War is also remarkable for its scope. The Confederacy alone encompassed an area larger than the combined size of Germany, France, Spain, Portugal and Great Britain. And, with populations of over 20 million in the north and 6 million in the south, this was no localized affair.[8]

Professor Cohen, a leading American strategic thinker, explains clearly how the Union's strategy was inspired. In Cohen's view, Lincoln was the war's principal architect, executing a strategic concept that rested on five interlocking propositions:

- First, the *political object* of the war was to restore the union, but only on the condition that slavery would not be expanded beyond the Confederate states.

- Second, Lincoln believed it inevitable that the South would not yield on this condition, but to achieve the *political conditions* for success, he judged that the war had to begin with acts of Southern aggression.

- Third, for *strategic reasons*, the war needed to be waged in a way that deprived the South of the support of other countries, particularly Britain.

- Forth, to gain the *political object*, the Union armies needed to crush their counterparts — the *military object* was thus to defeat the Confederate armies.

- Fifth, the best *strategy* would be a concerted offensive around the circumference of the South, which would play to the numerical and material strengths of the Union.

As is invariably the case in strategy, it was necessary to adapt these propositions during the course of the war, but as an example for us of clear-headed strategic calculation, they are instructive.[9]

As the war began, the Confederacy's talented generals, Lee and Jackson (both students of Napoleon's campaigns), were dominant in the field, at least initially. It was, however, not only the North's economic muscle that proved their undoing, but also the modern military facts on the ground:

The most skilful generalship thus could no longer achieve

against resolute enemies armed with rifles sufficiently favourable casualty rates and margins of victory in battle to make the results of any one battle decisive. There were no more Austerlitz or Jena-Auerstedt victories to be had.[10]

In other words, the technological developments of the *Industrial Transformation* were kicking in.

Meanwhile in Grant and Sherman, Lincoln had found the generals he needed. Skilled though both were, Lincoln had still to 'educate [them] about the purposes of the war and to remind them of its fundamental political characteristics ... not only to create a strategic approach to the war, but to insist that his generals adhere to it.'[11]

Interpreting this in the light of our earlier analysis and in particular seeing it through the lens of Clausewitz and Jomini, Lincoln had to judge the *political nature* of the war, determine the Union's *political object*, create a *strategy* to deliver the object and see to it that his generals *execute* the strategy. As such, Lincoln emerges as the master practitioner of the US Civil War. But equally the Lincoln and Grant team stands out as a notably strong politician-soldier partnership. As we shall see, in modern history the strength or otherwise of such partnerships seems to bear on strategic success.

Curiously Europeans drew few lessons from the US Civil War or, for that matter, from the Crimean (and there is little in the latter to entice us either). Of much more strategic interest is the practice and theory of a central figure in three Prussian Wars between 1864 and 1871, Moltke the Elder.

Serving for only five years with troops and commanding nothing larger in the field than a company, Moltke was nevertheless fortunate (from a soldier's perspective) to see active service as a military advisor with the Turks. Extremely well read and a talented writer with an abiding interest in politics, he was also a disciple of Clausewitz. After being selected (at the age of 65) as Chief of the General Staff, he would guide the Prussian Army through a period of conspicuous success.

Not only did Moltke study Clausewitz but in at least one area he improved on the great man's thinking: 'Moltke also endorsed Clausewitz's contention that the objective of war was the achievement of a satisfactory political result and that this required flexible and adaptive strategy'[12] The idea of a 'flexible and adaptive strategy' is not something that we usually attribute to Clausewitz. Clausewitz makes no mention of the thought in the third book of *On War*, which discusses strategy.[13] Nor for that matter does Jomini highlight the idea. It is very much a Moltkean thought, evident both in his writing and in practice.

Moltke accepted the Jominian idea of the need for a strategy that sought to break the opponent's will, but also the Clausewitzian idea of war as an irrational and unpredictable environment. Indeed he believed that, on the first major encounter of a war, new and unforeseeable conditions would be created and that 'all consequential acts of war are, therefore, not executions of a premeditated plan, but spontaneous actions, directed by military tact.'[14] As such, he subtly linked Jomini and Clausewitz through the military cliché and truism, 'no plan survives first contact with the enemy'. As we will see in Part II, the insight that we need 'flexible and adaptive strategy' because 'no plan survives first contact with the enemy' is simple but powerful and as relevant to strategy makers now as it was in the past.

Moltke's other less well recognized gift to strategy was the transformation of the Prussian General Staff. Formally created after the defeat of Napoleon, the core General Staff was an elite cadre of specially selected army officers, trained in the higher matters of war, according to a doctrine that owed much to Clausewitz. On taking over as Chief of the General Staff in 1857, Moltke welded this cadre into a unique instrument that combined 'flexibility and initiative at the local level with conformity to a common operational doctrine and to the intentions of the high command.'[15] Never more than a few hundred officers, under Moltke its purpose was twofold. First, it acted as the Army's brains, refining operational methods in peacetime and developing strategic plans for war. Second, it acted as the Army's nervous system in war. General Staff officers, trained to a common philosophy, would be attached to the main army formation HQs. And, when these HQs received the broad instructions that Moltke favoured, outlining the general objective and specific mission, these officers, trained to a common fighting doctrine, were able to interpret the orders for the HQs in the nature and spirit that Moltke intended.

As such, Moltke had developed a command and control organization that could create strategy, then communicate and execute it, yet retain the flexibility for modification in the field. He had thus solved the problem that had plagued Napoleon, namely that modern war's span was beyond the capacity of one commander's mind. The Prussian General Staff was not without its problems, particularly as it related to the political.[16] But by 1870-71, Moltke's system was already widely recognised for its impressive professionalism and its spectacular performance in action. Within three decades, it had been adopted, with modifications, by all major armies.

Moltke is not always viewed as one of the great strategic theorists, yet for me his insights on 'no plan surviving contact with the enemy' and the consequent need for flexibility, together with his transformation of the General Staff, mark him out. When his performance in the three Prussian Wars is judged against our three tests of strategic success — effectiveness, efficiency and endurability — then he, in partnership with Bismarck, ranks clearly as another of strategy's master-practitioners.

It is said of London buses that none arrive for ages, then suddenly you get two or three at once. In this (I think, sole) respect, strategic theorists seem rather like London buses, in that at the end of the 19th century, two more great thinkers emerged. Both were naval theorists, the first an American naval officer, Admiral Thomas Mahan, the second an English lawyer, Sir Julian Corbett (the first civilian to appear on our list of great theorists). Mahan tended toward a Jominian style of thinking, Corbett toward a Clausewitzian. And Mahan's thinking, like Jomini's, was more immediately influential, whereas Corbett's thinking, like Clausewitz's, has stood better the passage of time. But it was not until 1914, late in both their lives, that their ideas would be tested in practice. Trafalgar had removed the threat of Napoleon to the British Isles and it would be over a hundred years before another nation challenged Britain's maritime dominance. A maritime *Pax Britannica* was the context in which they thought and wrote: Mahan a naval officer of an emerging great power; Corbett a lawyer lecturing to officers of the maritime super-power.

Mahan's father, Dennis Hart Mahan, was a West Point Professor and Faculty Dean and a student and supporter of Jomini. It is thus no surprise that Mahan himself would 'one day become America's most eminent Jominian.'[17] Mahan's two great historical works, published in 1890 and 1892[18], were immediately popular because they explained (in Mahan's analysis) the central role of sea power in Britain's rise to greatness. Indeed Mahan's great strength was as an historian and, through this, an advocate for a powerful United States Navy.

But notwithstanding his fame, there is just one insight in Mahan on strategy that is useful to us, the concept of sea control. Sea control is the idea of controlling the sea so that you have freedom of action to use it and your enemy does not.[19] Mahan believed that securing sea control was central to success in naval warfare and could only be achieved through battle. It followed, he argued, that the primary mission of your fleet must be to destroy the enemy's. The use of ships to pursue a *guerre de course* against enemy merchantmen or to support an amphibious operation would, at best, serve a subordinate purpose and, at worst, divert you from winning sea control through battle. Today it would be old hat to suggest that sea control can be gained solely through battle, but the central idea nevertheless remains as important today as in Mahan's time.

Corbett, although less famous than Mahan, is a source of deeper insight. The first civilian amongst our theorists, after taking a first-class honours degree in law at Trinity College, Cambridge, he practised as a barrister. But he was wealthy enough not to need to work and, starting with an interest in Sir Francis Drake, by the turn of the century he had become a leading naval historian. In 1902, he was invited to lecture at the Royal Naval College, Greenwich; thus beginning an official relationship with the Royal Navy that would last until his death in 1922. In a forward to Corbett's seminal work, Professor Eric Grove describes him as 'Britain's greatest maritime strategist' and says of *Some Principles of Maritime Strategy* that there 'is simply no more classic exposition of the subject.'[20] Both judgments hold good today.

Corbett was famous for explaining the relationship between naval strategy and higher politico-military strategy. In particular, he argued that (top level) politico-military strategy and (subordinate) strategies for land, sea and air forces should be umbilically related. The latter had to be designed to contribute to the success of the former. But he was also a brilliant commentator on Clausewitz, simplifying and intelligently interpreting the great Prussian's writing as well as moving the thinking forward.[21]

For example, Corbett clarified Clausewitz's distinction between unlimited and limited war. What divided unlimited and limited wars was the nature of the political objects for which they were being fought. In unlimited war, the issue at contest was so vital that the whole weight of the nation-state would be brought to bear. Whereas in limited war the issues were not vital and this would influence your strategy, because politicians would not want to spend too much blood and treasure on limited objects.[22]

In unlimited wars, Corbett agreed with Clausewitz that you would need to defeat the enemy's armed forces and thus remove his ability to resist. Defeat of the enemy's armed forces would thus become your primary military object, whereas in limited wars it might not be. However, Corbett went on to suggest that in practice, in wars fought between continental neighbours, the distinction between unlimited and limited war was difficult to sustain. The shared boundary meant that a limited war could easily grow into an unlimited one. However, if the states were separated — by the sea — then the state commanding the sea could take as much or as little of the war as it chose.

We can develop this thinking further. Clausewitz and Corbett both seek to classify war by the nature of the political issue at contest. What neither brings out is that there will be occasions when a vital interest for one party to a contest is only a subsidiary interest to the other. In other words, there will be times when an unlimited war for one opponent may be a limited one for the other. As we shall see in Part II, understanding the balance of interest between the parties to the contest is key to understanding the nature of a war.

Corbett also dealt decisively with the flawed ideas of Napoleonic warfare as a panacea and manoeuvre in war as a substitute for battle. Napoleonic warfare was, as he correctly pointed out, a method of war, not a universal solution to all war's problems. For example, criticising a German Staff history of the actions of the Japanese in the

Russo-Japanese war, Corbett concluded that the misinterpretation could only be explained by:

> The domination of the Napoleonic idea of war, against the universal application which Clausewitz so solemnly protested. It is the work of men who have a natural difficulty in conceiving a war plan that does not culminate in a Jena or a Sedan. It is a view surely which is a child of theory, bearing no relation to the actuality of the war in question and affording no explanation of its ultimate success.[23]

Just so. And on classical manoeuvre warfare[24], Corbett was equally sure footed:

> Whatever the form of war, there is no likelihood of our ever going back to the old fallacy of attempting to decide war by manoeuvres. All forms of war demand the use of battles. By our fundamental theory war is always 'a continuation of political intercourse, in which fighting is substituted for writing notes.' However great the controlling influence of the political object, it must never obscure the fact that it is by fighting we have to gain our end. [25]

Corbett closed his analysis of the General Theory of War thus and shifted target to naval strategy. For now, we must part company with him, but we will meet again with his thinking.

The *Industrial Transformation* drew to a close with the start of the First World War. The political consequences and its strategic lessons would be mulled over after 1918 and so we will leave our analysis of The Great War's impact on strategy to Chapter 4 and *The Modern Epoch*.

Conclusion

Beginning with the US Civil War, the *Industrial Transformation* was a time of profound change in warfare, culminating in The Great War. As the complexity of armies and fleets grew beyond the capacity of a single commander's mind, Moltke's General Staff and explicit strategy allowed leaders to maintain executive control. Political views on the utility of war diverged significantly over the period. One pole came to see war as morally wrong and economically illogical. The other came to see war as a political philosophy in its own right. Those in the middle ground retained the classical instrumental view, but with an increasing sense of foreboding.

The US Civil War and the Prussian Wars had similarities and contrasts. The victorious states in these conflicts were led by talented teams of politicians and soldiers. In the US Civil War we see a modern form of strategy making in a political sense, with a fusion of political and military leaders' thinking. In the Prussian Wars, we see a modern form of strategy making in an organizational sense with the General Staff the means for creating and executing Prussian strategy.

But as World War I approached, political and military leaders dispensed with the practice of making strategy based on clear political objectives. The General Staffs that had evolved to deal with war's scope and complexity thus became politically rudderless. And it was unsurprising that their focus should alight on the essential need, revealed in railway timetables, to mobilize quickly to avoid defeat. Hence the hair trigger situation in Europe in August 1914. With no clear political objects in either coalition the result was the de-rationalisation of war — as much through political omission as through military commission.

Of the practitioners and theorists, three stand out, Lincoln, Moltke and Corbett. Both Lincoln and Moltke emerge as great practitioners with Moltke also a leading theorist — the first conscious advocate of flexible strategy and the source of the central idea that no plan survives contact with the enemy. And Corbett, although famed for encompassing land and naval warfare in strategy, is important to us for his interpretations and improvements on Clausewitz.

As with the previous chapter, let us conclude by summarising the key insights encountered on this canter through the *Industrial Transformation*, re-ordering them to suit our purposes:

- The nature of a war critically depends on the nature of the political issue at contest.

- Nation states will be less willing to expend blood and treasure over wars with limited objects.

- A limited war for one party may be unlimited for another and this will critically influence the nature of the war.

- The quality of the political *and* military leaders is a key factor in successful strategic performance.

- The span of modern warfare is too great, in time, space and method, for one mind to exercise control. A General (or Air or Naval) Staff of one form or another is essential for the direction and command of modern operations.

- Top level politico-military strategy and subordinate strategies for land, sea and air forces should be umbilically related. The latter must be designed to contribute to the success of the former.

- In war, it is generally through fighting that we achieve our objects.

- No plan survives contact with the enemy. Because of this and because of the unpredictable nature of war, flexible and adaptive strategy is required.

- Ideas and theory matter in war because they shape our thoughts and actions.

- No particular idea or theory — such as the Napoleonic warfare or classical manoeuvre warfare — should be universally applied.

Herewith the second tranche of insights for our jigsaw box. Again some of the ideas may seem obvious to us now, but this was not so in their time.

What brought the *Industrial Transformation* to a close, crystallising military developments and clarifying political trends, was World War I. This bloody experimental cauldron of warfare cauterized Europe — politically and economically — and shocked the rest of the world. It changed, probably for ever, political and popular views on war, in particular on war's political utility and moral legitimacy. It is thus to the *Modern Epoch*, starting with the 'Great War', that we now turn.

Chapter 4

The Modern Epoch: 1914-1991

*[The Joint Chiefs of Staff] and McNamara became fixated on
the means rather than the ends, and on the manner in which the
war [in Vietnam] was conducted instead of a military strategy
that could connect military actions to achievable policy goals.*

H.R. McMaster

Introduction

With the exception of nuclear bombs, the weapons systems and
operational techniques that have dominated modern warfare were
all present in World War I — what we see over the *Modern Epoch*
is their incremental refinement.

Politically, two great contests provided the Epoch's backdrop.
Liberal democratic philosophy had the blue corner while the red
was occupied by two totalitarian opponents, the first Fascist, the
second Socialist. Of course, to describe this summary as even a crude
generalisation of the international politics of the *Modern Epoch*
would be far too complimentary. However, although both contests
sat within a more complex political milieu, they were evidentially
the wellspring of many of the *Epoch*'s wars. Within this milieu, views
on the political utility of the instrument of war had been shaken to
their foundations by World War I. And in 1945, Hiroshima and
Nagasaki provided a second Richter moment.

The *Modern Epoch* contained events that crucially shaped our thinking on strategy. There were great practitioners, such as in the World War II alliance of Roosevelt, Churchill, General Marshall and Field Marshal Alanbrooke. There were also important theorists albeit none to rival Clausewitz. And last but not least, half way through the period the academic discipline of strategic studies was borne, albeit with a dominant infant interest in nuclear (rather than general) strategy.

Military Means in the Modern Epoch

The navies, armies and air forces that emerged from World War I, at the start of the *Modern Epoch*, shared a number of common characteristics.

First, all three had become more complicated. We see this complexity in the sheer range of fielded weapon systems. For example, armies had introduced light, medium and heavy tanks; light, heavy and, later, mechanized artillery and as counters, anti-aircraft and anti-tank guns. Navies had introduced aircraft carriers, torpedo boats and submarines; and as counters, torpedo-boat destroyers, anti-submarine corvettes and frigates. The new air forces had introduced light and heavy bombers, fighters and reconnaissance aircraft. Other aircraft types, such as maritime patrol and air transport, would follow soon. This complexity was also reflected in the organisations which evolved to marshal their new forces and weapons systems. The hierarchies — 'force structures' in the jargon — of all three services emerged from World War I more intricate and layered and this changed little in later years.

Second, because the munitions they fired were not guided, but instead generally relied on ballistic prediction, weapons were not precise — most thus relied on volume of fire to achieve their effect.

Examples include machine guns, anti-tank and anti-aircraft guns, torpedoes and depth charges, heavy naval guns, artillery and bombers. It was not until late in World War II that the Germans developed bombs that were actively guided to the target.[1] And it would take another thirty or so years before reliable guidance technologies were introduced into naval and air weapons systems and even longer for land-based weapon systems.

Third, to deliver fire in volume, weapons and forces needed to be massed — Jomini's century old principle of massing forces to deliver overwhelming firepower at the decisive point was still relevant. Indeed his principle would continue to guide commanders through World War II and the conventional wars of the Cold War.

Fourth, in a negative sense, the technical ability to command navies, armies and air forces failed to keep pace with their destructive potential. The brain and nervous system of the military machine failed to keep pace with the brawn. As weapons ranged over the horizon, our ability to see — with intelligence, surveillance and reconnaissance — beyond the horizon lagged behind. In parallel, as our forces occupied greater areas spreading out of sight of their commanders, our ability to monitor and command them also lagged behind.

This is not to say there was no progress. Reconnaissance and surveillance forces evolved, as did our ability to collect intelligence. But without the support of computers, intelligence collation and analysis was laborious and manpower intensive. The exchange of information between friendly units, particularly across the air, sea and land boundaries, was also difficult and hindered their cooperation. Worse still it led to mistaken attacks on friendly forces — 'blue-on-blue' in military parlance — throughout the Epoch.[2] The fundamental command and intelligence problem was that we were unable to collect organize and distribute information and then dispatch orders in real time.

For these reasons, warfare in the *Modern Epoch* was quite unlike the past. 'Area campaigns' replaced the 'point battles' of the *Classical Epoch* as the currency of strategic exchange. Battle still counted, but less so as a culminating point of strategy. Instead a battle's value was judged by its contribution to the area campaign. Disruption of the enemy command and support structures and their lines of communication might be deemed more important than attritional battle on the front line. For navies and air forces, freedom of action to use the sea or air or to deny its use to the opponent, became a defining reason for battle, more important than the destruction of the enemy air and naval forces. More generally, with the greater geographic scope, organizational scale and military complexity of the forces, the importance of logistics planning also increased. Ultimately, as armed forces became more complex, so too did warfare and war.

And because of all of this, strategy became more important. Strategy making became the vehicle for thinking through how these complex wars would be fought. Once created, strategy provided the conceptual framework to guide planners and provide purpose and direction for subordinate commanders and their operations once begun.

Strategic success rested increasingly on the ability to use all levers of national power in harmony, so strategy makers began to look upward to the political and outwards to adjoining areas of government, as well as downward to the operational levels. To generate the firepower and mass needed to succeed at the tactical level, nations needed to harness their economic and industrial means to deliver the raw materials and sustain the production required. And in a circular way, because of this, operational objectives to secure the possession of territory that included key strategic resources, such as oil, would become central objectives in campaign plans in the great wars of national survival of the 20th century. The use of the idea of grand strategy in the 20th century was thus an essential response to the new nature of modern warfare.

Political Ends in the Modern Epoch

The Great War's political impacts echoed loudly through the *Modern Epoch*. What made the war different from all those before it were the costs, none of which were foreseen. Indeed, in the light of this it is curious that, after the war, strategic thinkers focused mostly on war's operational and tactical lessons and gave little thought to the political and strategic ones whereas political thinkers, politicians and nations saw the matter from a wholly different perspective.

Politicians proved more alert to the philosophical implications because they understood better the war's visceral political costs.

> The politicians did show themselves much more sensitive than their military brethren to the price being exacted for the undefined 'victory'. They sensed that the common soldier was not merely a means for fighting but also one for whom the fight was being waged. They recognized that the state is its people and not some disembodied abstraction. In the beginning no one had any idea what the ultimate price would be, but as the war progressed the generals tended by and large to accept and the politicians by and large to resist the notion that competitive attrition in manpower could be adopted as a valid standard of military success.[3]

The urgent political question was how to avoid a repeat performance. Different explanations of the war's causes led to different answers. The US President, Woodrow Wilson, blamed the European state system and deduced the need for a new world order based on the League of Nations. For Clemenceau, France's neighbour was the problem — for France to be secure, Germany had to be neutered. Lloyd George and the British, however, in large part due to national exhaustion and the burden of over-extended empire, tended toward a policy of pragmatism — or appeasement, depending on your taste. The roots of World War II were to be found in all these attitudes.

Ultimately World War I was the defining war of the century, possibly of all time, because of its profound impact on popular and political views on war. And yet, despite the slaughter, the divergent political views that were evident in the *Industrial Transformation* survived and indeed, in a sense, prospered during the inter-war years. Now though, they were more clearly associated with particular nations and philosophies. Amongst the Western victors, the war-as-irrational view strengthened. To paraphrase Brodie, the idea was not new that war had consequences that were hideous and evil but rather what was new was the idea that war was *intrinsically* evil.[4] Whereas we see the opposite camp at its most extreme in Adolf Hitler's philosophy of war as an inevitable and healthy political condition.

The nature and distribution of wars in the inter-war years reflect these opposing views. A third or so of the inter-war wars were fought by the (soon-to-be) Axis powers. Another third were fought by the Soviet Union. In both cases the political objects sought were generally expansionist. The last third were a ragtag mix of minor territorial wars, sprinkled around the globe. But most revealing was the low frequency with which Western powers waged war in these years. The British took up arms just twice, against the Soviets in 1918-20 and the Afghans in 1919, the French and Americans once each, the former fighting the Druze in 1925-27 and the latter supporting the Nicaraguan rebels in 1927-33.

But World War II provided a political wake up call to the Western powers as protectors of the liberal democratic centre. War may have been morally repugnant but, if others intended to advance their extreme political interests with force, the West would need to respond in kind. Freedom would need to be protected. Thus after World War II, the use of armed force for (generally defensive) political objects, was accepted again as legitimate by the West's leaders and nations. And whereas Britain, France and United States fought just four times in the inter-war years, their total for the three decades after World War II rose to fourteen.

The two defining wars of the Cold War period were perhaps the respective interventions of the superpowers in Vietnam in 1965 and Afghanistan in 1979, because they demonstrated the limits of a superpower's power. The Vietnam experience caused more soul searching amongst the US bodies politic and military than any other Cold War event. The Soviet experience in Afghanistan was equally chastening. But the result was a better collective understanding of the possibilities, risks, limitations and costs of using conventional armed force in pursuit of political objects.

In short, having diverged before World War II, political views on conventional war began to converge afterwards. War was accepted, reluctantly by many, as a legitimate political instrument to secure political objectives. But it was an instrument with clear limitations, as Vietnam and Afghanistan demonstrated.

Strategy in the Modern Epoch

After World War I, strategy theorists ruminated at length on conventional strategy. But after World War II, the thinking started to dry up. Hiroshima, Nagasaki and the need to get to grips with nuclear strategy help explain this. So too, more subtly, does the more political nature of the limited wars of the Cold War, where strategy was difficult. Nevertheless with the practice of great statesmen and soldiers, such as Churchill and Marshall and the theory of great thinkers, such as the American political scientist Bernard Brodie and the French soldier-scholar General André Beaufre, for us to ponder on, the *Modern Epoch* is rich in insight.

World War I

Bernard Brodie asks the simple question of World War I: 'Why, over more than four long and ghastly years, did it prove impossible to stop it?' The answer, he suggests, was 'a fierce dedication to the goal of victory, which none in power [would] permit to be shaken.'[5] And because, in Brodie's view, neither coalition was fighting for a clear political objective, then victory could only be measured against their (shared) military objective of defeating each other's armies. As Brodie observes:

> The war created its own objectives ... No doubt the immense tragedy of World War I, in a real sense a war without purpose, is to be explained on grounds other than mere forgetfulness of Clausewitz's admonitions about relating means to ends; but it is nevertheless remarkable that no military leader on either side of the conflict — and for that matter few besides the historian Hans Delbrück among noteworthy civilians — seemed to be aware of and protest against the ongoing obliteration of this all-important idea.[6]

Was Brodie right? Was this a war that created its own objectives? Dr Gary Sheffield is one of a number of military historians who take a different view.

They see the war as an inevitable consequence of fatal changes in German foreign and military policy, after the departure of Bismarck and Moltke the Elder and their policy of *status quo*. With the new world policy, *Weltpolitik*, Germany's political and military leaders sought hegemony in Europe and, under Kaiser Wilhelm II's leadership, were prepared to risk war to achieve it. The Triple Entente were prepared to go to war to prevent it. The Kaiser's decisions to challenge Britain's maritime dominance and then, once war had begun, to declare unrestricted submarine warfare, notwithstanding that this would likely drive the US into the arms of the Allies, were grand strategic own goals. So although unfashionable, Dr Sheffield's case is persuasive.[7]

The war was also a source of hard strategic lessons. It exposed the central flaw of the German system where, once war had begun, strategy and the generals reigned over policy and politician:

> Ludendorff was not an aberration but, rather, the product, if an extreme case, of a specifically German mentality and milieu that believed that, especially in time of war, the military ought to take command of the state and absorb its other agencies.[8]

It also caused practitioners and theorists to revise their views in a wide range of areas: the danger of a mindless preference for the offensive was exposed; the potential of modern manoeuvre warfare was highlighted; the role of air power in future wars was debated. And so on.

But for us, against the tests of superior strategy making — effectiveness, efficiency and endurability — World War I was a strategic failure, even for the victors. The costs of victory were catastrophic and the results did not endure.

Of more use to us are the post-war lessons deduced by post-War commentators. We will start with an Englishman, Basil Liddell Hart and then consider the thinking of a German soldier, an Italian airman and a French sailor, respectively Hans von Seeckt, Giulio Douhet and Raoul Castex.

The inter-war years

Captain Basil Liddell Hart is the second (Cambridge educated) Englishman amongst our influential theorists. Born in 1895, Liddell Hart went up to Corpus Christi College, Cambridge, in 1913 to read modern history, but then volunteered for the British Army as the Great War began. On 1 July 1916, the first day of the Somme, his battalion lost all but two of its officers. This and later field experiences surely influenced his revisionist thinking on the war.

Although Liddell Hart wrote prodigiously, we are interested in him for just one idea, that of the 'indirect approach'. He illustrates the notion in this analysis of the psychological impact upon the German Chief of the General Staff, Ludendorff, of his unexpected reverses in the Summer and Autumn of 1918:

> Rather does the record of the last 'hundred days', when sifted, confirm the immemorial lesson that the true aim of war is the mind of the hostile rulers, not the bodies of their troops; that the balance between victory and defeat turns on mental impressions and only indirectly on physical blows. It was the shock of being surprised and the feeling that he was powerless to counter potential strategic moves, that shook Ludendorff's nerve more than the loss of prisoners, guns and acreage.[9]

Liddell Hart coins the term 'indirect approach' to describe the idea of achieving a psychological shock effect by doing what your enemy least expects, rather than confronting him head on. And, based on this analysis, Liddell Hart sets out his thinking on strategy:

> [The strategist's] true aim is not so much to seek battle as to seek a strategic situation so advantageous that if it does not of itself produce the decision, its continuation by a battle is sure to achieve this. In other words, dislocation is the aim of strategy; its sequel maybe either the enemy's dissolution or his easier disruption.[10]

But here we see Liddell Hart making the same mistake as Jomini, namely presenting us with his holy grail for strategy. How could the idea of dislocation as strategy's aim have been applied to, say, the grinding encounters of the Battle of Britain or Battle of the Atlantic?

What Liddell Hart has given us is an important strategic technique, very useful but not a panacea for making strategy.

Our next individual, General Hans von Seeckt, is less well known. Although the *blitzkrieg* doctrine[11] is commonly accredited to the influence of inter-war writers, such as Liddell Hart and de Gaulle and the practice of German generals, such as Rommel and Guderian, this received wisdom is flawed. The key driving force was von Seeckt, one of the most successful German generals of World War I, Chief of the General Staff from 1919 to 1920 and then commander of the German Army from 1920 to 1926. 'Most of the tactics that comprised *blitzkrieg* in 1939 and 1940 sprang directly from the initiatives instigated by von Seeckt and the General Staff committees after World War I.'[12] Geyer gives a sense of the philosophy that resulted:

> *Blitzkrieg* ... was not new. The core of these operations [consisted of] a kind of operational opportunism that knew no pre-set and standardized methods, only the fullest possible exploitation of success with all available means in pursuit of the ultimate goal of overthrowing the enemy by breaking the will of its leadership, *Blitzkrieg* lived off the destruction of a systematic approach to military command decisions. It was the opposite of a doctrine. *Blitzkrieg* operations consisted of an avalanche of actions that were sorted out less by design than by success.[13]

The ideas would be successfully tested by the Germans in World War II. General Guderian's actions in the French campaign in 1940 are seen by many as the defining example. The arrival of Guderian's XIX Panzer Corps on the banks of the Meuse on the fourth day of the offensive was wholly unanticipated by the French, as was his surprise crossing and breakneck dash to the English Channel. Liddell Hart has perceptively noted: 'The vital weakness of the French lay, not in the quantity nor in quality of equipment, but in their theory'[14] — testament to the broader importance of theory in war. But key was the cumulative impact of these shocks on the French High Command, a classic case of a victory through the psychological dislocation and disruption of an enemy's higher leadership.

It was von Seeckt who had laid the ground work for this performance. James Corum's view of von Seeckt as 'an original military thinker, whose clarity of vision, comprehensive view of future warfare and ability to impose these views on the German Army made him one of the most important military thinkers of the 20th century'[15] may not be fashionable, but it is persuasive. But what is there in von Seeckt's *blitzkrieg* for strategy?

Blitzkrieg was operational and tactical technique, not strategy. And, as the history of World War II demonstrates, the best tactics and operational doctrines are nothing without superior strategy. But a key strategic insight lies hidden in *blitzkrieg's* command doctrine. Front line commanders were encouraged to exploit success as it developed before them, planned or otherwise, rather than rigidly adhere to original plans or refer to higher authorities. And in a real sense, this was a logical development of Moltke's view that flexible strategy was the answer to the conundrum that 'no plan survives contact with the enemy'. A key feature of flexible strategy would be the empowerment of front line commanders, so that they could adjust strategy in the light of events and success. As we shall see, the 'learning school' of corporate strategists promotes something very similar and such thinking is equally relevant to modern politico-military strategy. The lesson for us is that flexible strategy needs two things: first, adaptability must be 'designed in' when the strategy is being created; second, there needs to be a corresponding adaptability in the organization and mindsets of those who will execute the strategy.

Looking elsewhere, we find that early air power thinking was not quite as imaginative, not least because its early advocates were just that, advocates. These were men fighting for their fledgling air services under the covetous gaze of senior army and navy officers. Of them, just one, the Italian airman, General Giulio Douhet, stands out. Born in 1869, Douhet's army career was chequered, through contretemps with higher authorities unable to see the potential of the aeroplane. Brodie observes that, in Douhet's writing in the 1920s, 'the few ideas that [Douhet] elaborated were not altogether his own creations ... but he was the first to weave them into a coherent philosophy.'[16] MacIsaac succinctly summarizes his key tenets:

> Douhet's theory of war broke down into view points that might be abbreviated as follows: (1) modern warfare allows no distinction between combatants and non-combatants; (2) successful offensives by surface forces are no longer possible; (3) the advantages of speed and elevation in the three dimensional arena of aerial warfare have made it impossible to take defensive measures against an offensive aerial strategy; (4) therefore, a nation must be prepared at the outset to launch massive bombing attacks against the enemy centres of population, government and industry — hit first and hit hard to shatter the enemy civilian morale, leaving the enemy government no option but to sue for peace; (5) to do this an independent air force armed with long range bombardment aircraft, maintained in a constant state of readiness, is the primary requirement.[17]

These ideas were tested during the British and American strategic bombing offensives of World War II and later over Vietnam with largely inconclusive results, notwithstanding the huge weight of resources, blood and treasure expended in their pursuit.

Air power theory would have benefitted from the scrutiny of a mind like Corbett's. In this quote, I have adapted his thinking, by replacing 'at sea' with 'in the air' and 'navy' with 'air force', so as to get to the key issue for air power theorists:

> Since men live on the land and not [in the air], great issues between nations at war have always been decided — except in the rarest cases — by what your army can do against your enemy's territory and national life or else by the fear of what your [air force] makes it possible for your army to do.[18]

And to further develop this thinking, I have replaced the words 'sea' and 'naval warfare' with 'air' and 'air warfare' in Corbett's words here:

> The object of [air] warfare must always be directly or indirectly either to secure the command of the [air] or to prevent the enemy securing it.[19]

> The common situation in [air] war is that neither side has the command; that the normal position is not a commanded [air space], but an uncommanded [air space].[20]

> Command of the [air] is not identical in its strategical considerations with the conquest of territory.[21]

Notwithstanding the replacements, the underlying logic holds good. Men and women generally pass through, rather than live on, the sea and in the air, so warfare in both is different from that on land. In the air and at sea, it is not possible to 'hold territory'. Rather the freedom of action to use the sea or air or to deny their use to your opponent — termed, in the jargon, 'sea control' and 'air superiority' or 'sea denial' and 'airspace denial' — is key and this point holds good even now. If this type of thinking had been interwoven with the strident views of the early air power theorists, then we might by now have a more balanced and logical body of air power theory than the current meagre showing.

The last of our inter-war theorists, Admiral Raoul Castex, was a leading 20th century naval thinker. Buried within his main work, *Théories Stratégiques*, are significant insights into general strategy and its relationship with both tactics and policy.[22]

Castex's reflections on policy and strategy are particularly informative — he sees the two as routinely interactive:

> Policy intervenes to orient strategy in specific directions. Such interventions can be positive, that is, prescribing actions or negative, forbidding specific enterprises. Obviously, political demands are not always the most judicious; their inspiration can be good or bad; they may be lacking in foresight. Frequently policy comes to trespass on the domain of strategy and intervenes excessively in the conduct of operations and in other matters that do not concern it. Nonetheless, the demands made by policy cannot be neglected or distrustfully dismissed; they have a preponderant weight. Consequently, strategy cannot abstract itself from policy and work in isolation.[23]

In other words, it is policy — which is the province of political leaders — that must direct and, on occasion, shape and adjust strategy in response to political necessities. Frustrating though it can be for military officers and much as they may abhor such interference, Castex is right and even more so in today's modern politicized wars.

Castex ponders at length on the relationship between government and politicians on the one hand and strategy and commanders on the other. Government action 'rarely begins with premeditated, methodically analysed long term prognostications developed through a process of leisured thought and implemented with consistency and perseverance.'[24] But one should not be surprised by this, because:

> Politicians do not generally operate in conditions permitting

the development of large-scale plans of action or war plans. Most of them lack the special training, both technical and moral. ... However good their intentions, politicians find their ephemeral periods in office dominated by current affairs, by political struggles, by agitations in the parliamentary assemblies, etc. Such an atmosphere is not conducive to devising a major political and military plan.[25]

These words have a modern resonance. Indeed, the lack of training that he identifies for politicians is equally applicable to civil servants and diplomats. It worries me that, although diplomats and officials are expected to shape and politicians sanction, the policy that rules over strategy, few, if any, are trained in the theory of strategy or military affairs.

Although rarely cited in modern texts on the relationship between policy and strategy, these ideas put Castex into a class of his own. He may not have been influential — in part because of language and in part because of his assumed naval focus — but we will return regularly to his thinking in future chapters. Before this we have the 'minor aberrations' of World War II and nuclear weapons to consider.

World War II

I use the term 'aberrations' in a way that is not wholly ironic. At least I hope that a war that encompassed the globe and included the strategic bombing of Germany and Japan, the Holocaust, the death of over 60 million people and the use of nuclear weapons, was an aberration. I am not suggesting that such a war is not possible in the future. But, for the positive reason of the reduction in the number of totalitarian governments and the negative reason of the great powers' retention of nuclear weapons, the likelihood of a war on a similar scale and intensity has shrunk appreciably, even if not yet quite to zero. I will focus on just one specific but informative area of the war: the successful creation and execution of strategy by the two Western Allies, the US and Britain.

The US and Britain formed the 'inner web of the Grand Alliance' and the similarities and contrasts of their strategy making approaches are instructive.[26] As the war partnership began, on 11 December 1941, Britain had been fighting a defensive war for over two years and was approaching full mobilisation. Churchill and the British Army leaders had recognized that, thanks to von Seeckt, they were facing a German Army that was formidable — an army that many would come to regard as, unit-for-unit, the most effective fighting force of the war.

Shortfalls in the British forces, particularly its army, had been exposed. The historian Williamson Murray thinks that 'training and doctrine were the source of Britain's battlefield deficiencies'[27] but he overlooks two more important factors. First the failure to seize on the possibilities in air and armoured warfare that Liddell Hart and Fuller espoused, von Seeckt inspired and Guderian and the *Wehrmacht* made good, suggests a lack of strategic vision amongst senior British officers. Second the shortage of high quality operational leaders — Slim in Burma was a notable exception   was a concern for Churchill and Alanbrooke and would remain so throughout the war.

Meanwhile, America had been preparing for the coming war for some time. The US strategic thinkers were pragmatically self-confident. Their approach was based on a Jominian style of decisive mass, which the United States had the economic and industrial muscle to deliver. Furthermore they would soon be in a position to deploy new and powerful operational capabilities, such as carrier air power. And, perhaps critically, 'at the deepest psychological level, the American high command appears to have escaped the emotional scars that the World War I slaughter inflicted on Britain.'[28]

Crucially, from the start of the Alliance, the US and British were pursuing different political objectives. In the short term, if the British Isles fell, this would have had a catastrophic impact on the war — so the short-term objective for both allies was Britain's successful defence. But Britain's long term objectives, deduced by Murray as 'preservation of the Empire and maintenance of economic and political power,'[29] were in marked contrast to those of the United States:

> American decision makers came to see ... the spread of militaristic and totalitarian regimes a confirmation of Wilson's basic view that a liberal world order was the only guarantee of American safety. For that reason, their long-term objective became the removal of the causes of war by creating such an order. American strategy in World War II is understandable only within the context of such a vision. The United States sought not merely to defeat particular enemies, but to reconstruct enemy polities and the larger world order. ... In Roosevelt's casual words, ... America's objective became the 'unconditional surrender' of the Axis Powers. Yet it soon became apparent that — with occasional exceptions — the United States sought not the obliteration of its opponents but their reconstruction in its own image.[30]

Allied arguments over strategy were intense. For example, to confront Germany the British preferred an indirect approach, from the Mediterranean into the 'soft underbelly' of Southern Europe. In contrast, the Americans preferred a direct approach across the Channel. Their different national objectives help explain these differences, but so too do the contrasts in their strategic cultures.

The British had re-armed reluctantly. Arguably theirs was a defensive mindset, notwithstanding Churchill's personal inclination to carry the fight to Germany. This was no doubt a result of the Great War experience, but also critically conditioned by two things. First,

Churchill and the British knew that they lacked the resources to execute anything other than an indirect strategy. Second, at the operational level, their record against the German Army had been dismal. Cohen's view that, by the end of 1941, Britain had 'nearly bankrupted itself as its forces were driven from the Continent in one debacle after another'[31] is unfair and in particular misses the strategic efficiency of Britain's mobilisation when compared to Germany's, but it nevertheless contains more than a grain or two of operational truth.

In contrast, the US strategic culture was increasingly self-confident. The Americans 'intended to fight a mobile, aggressive war on fronts of their own choosing, to draw more thoroughly on the vast industrial productive capacities of the nation and not to fall prey to the duplicity of wily European allies.'[32] Given the Axis regimes' totalitarian politics, Americans judged that to deliver their objectives they would need to confront and comprehensively defeat the Axis powers militarily, with the priority being to defeat, first, the German Army and Luftwaffe and then the Japanese Navy and Army. But in a modern democracy, time would be an issue. They would need to win quickly. Consequently, they would need to play to their strengths, operational and industrial. American strategy making rested on these judgements.

As Cohen concludes, World War II both shaped and revealed American strategic culture as no other war with the exception of the Civil War. Two dominant characteristics stood out: 'the preference for massing a vast array of men and machines and the predilection for direct and violent assault.'[33]

Of particular interest for us is the time that British and Americans leaders dedicated to strategy making:

> It was the American military that succeeded in establishing the Combined Chiefs of Staff organisation and rooting it in Washington during the ARCADIA conference of 1941-42. ...

The Anglo-Americans conferred most frequently in 1943 and the four conferences of that year were the longest of the war, ten days or more, remarkably protracted periods of strategic deliberation. ... throughout the war, the Combined Chiefs of Staff alternated between their own meetings and meetings in the presence of Churchill and Roosevelt, who also conducted their own private discussions. ... the President and Prime Minister did not confine themselves to issuing sweeping policy guidelines. Rather they were civilian leaders who believed that victory was possible only by weaving strategic decisions, thread by thread, into a cloth of their own unique design. ... Once top civilian and military leaders had made the strategic decisions, the services implemented them as executive agent[s].[34]

These protracted conferences were testament to an oft unrecognized fact. Notwithstanding views to the contrary, strategy making was hard work and it took time and effort for strategic leaders to hammer out strategy. But by investing time in this way, British and American political and military leaders gained a second crucial benefit. They established the personal relationships that were essential for oiling the coalition wheels and maintaining unity of purpose as the strategy was executed.

There are modern lessons for us here. If political and military leaders in future coalitions do not invest adequate time in strategy making, strategy will surely suffer — as will the prospects of political and strategic success.

In the final analysis American strategy was a resounding success. Generally there was a clear sense of the ends sought, of the means available — in particular, the lack of time — and a well conceived strategy to deliver these ends. Against our three tests — effectiveness, efficiency and long term durability — US strategy was successful. Britain only partially achieved her objectives and at very significant long term cost. Her freedom of action had, of course, been constrained by her circumstances. But then arguably some of the seeds of her circumstances lay in strategy making shortfalls in World War I and its immediate aftermath.

Nuclear strategy

Our discussion on World War II omitted two seismic events, but this is because Hiroshima and Nagasaki seem to sit more naturally in the Cold War. The historical dawning of the nuclear age was soon followed by the theoretical dawning of nuclear strategy. This may help explain the theoretical twilight cast over general strategy and why World War II's conventional lessons were not more widely reflected in theory in the Cold War.

In the long view, the use of nuclear weapons in 1945 and the West's recognition of Soviet socialism's malign nature in 1947 were simultaneous events. They caused strategic theorists to think about nuclear strategy and the counter-revolutionary warfare they judged would be needed to contain socialism.

Nuclear war was the clear and present danger. 'Strategists struggled to make sense of new weapons that seemed to turn conventional military wisdom upside down. ... the widely accepted Clausewitzian idea of war as an instrument of policy began to look decidedly odd.'[35] New thinking was needed to complement, rather than replace, the old theory; and new thinking was also needed to help execute a US grand strategy of containment to deal with the Soviet Union. Therefore, the scholars of the newly born strategic studies departments and think tanks had much to keep them busy. And they were industrious. In the years that followed, they produced three closely related bodies of theory on deterrence, arms-control and limited warfare (with a counter-revolutionary bias), that guided us through the Cold War years.

Thankfully theories of nuclear strategy were never put into fighting practice. This helps to explain why academics came to dominate thinking on nuclear strategy. Theorists from other academic disciplines were also drawn to the subject. They included political scientists, economists, mathematicians, physicists and psychologists and the body of nuclear theory they produced reached theological levels of abstraction. The strategic thinker Professor Colin Gray describes the period from 1955 to 1965 as the Golden Age of strategic studies, both because of the growth in the academic strategic studies community and because of its success in addressing the strategic problems of the nuclear age, such that they passed from 'a theoretical *terra incognita* to apparent understanding or resolution — or both.'[36] But by institutional default, these academics came also to dominate thinking on conventional politico-military strategy — which was perhaps not such a good thing.

The writing of Thomas Schelling, the influential economist, illustrates the problems of introducing thinking from other disciplines. As Schelling explained, his great work, *The Strategy of Conflict*, was not actually about strategy:

> 'strategy' is taken, here, from the theory of games, which distinguishes games of skill, games of chance and games of strategy, the latter being those in which the best course of action for each player depends on what the other players do.[37]

But the principal assumption in Schelling's analysis was flawed: 'the assumption of rational behaviour is a productive one ... [it] gives a grip on the subject that is peculiarly conducive to the development of theory.'[38] Any theory founded on the idea of rational behaviour in war was — and is — flawed because, as Clausewitz explains and the record shows, armed conflict and war are political conditions where human behaviour is often at its most irrational.

More generally, the essential diversion of most of the strategic intellectual horsepower toward nuclear strategy explains why the theory of general strategy advanced little during the Cold War and why no successors to Clausewitz emerged. But Liddell Hart was wrong to say that 'old concepts and old definitions of strategy have become not only obsolete but nonsensical.'[39] As the Cold War's history reveals, when you fought conventional wars you ignored older concepts of strategy at your peril.

The Cold War

Although I have sounded a note of caution on the influence of nuclear theorists, such as Schelling, on conventional strategy, the Cold War is nevertheless an important source of insights for us. There is an all-too-rich vein of conventional wars to study but we will set to one side classic conventional conflicts, such as the Korean, Arab-Israeli, Iran-Iraq and Indo-Pakistan Wars. Instead we will focus on two more complex conflicts — the Malayan Emergency and the US intervention in Vietnam. Of the leaders, there are insights in General Templer's leadership in Malaya. And of the thinkers, three stand out: the American political scientist Bernard Brodie, Rear Admiral Wylie, USN and, last but not least, General Beaufre, French Army.

When the Malayan Communist Party's (MCP) insurgents began to fight in 1948, Britain was caught off balance but the position was not disastrous. Ethnic Chinese predominated in the MCP and the insurgents enjoyed little support among the majority ethnic Malays. Furthermore, government worked well and the security forces' experience of jungle warfare had been honed during the Burma campaign of World War II.

Early on, Britain declared that Malaya would be granted her independence. This undercut the political logic of the MCP's cause, but also gave British leaders a clear political object. Lieutenant General Sir Harold Briggs commanded the security forces and the 'organisation and arrangements that Briggs put in place to deal with the growing conflict addressed and countered the key elements expounded by Mao Tse Tung as essential to the success of a revolutionary war.'[40] Briggs' strategy aimed to secure the government bases and population centres. It created new villages and planned to re-locate half a million people. In modern parlance, it was an exercise in 'managed development'. More importantly, the strategy was not solely a military strategy, but rather an integrated politico-military strategy, in our parlance a proper campaign strategy. But despite the strategy, guerrilla actions increased during the first three years of the campaign, culminating in the murder of the High Commissioner, Sir Henry Gurney, in late 1951.

When General Sir Gerald Templer took over in Malaya, in early 1952, a coherent strategy had been created and was already being executed. The question for Templer was simple: was it the right strategy? Appointed by Churchill as both High Commissioner and Director of Operations — thus combining the civil and military leadership roles — Templer's first step was to examine Briggs' strategy. Having judged it workable, with minor refinements, he then set about executing it — with exceptional vigour. Key to successful execution was his assessment that:

> Any idea that the business of normal civil Government and the business of the Emergency are two separate entities must be killed for good. The two activities are completely and utterly inter-related … The answer lies not in pouring more men into the jungle, but in winning the hearts and minds of the people.[41]

In other words, he recognized the political nature of the insurgency and the fact that 'if an insurgency represents anything other than a very minor disturbance, … the sum of the political and economic measures to combat it as a whole will involve the whole business of government in one form or another.'[42] This reinforces the need not only for a coherent politico-military strategy, but also for a coherent politico-military approach when executing that strategy.

The strategy rested on strong political foundations: Templer and the Colonial Office Minister, Sir Oliver Lyttelton, understood the political issue at contest — the need for Malaya to gain democratic independence was clear from the outset. The strategy drew on a range of strategic techniques, but, critically, recognized the need for a comprehensive and patient counter-insurgency approach. Templer understood there could be no quick fixes in a war of this nature.[43] Whitehall's armchair experts called regularly for different approaches but were held at arm's length by Lyttelton. And when Templer departed the theatre, in 1954, the insurgents were a spent force. Elections were conducted in 1955, Malayan independence declared in 1957 and, in 1960, the Emergency was over. Templer's brilliant execution in the field was intelligently and stoutly supported by his political master, Lyttelton. And against our three tests of superior strategy — effectiveness, efficiency and durability of political result — theirs was a complete success.

Although Sir Robert Thompson would later draw the counter-insurgency techniques together in his thoughtful book *Countering Communist Insurgency*, he perhaps missed a central point. It was not the techniques, *per se*, that won the campaign, but the strategy.[44] We will return to Malaya later, as examples of superior strategy making such as this were not plentiful in the Cold War.

Brodie

Before turning to Vietnam, I want to discuss a key Cold War strategic theorist, Professor Bernard Brodie, in part because his analysis helps us to prise out key lessons from the Vietnam War. A political scientist, Brodie lectured and researched at Chicago, Princeton, Yale,

Dartmouth College, the RAND think tank and also spent short advisory spells with the USAF and the USN.[45] The 'quintessential strategist of the first generation of the nuclear age', he published widely on nuclear strategy. He too judged that conventional strategy had 'been generally ignored by the strategic community, perhaps because of the relatively small attention it pays to those nuclear matters which have remained the professional preoccupation.'[46] But unlike his peer group, he took a close interest in conventional politico-military strategy, as reflected in his two seminal works, *War and Politics* and *Strategy in the Missile Age*.[47]

Brodie studied Clausewitz closely, usefully interpreting the great Prussian's thinking, but also, like Corbett, moving it forward. An illuminating example is this discussion on vital interests, so often the source of inspiration — positive and negative — for war-making decisions:

> Vital interests, despite common assumptions to the contrary have only a vague connection with objective fact. A sovereign nation determines for itself what its vital interests are (freedom to do so is what sovereign means) and its leaders accomplish this exacting task largely by using their highly fallible and inevitably biased human judgement to interpret the external political environment. To save wear and tear on their always overburdened and frequently limited analytical powers, they cling obsessively to common accepted axioms, some of which may be old enough to have the aura of 'traditional' policy.[48]

This thought leads us to a straightforward but important deduction about political calculations — about foreign policy, national security, vital interests and so on — prior to a decision to use armed force. Put simply, these prior political calculations need as much if not more rigour as the strategic calculations to create strategy and guide the use of force. Otherwise the strategy will be built on weak foundations.

The international relations theorist Professor Booth suggests that whilst 'Clausewitz helped coin our clichés for the age when wars were rational, national and instrumental ... Bernard Brodie helped coin our clichés for the age of nuclear deterrence, when the threat and use of force as an instrument of statecraft for the great powers became more problematic and when general war became functionally (though not practically) obsolete.' Booth concludes that no modern scholar has matched Brodie. I agree and we will draw regularly from his thinking in the chapters that follow.[49]

Vietnam

Few wars have been more studied than Vietnam. Fought, if you like, as a 'campaign' in the US grand strategy of 'containment', the historical sense is of the political hand being consciously pushed into the strategic mangle, notwithstanding numerous warnings. George Kennan, the great US diplomat, testified to the Senate Foreign Relations Committee just one year into the campaign: 'Vietnam is not a region of major military, industrial importance [and] it is difficult to believe that any developments of the world situation would be determined in normal circumstances by what happens on that territory.'[50] Furthermore, as Brodie noted:

> [The US engagement in Vietnam should have been guided by] a conception that ought to be utterly commonplace in strategic discourse and in related national policy decisions but that seems on the contrary to be often neglected or omitted. It is the conception of reasonable price and of its being applied to strategy and national policy — the idea that some ends or objectives are worth paying a good deal for and others are not. The latter include ends that are no doubt desirable but which are worth attempting only if the price can with confidence be kept relatively low.[51]

Americans were thus fighting a war in a country of peripheral value to their grand strategy of containment and the costs were disproportionate and growing.

The factors cited that led to the defeat are many. In John Nagl's view, a key feature was the US Army's inability to adapt its Jominian concept of warfare based on mass, firepower and manoeuvre warfare to one suited to the politically nuanced needs of counter-insurgency warfare.[52] In H.R. McMaster's view, strategic issues played a crucial part. In particular, he argues that US President, Lyndon B. Johnson's desire to protect the national political consensus needed for his domestic 'Great Society' programme led him to deceive Congress and the American people about the true nature of the war. His Secretary of Defence, Robert McNamara, supported this deception and promoted a strategy of graduated military pressure, deliberately suppressing military and intelligence advice that argued against the strategy. The Joint Chiefs of Staff were too beset with inter-service wrangling to offer and promote strongly a coherent alternative.[53] And in Colonel Summers' view, Vietnam was lost, above all, because of a failure of strategy. If so, then Vietnam was the antithesis of Malaya.

The US had also ignored Clausewitz and committed a classic mistake by failing to understand the nature of the war. Summers judged this failure due in part to the ideas of 'such limited war theorists as Robert Osgood and Thomas Schelling' who shared in the:

> happy belief that the study of limited war in no way depended on any actual knowledge about war ... military problems are no proper part of a theory of limited war because limited war is an essentially diplomatic instrument, a tool for bargaining with the enemy ... military forces are not for fighting but for signalling.'[54]

Testimony again to the influence — positive and negative — of ideas in war, this was a costly conceptual mistake, because the US were dealing with an enemy who was 'playing by the old rules, where the very object of war is victory ... and these old rules proved decisive.'[55]

With weak thinking in both the political and pseudo-military camps and a war that was hard to justify at home, it is not difficult to spot the seeds and fertilizer of the failure. Brodie, Nagl, McMaster and Summers come at Vietnam from different perspectives and no one is likely to be able to pin down the exact causality but their views combined provide an excellent insight into the pathology of the failure. Ultimately, success or failure hinged on political and military leadership. Johnson and McNamara and their advisors, military and civil, parented a strategic defeat.

Wylie and Beaufre

We will close our discussion of the Modern Epoch by looking at the insights of two Cold War officers, an American sailor-scholar and a French soldier-scholar.

Rear Admiral Wylie's overarching desire was to bring order to the art of strategy making. After Clausewitz's *On War*, Professor Gray regards Wylie's incisive book *Military Strategy: a general theory of power control*[56] as the best book on strategy. Gray overstates the case but Wylie's writing sets the standard for clarity.

Wylie cautions us about using 'principles of war' — 'no one that I know of has ever discussed the very practical matter of how the principles are used to generate a strategy.'[57] But his key insight is on different patterns in strategy, which he describes as 'two hitherto unrecognized general operational patterns of strategy ... sequential and cumulative patterns.'[58] Sequential strategies unfold step by step. Each new step can be taken only after the previous step has been successfully negotiated. The strategy succeeds when the chain is complete. Whereas in cumulative strategies, individual actions are independent of one another, but add up to a collective result. An example of a sequential strategy in practice would be the American's approach to the Pacific campaign between 1943 and 1945. An example of a cumulative strategy would be Britain's approach to the Battle of the Atlantic between 1939 and 1944. In practice, strategy tends to incorporate both patterns, but the distinction is useful and we will return to Wylie's idea in Part III.

General André Beaufre's experience was as a soldier in both World Wars, Indochina, Algeria and as commander of the French land forces at Suez. Written in 1963, his great book, *An Introduction to Strategy,* is described by Liddell Hart as 'the most comprehensive and carefully formulated treatise on strategy, brought up to date, that has appeared in this generation — and in many respects surpasses any previous treatise'.[59] Warm words but deserved because Beaufre's work is a rich source of insight.

Beaufre's great contribution is to highlight war's fundamental dialectical nature and strategy's role of guiding the action of opposing social forces.[60] He sets out the matter thus:

> It is the art which enables a man, no matter what the techniques employed, to master the problems set by any clash of wills and as a result to employ the techniques available with maximum efficiency. It is therefore the art of the dialectic of force or, more precisely, the art of the dialectic of two opposing wills using force to resolve their dispute.[61]

We will return to this key quote in later chapters, but Beaufre also has other important insights for us. Strategy must always be designed to suit the circumstances of the case. Military decisions come about through the moral disintegration of the enemy.

His final insight is very much in keeping with our Darwinistic view of strategy and strategy makers and a particularly appropriate ending for the *Modern Epoch*: 'In war the loser deserves to lose because his defeat must result from errors of thinking, made either before or during the conflict.'[62]

Conclusion

There has been much to cover in the *Modern Epoch* and I am grateful to the reader for having stayed the course. In return, the chapters that follow may not be easier but they will be shorter.

And so to conclude, the key politico-military events of the *Modern Epoch* were the two World Wars, unprecedented in geographic scale and the destructive power of the fighting forces. Navies, armies and air forces fielded diverse arrays of weapons and the resulting complexity required equally complex military hierarchies for command and control. The forces were also short-sighted in comparison to their reach and thus proved to be rather ponderous strategic instruments.

Politically, the divergent views, apparent before the First World War, on the use of war as a political instrument persisted into the inter-war years. But now they aligned more closely with the dominant political philosophies. The left and right wing dictatorships of the Axis powers and the Soviet Union fought wars for political purposes in the inter-war years. But in the centre, the great Western democracies adopted a more pacific approach, albeit in isolationist and appeasement guises. World War II changed this. Having defeated totalitarian Fascism, the great democracies now found themselves in (what they perceived to be) a Third (Cold) World War against totalitarian Socialism. By the mid-1970s, with the former old world colonies largely independent, war assumed two political guises: either proxy war between the two superpowers; or a ragtag of wars in the third world. Vietnam (and Afghanistan) showed us the limits of the superpowers' power. But the key point is that, apart from the early years after World War I, throughout the *Modern Epoch* the willingness to use armed force for political purposes persisted.

What of strategy? And what of the ideas in the growing literature on strategy? As we have seen, sometimes these ideas were ignored. And other times they were applied unintelligently and their influence was unhelpful. But this should not cause us to ignore such thinking, rather we should use it in a more informed and critical way.

To help this, as in the previous two chapters, let us summarize the key insights encountered during this tour of the *Modern Epoch*, re-ordered to suit our purposes:

- A clear and sober analysis of your vital national interests is essential in order for your higher policy to have firm foundations.

- The political purpose for an operation or war must satisfy some rational criteria and thus be based on a rational calculation. But you need also to keep in mind the concept of reasonable price, noting that some objects are worth paying a good deal for and others are not.

- Making strategy is hard work and requires the dedicated time of the political and military leaders who will execute it.

- The political environment in which politicians operate is evidentially different from the strategic environment of diplomats and military officers and less conducive to longer term planning and thinking. A specific example is that partners in coalitions may not share common objectives in war and this may lead to different views on the right course of action.

- Flexible strategy needs to have adaptability 'designed in', but also requires a corresponding adaptability in the organizations and mindsets of those who execute it.

- The psychological impact of your actions can be as important as the physical impact. Actions that shock the higher leadership of your opponent may have a disproportionate value.

- Your ability to exercise command of the sea or air or to deny its use to your opponent, is a key factor in overall strategic success.

- Politico-military strategy is fundamentally dialectical in nature. Thus communication with your enemy never absolutely ceases during a war.

- In as much as it influences operational performance, theory is a key factor in the pattern of events in war. Some principles of war have an enduring quality but there are no invariable principles and the relevance of each must be judged according to the context of the time and the circumstances of the case.

- Ultimately, failure in war is due to errors in thinking, made either before or during the conflict.

Again many of these ideas may seem obvious to us now, but the record shows that political and military leaders of the *Modern Epoch* regularly ignored them, sometimes with grave results. This is because, after World War II, strategy lost its way. In part, this was because of the urgent need to develop theory for nuclear strategy but also because, in the very act of developing nuclear theory, ideas from other academic disciplines were introduced into conventional strategy, many of which proved unworkable in real war. Yet nothing in the analysis so far seems to undermine my view that superior strategy is a key factor in success in armed conflict and war. If so, then the lack of a modern theory of strategy making should be of concern to those of us who believe that, when we use force in the 21st century, we should do so wisely.

Chapter 5

Modern Theory
Contemporary Thinkers, Military Doctrine & Corporate Theory

We should not deceive ourselves that we have the ability to start from scratch with completely fresh ideas and, guided merely by logic, to fashion a strategy according to the needs of our time ... For better or for worse we shall be applying our intellects, as presently furnished, to new and baffling problems and whether the results will be good or bad depends on some extent to the character of the furnishings — whether they are mere habits of which we have not reconsidered for a long time or on the contrary, ideas which are old only because they have a deserved long life.

Bernard Brodie

Introduction

General Beaufre observed in 1963 that the number of general treatises on strategy making was remarkably small and this remains true today.[1] Why is this so? The public scrutiny of events in Afghanistan and Iraq is intense and unremitting. So too is the responding blizzard of research articles from strategic studies departments of universities and political think tanks. So why is there so little thinking on strategy making? Perhaps the answer is simple. Strategy makers have been too busy to step back and reflect and scholars too far removed from the decision making to understand the gap and recognize the likely link between theoretical shortfall and operational setback. But this is speculation — what matters now is to address the shortfall.

Modern military doctrine is an obvious first place to search for insights. Military doctrine is the language of combat and should, one would have thought, have much to say about strategy. And yet, at the strategic level, the doctrine cupboard is strangely bare. Doctrine is nevertheless important, not because of the strategic insights, but rather because it conditions military minds — and thus has an indirect effect on strategy making.

A second potential source is the work of modern scholars of strategy, but in these the insights tend to be tucked away as tantalising snippets in broader analyses on war, general strategy and campaign histories. Indeed, only one significant author, the former US soldier Professor Dick Yarger, has written a general theory for *making* strategy.

There is a third potential source, the corporate world where there is a large body of thinking on corporate strategy making. Indeed, according to Professors Mintzberg, Ahlstrand and Lampel, there are ten different schools of corporate strategy making. Although modern business jargon is as impressively impenetrable as modern military jargon, the competitive philosophy in corporate literature resonates with that of politico-military strategy. For me, the potential for read-across is clear, albeit the actual read-across is not always exact. As we shall see, we need to be selective and thoughtful when we do so. Some areas of business theory are very relevant in the politico-military arena, others less so or not at all.

Military Doctrine

Military doctrine is our first potential source for modern theory. Doctrine draws from historical and contemporary practice but is also significantly influenced by the theory of the great strategic thinkers. For instance, important aspects of the thinking of Clausewitz and Jomini can be identified within modern military doctrine. It is defined thus:

> Put most simply, doctrine is 'that which is taught'. Military doctrine is defined by the North Atlantic Treaty Organisation (NATO) as 'fundamental principles by which military forces guide the actions in support of objectives. It is authoritative, but requires judgement in its application'. ... Its purpose is to guide, explain and educate and to provide the basis for further study and informed debate.[2]

What sets military doctrine apart from other theory is that it has, at its heart, the idea of contest. It is broad in its scope and seeks to inform the totality of military operations, from strategic down to tactical, across the spectrum of conflicts and throughout the different military environments, be they land, sea or air.

That said, military doctrine says less about high level strategy making than one might have expected — its focuses more at the lower operational and tactical levels. But it nevertheless influences politico-military strategy making in three interrelated ways:

- First, doctrine establishes a common technical language for use when talking about military operations.

- Second, doctrine draws the lessons of history and modern campaigns into a common body of knowledge that is a key source of reference — conscious and unconscious — for military strategy makers and planners.

- Third, because doctrine tends — for better or (sometimes) worse — to shape the thinking of young military officers early in their careers, it inevitably influences the way they think later.

Because of its influence on military minds when strategy making, I want to draw out here those terms and ideas within contemporary doctrine that have the most influence on strategy making. This is not a lengthy examination. For the budding doctrine masochist, there is a lifetime's worth of punishment out there in the doctrine literature. My aim, instead, is to introduce the reader to some of the important terms and explain how they are used. I am not seeking to provide detailed derivations of the terms but rather some simple translations of this vocabulary of war. But I hope that, through this brief introduction, the reader will also get a sense of military doctrine, of how the language is used and in particular of its conditioning influence on the military mind when in the problem-solving mode.

I have selected the enduring terms that seem to me most likely to influence strategic thinking. Although my sources are mostly British, the differences in definitions between Western countries, particularly NATO countries, are not generally significant:

- **The Principles of War** — military organizations in Western nations routinely maintain a list of 'principles of war', as a simplified distillation of theory and experience for military officers to draw on. The doctrine authors point out: '[Principles of war] are not a checklist which guarantees success. However, if applied with judgement, they provide guidance in the planning and conduct of operations at all levels and they offer criteria against which a proposed course of action may be tested.'[3] Recall that, as we saw in Chapter 2, the idea of principles of war is a Jominian one, as indeed are two of the individual principles, further evidence of the influence of ideas on war throughout history.[4]

- **The Aim** — the first principle of war is the one with the greatest claim to universal applicability — 'selection and maintenance of the aim'. The point is simply that in war, as in any of life's great endeavours, success rests on selecting and defining your aim and then pursuing it relentlessly, notwithstanding competing pressures. At our strategic level, this principle translates into the need to understand clearly what your political objective is and then keep it in the front of your mind as you create and execute your strategy.

- **Centre-of-Gravity** — 'Success in conflict can be achieved through identifying and controlling or destroying the enemy's centre of gravity. The centre of gravity was defined by Clausewitz as, "the hub of all power and movement on which everything depends ... the point at which all our energies should be directed." A more modern description is that characteristic, capability or location from which a military force, nation or alliance derives freedom of action, physical strength or the will to fight.'[5] Although Clausewitz is generally seen as the originator of the idea of centre of gravity in war, recall that he was writing at a time when Newtonian physics was ascendant. So, as with all doctrine, we must use the centre of gravity metaphor with care and recognize that it will not always be useful in problem solving. For example, in a worldwide terrorist network such as Al-Qaeda, it is harder to pin down a centre of gravity or at least one that is tangible and susceptible to force.

- **Lines of Operation** — 'in a campaign or operation, a line linking decisive points in time and space on the path to the centre of gravity'[6] is described as a line of operation. Again, the idea has historical form and was clarified by Jomini as *lignes d'opérations*. Today we use the term to describe a particular work stream of inter-related activities in a campaign. For example, today's military-strategic campaign plans for Afghanistan will typically (although not necessarily correctly) be based around three to five classic 'lines of operation.' Earlier plans tended to encompass three — *security, development, governance* — whereas in later plans these had grown to five — *combat operations, train & employ indigenous security forces, essential life support services, governance* and *economic development*. The key to choosing particular lines of operation is to, first, create your strategy, then decide what streams of activity critically support your strategy and group them in a coherent way.

- **Manoeuvrist Approach** — the ugly term *manoeuvrist* is important because it is fashionable and guides much Western military thinking at the operational and tactical levels — not always for the good. 'The *manoeuvrist* approach to operations is one in which shattering the enemy's overall cohesion and will to fight, rather than his material, is paramount.'[7] The concept draws on various sources of inspiration, but Napoleon's actions, the thinking of Jomini and Liddell Hart, Von Seekt's analysis of Germany's defeat in the World War I and the operational success of *blitzkrieg* in World War II all play important parts. The key point is that manoeuvre is an alternative to attrition — if battles can be fought which disrupt and defeat the enemy psychologically then this must be less costly than the attritional affairs of World War I. The problem is that the idea is attractive in theory, but not always easy to use in practice. We examine manoeuvre in more detail Chapter 8.

- **Momentum** — 'In military terms, momentum is the measure of effect that a formation or unit that is moving at speed can have. It is the product of that moving force's size and speed (mass x velocity).'[8] The term momentum is most usually used in land operations and, as this quote shows, is another example of Newtonian metaphors in use.

- **_Tempo_** — 'Tempo is the rate at which events are driven in relation to the enemy and the situation'[9] and is an important term in _manoeuvrist_ warfare:

  'Forces that can maintain high tempo, with fast decision making cycles, can seize the initiative and exploit weaknesses of the enemy.'[10]

We see here the encouragement to operate more quickly, in both an intellectual and physical sense, than the enemy, deduced from the idea of manoeuvre — again useful, but not always easy to employ in practice.

- **_Main Effort_** — 'A concentration of forces or means, in a particular area, where a commander seeks to bring about a decision.'[11] There is, in the term 'main effort', a sense of mechanics and leverage, but the phrase is also used more loosely to describe something that is the top operational or tactical priority in a battle or campaign.

- **_Mission Command_** — is the term for a style of command in which subordinates are given a clear understanding of their commander's higher intentions, together with their place in the plan, but then left to carry out their mission with the maximum freedom of action.

This technical language that military doctrine creates is both a strength and a weakness. It is a strength because it provides an excellent shorthand for clipped operational and tactical discussions where time is of the essence. For example, when I talk to an Army or RAF or NATO colleague about the 'main effort', we both know that I am talking about 'a concentration of forces or means, in a particular area, where a commander seeks to bring about a decision.' But it is also a weakness because, whilst the terms are (generally) well understood in the military club, to outsiders they are at best semi-intelligible and at worst impenetrable military gobbledegook. At the strategic level, where the roles of political, military and diplomatic strategy makers are so interleaved, the language thus has the potential to confuse and needs to be used intelligently.

Military doctrine also suffers, like business theory, from fashion and fad. Two contemporary examples illustrate the point. First, a new notion of 'effects-based warfare' is fashionable in modern Western doctrine. The idea behind this is that you have to decide what military effect you are seeking to achieve before deciding which military means to employ to achieve the effect. Rather a blinding glimpse of the obvious, but rafts of paper and years of thinking and conferences have been sacrificed in its honour. Second, there is much official literature on the idea of 'network' warfare — 'network centric warfare' in the US and 'network enabled capability' in the UK. These words simply spice up the idea of using military internets to share and manage information in real time. The wise military commander is the one who is able to delineate fad from enduring substance in doctrine and see these fashions through a common sense lens. Like all new ideas, some fade quickly and others stand the test of time.

But these cautions accepted, doctrine is the language of contest and combat — which, ultimately, is what politico-military strategy is about. And it guides the way that the military operates. As I write, one of the key documents that is guiding contemporary operations in Afghanistan is the US Army and US Marine Corps' Counter-insurgency Field Manual.[12] The doctrine therein has critically shifted the US approach in both campaigns from one based on killing insurgents to one based on providing security for local populations.

So doctrine matters. It is an important reference for us as strategy makers — politicians, officials and diplomats, as well as military officers — when we think about current or future operations. But the key point is that doctrine is a source of guidance, not a source of inspiration. When doctrine leads, as it very often does — even now — to indoctrination, then we will get into trouble. The French Army's rigid adoption of the doctrinal principle of the offensive prior to 1914 and its messianic application in early World War I is a classic case in point — the precise costs are difficult to estimate, but run easily into tens of thousands of squandered French lives.

Contemporary Strategy Making Theory

Turning to modern writers, the general lack of thinking and writing on politico-military strategy is perplexing. An explanation might be that politico-military strategy in the *Information Transformation* is inevitably work in progress.[13] There are certainly those who have made singular contributions on strategic issues — Sir Michael Howard and Sir Lawrence Freedman are two of the field's great historians and Professor Colin Gray stands out as a prolific purveyor of insights on strategy. But few, if any, seem to have written on theory in strategy *making*. Indeed, there are just two exceptions worthy of discussion, Edward Luttwak and Harry Yarger.

Edward Luttwak, an influential war theorist of the 20th century, is of interest to us for a single idea, the notion of paradox in strategy, captured in the first paragraph of his book, *The Paradox of Strategy*:

> Consider an ordinary tactical choice, of the sort frequently made in war. An advancing force can move toward its objective on one of two roads, one good and one bad, the first broad, direct and well-paved, the second narrow, circuitous and unpaved. Only in the conflictual realm of strategy would the choice arise at all, for it is only if combat is possible that a bad road can be good precisely because it is bad and may therefore be less strongly held or even left unguarded by the enemy.

This simple idea is closely related to Liddell Hart's *indirect approach*, the idea of doing what your opponent least expects. Implicitly Luttwak warns us to be thoughtful when using linear thinking and cause-and-effect logic to shape strategy for war. The important deduction is that rationally conceived and executed strategies will not always lead to rational war outcomes, not least because 'the enemy gets a vote'.

There are more insights in Professor Yarger's work — but this is not surprising because he is the only modern writer on military strategy *making*. A US Army Colonel and Vietnam veteran, Professor Yarger's first monograph, *Strategic Theory for the 21st century: the Little Book on Big Strategy*[14] is just 71 pages and the tenor of his thinking is clear early on:

> Why study a theory of strategy? Theory's value lies not in a prescription for success but in how it helps us expand and discipline our thinking.[15]

> Strategic thinking is difficult. It is best viewed as both art and a science. … History's great strategists possessed 'a very highly developed mental aptitude' for both art and science.[16]

> It is useful to consider the roles of strategists today[:] … leader, practitioner and theorist. … The leader provides the vision, inspiration organizational skills, direction and personal impetus … The practitioner thoroughly comprehends the levels of strategy and their relationships and develops strategy. He translates broad policy guidance into integrated strategies that lead to policy success. The theorist develops theoretical concepts through study and thought and teaches and mentors others. A master of the strategic art is proficient in all three areas [17]

The last sentence echoes a conclusion from the historical analysis of our earlier chapters. When the strategic leader is also a first class strategist and an historical scholar, the combination is powerful — witness Frederick and Moltke.

Like Clausewitz, Yarger seeks to improve judgement, not provide recipes for success. He suggests fourteen premises for a theory of strategy, five of which I highlight here:[18]

- Any strategy creates a dilemma for the strategist and other actors, because it introduces change into the strategic environment even when it seeks to maintain the *status quo*.

- 'Friction' is the difference between the ideal strategy and the applied strategy — how it is supposed to work versus how it actually unfolds.

- Strategy has a symbiotic relationship with time — a key component of strategic competency is thinking in time.

- Strategy is cumulative — once enacted, its effects become part of the play of continuity and change.

- In strategy, efficiency is desirable but subordinate to effectiveness, which is not to say that efficiency is not desired.

These are important thoughts and evidence of the coherence of Yarger's work.

One final thought from Yarger is worth exploring. As we have seen earlier, strategic thinkers often seek to organize events and actions into tidy levels: political, military-strategic, operational and tactical. But as Yarger explains, the modern reality makes this increasingly difficult:

> With advances in transportation and communications, there has been a spatial and temporal convergence of strategy, operational art and tactics. Increasingly, in part due to increasing communications capabilities, events at the tactical

level have strategic consequences.[19]

Indeed, I would take Yarger's thinking further and note that, as well as having strategic consequences, events at the tactical level increasingly have political consequences. A key political feature of the *Information Transformation* is the increased politicization of war, in no small part due to the media's own transformation — as such, Clausewitz was remarkably prescient in his seminal observation of war as the continuation of politics with the addition of other means.

Corporate Strategy

As we turn to our third potential source of modern theory — from politico-military strategy making famine to corporate strategy making feast — I will draw particularly on the excellent overview of the corporate strategy making schools, *Strategy Safari*,[20] by Patrick Mintzberg, Bruce Ahlstrand and Joseph Lampel. And to help give context and colour, I will also draw out similarities and contrasts between the two forms of strategy using examples from the politico-military past. The evolution of thinking in the discipline is complex but there is no need here for anything more than a short introduction.

The historical linkage between corporate strategy and military strategy is closer than one might first expect. In a seminal text, Igor Ansoff, one the earliest of the corporate strategy thinkers, tracks the discipline's origin to the years after World War II, noting that:

> The concept of strategy is relatively new to management literature. Its historical origin lies in the military art, where it is a broad, rather vaguely defined, 'grand' concept of a military campaign of *application* of large-scale forces against an enemy. Strategy is contrasted to *tactics*, which is the specific scheme for the *employment* of allocated resources. The bridge to business usage was provided in 1948 by Von Neumann

and Morgenstern in their now-famous theory of games.[221]

Ansoff acknowledges the corporate debt to the 'many years of thought and study in the United States military services which led to the development of a doctrine and methodology of military decision making.'[22] Note that Ansoff is referring, in this quote, not to strategy's great theorists, such as Clausewitz, but rather to the US Army Field Manual of 1954, that is to the military doctrine of his time.[23] The influence of military doctrine is, it seems, more pervasive than one might have thought. Fundamentally, though, corporate strategy grew out of military strategy, drawing on the ideas of military theorists, military doctrine and, no doubt, the World War II experiences of military officers demobilising into corporate life.

But before we start to think about the implications in corporate theory for the politico-military world, two cautions need to be borne in mind. First, corporate strategy focuses generally on the whole firm as an entity — it is about the firm's very survival and prosperity. Indeed, in the theoretical sense, the entity of the firm or corporation in the corporate strategy literature corresponds to the entity of the nation-state in the politico-military literature. Christensen *et al*'s seminal Harvard Business School work, *Business Policy: Text & Cases*, sets out the perspective:

> Corporate strategy is the pattern of decisions that (1) determines, shapes and reveals its objectives, purposes or goals (2) produces the principal policies and plans for achieving these goals; and (3) defines the business the company intends to be in, the kind of economic and human organisation it intends to be and the nature of the economic and noneconomic contribution it intends to make to its shareholders, employees, customers and communities.'[24]

And so, whereas in politico-military strategy making the political objective should be known at the outset or at least only need clarification, in corporate strategy, strategy making calculates what the corporate objectives should be, allocates the resources and designs the courses of action, all under one banner. In other words, corporate strategy does *ways*, *means* and *ends*, whereas politico-military strategy tends to focus on *ways*.

Second, politico-military strategy works in armed conflict or war. And as we shall see later, armed conflict or war is an irrational political environment, indeed uniquely so. Thus although the conceptual work for politico-military strategists may initially seem easier — we focus just on *ways* — the nature of the war environment in which we and our agents fighting in the field, operate tests us like no other human activity.

These cautions accepted, there are many useful insights in the corporate literature and my aim in this short corporate overview is to complete our fishing trip for insights. But I also hope to stimulate thinking and help us focus on the creative act of making strategy, prior to our getting to grips, in Part II, with the heart of the matter, the creation and execution of politico-military strategy. So 'now for something completely different.'

Thinking about Strategy Formulation and Formation

In their popular and informative corporate strategy text, *Strategy Safari*, Mintzberg, Ahlstrand and Lampel identify ten different schools of strategy formulation and formation. As we shall see, some schools are more relevant to us than others but, before we examine them more closely, we need to understand the important distinction that the authors make between strategy *formulation* and strategy *formation*.

Mintzberg, Ahlstrand and Lampel's use of the term strategy formation rather than strategy formulation is deliberate; their point being that a strategy is not always consciously formulated, but sometimes forms as a result of the individual actions of the different actors on the strategic stage.[25] As such, strategy can be thought of both as *plan,* that is a direction or guide or course of action into the future and also as *pattern,* that is a consistency of behaviour over time.[26] From personal experience and historical analysis, this distinction is equally pertinent in the politico-military world and worth exploring in more detail. For convenience, from here on I will use the term 'strategy making' to include both 'strategy formulation' and 'strategy formation', but distinguish between formulation and formation when necessary.

The central idea is brought out in Mintzberg's diagram at Figure 5.1. This is an important diagram for us and understanding it will help us in later chapters. You start in the top left hand corner by creating a strategy, our *intended strategy.* As you execute this strategy, some parts of it succeed and other parts fail. The authors term the parts that succeed *deliberate strategy* and the parts that fail *unrealized strategy.* But as you execute the strategy, you also find — in the bottom left hand corner — from field experience that other approaches also succeed on the ground, notwithstanding that you did not envisage them when you first created the intended strategy. The authors term these approaches as *emergent strategy.* And if you're are a competent strategic leader, you progress to the right in the diagram by discarding your *unrealized strategy* and integrating your *emergent strategy* into your *deliberate strategy,* so as to create a *realized strategy* that takes you to your objective. Put more simply, you start with a broad sense of direction, build on the things that do work, discard the things that do not and also integrate new ideas from the field.

There are obvious parallels with politico-military strategy. For example, we can explain both Moltke's axiom that 'no plan survives contact with the enemy' and the command doctrine used in *blitzkrieg* using Mintzberg's framework.

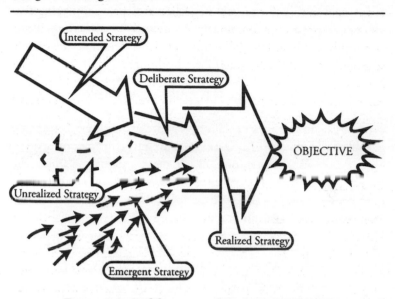

Figure 5.1: Deliberate and Emergent Strategy

Moltke argues that, whatever your starting strategy, after the cataclysm of the first collision of forces in battle, new conditions are created for which strategy must adapt. Or in Mintzberg's terms, because the first contact with the enemy will violently change your assumptions, some of your *intended strategy* must inevitably become *unrealized strategy*.

In *blitzkrieg*, the command approach is based upon the idea that your starting strategy represents only the very broadest of guidance. As the strategy is executed you assume that your field commanders will seize opportunities guided by front line success, rather than rely on detailed direction from on high. Or in Mintzberg's terms, in *blitzkrieg* when you create your *intended strategy* you assume the strong likelihood of *emergent strategy*. Indeed you go further, making conceptual space for *emergent strategy* and then encouraging it to flourish and become the primary source for your *realized strategy*.

Mintzberg, Ahlstrand and Lampel use the formulation-formation distinction to divide their ten strategy making schools into two groups. The first three are strategy formulation schools — the *design school*, the *planning school* and the *positioning school* — and are prescriptive, in that they explain how strategy should be formulated in theory and practice. The last seven are strategy formation schools — the *power school*, the *cultural school*, the *environmental school*, the *entrepreneurial school*, the *cognitive school*, the *learning school* and the *configuration school* — and are descriptive, in that they describe how strategy actually forms in practice.

In what follows, we will use Mintzberg, Ahlstrand and Lampel's taxonomy, but concentrate predominantly on the three schools — *design*, *power* and *learning* — that seem the most relevant to politico-military strategy.

Corporate strategy formulation schools

The design school is the most of influential of the corporate strategy schools and its concepts have formed the basis for undergraduate and MBA corporate strategy courses and for much corporate strategy practice.[27] The school's origins can be traced back to the mid-1950s, but the definitive text — *Business Policy: Text & Cases*[28] — was written at Harvard Business School in 1965. The broad approach is based on seven premises:

- Strategy making should be a deliberate process of conscious thought. Action must flow from reason.

- Responsibility for strategy making should rest with the CEO, who should be the strategist.

- The strategy making model must be simple and informal.

- Only one strategy will be appropriate to a specific situation.

- The design process is complete when strategies appear fully formulated. Mintzberg, Ahlstrand and Lampel describe this lyrically: 'Here ... we find not a Darwinian view of strategy formation, but the biblical version, with strategy as the grand conception, the ultimate choice ... the strategy appears ... at some point in time, fully formulated, ready to be implemented.'

- Strategies should be explicit, so they have to be simple.

- Only when the strategies are fully formulated can they be implemented. Here the authors make a central point: 'Consistent with classical notions of rationality — diagnosis, followed by prescription and then action — the design school clearly separates thinking from action.'

Design school thinking is still highly influential in corporate strategy. It is, for example, the source of the analytic framework of SWOT — 'the assessment of the [internal] Strengths and Weaknesses of the organisation in the light of the [external] Opportunities and Threats in its environment.'[29] But Mintzberg, Ahlstrand and Lampel explain that, although the design school gives us analytic tools, such as the SWOT framework, to help us prepare the ground for the 'creative act' of strategy making, it says very little on the central question of how strategies are actually created. In other words, there is little here to help us work out how to think things through as we go about our strategy making.

But more importantly, in the seventh premise above, Mintzberg, Ahlstrand and Lampel introduce a key general issue for us — the relationship between thinking and action in strategy making. Essentially the design school splits thinking and action — strategy creation and strategy execution are separate acts. But there is no logical reason why this should be so. Indeed common sense and experience tell us that a theory that sees thinking and action as separate will be flawed. In the real world, we know that thinking and action constantly interact. As strategy is created and executed, so new information arrives and events occur that cause us — or should cause us — to re-examine and adapt our strategy.

At least this is how we try to work in the politico-military world. Indeed, if we accept Moltke's tenet that 'no plan survives contact with the enemy', then there is a simple but powerful theoretical argument to say that thinking and action must constantly interact. Because at the heart of the Moltke truism is the idea that when strategy is executed, new conditions are created that force a reappraisal — and very likely an adjustment — of our strategy. Therefore, strategies can never be 'fully formulated', but rather are always being fine-tuned or refined in response to the results of action.

It is perhaps because of this reality that the idea of a feed-back loop between military strategy and action has been prominent for some time. Indeed Colonel John Boyd, one of the leading air power theorists, went so far as to systemize such thinking, with the concept of the 'OODA loop' — observe orientate, decide, act.[30] Introducing the OODA concept, based on his thinking about air combat during the Korean and Vietnam wars, Boyd proposed that success depended not on understanding and using the OODA feedback loop, but rather on your ability to use it more quickly than your enemy. In the jargon, the key to strategic success is to be able 'to operate within the enemy decision cycle.'

Turning briefly to the first of the design school's two children, Mintzberg, Ahlstrand and Lampel suggest that what distinguishes the planning school is its assumption that strategic planning will deliver strategy mechanistically, 'analysis will provide synthesis.'[31] But for me as a military professional, there is another equally important distinction. The school's title tells me that what is being described is a *strategic-planning process* — not a *strategy making process* — and this is an occasion where politico-military and corporate thinking appear to be at variance.

In the politico-military world, planning has real value. Without planning, it would be near impossible to mount even the most modest of military operations. But the key point is that we see strategy making and planning as different things. Plans turn strategy into action. Planning is strategy's servant, not its creative parent, nor its terminological twin. As Yarger explains:

> *Strategy is not planning.* ... it partakes of a different mindset. Planning makes strategy actionable. ... Planning is essentially linear and deterministic. ... The purpose of planning is to create certainty so that people and organisations can act. ... Strategy lays down what is important and to be achieved, sets the parameters for the necessary action.[32]

Just so. A *planning* process should surely produce *plans,* whereas a *strategy making* process should surely produce *strategy.* And if, as Mintzberg, Ahlstrand and Lampel suggest, a lot of businesses got into trouble and lost large amounts of money in the 1980s and 1990s using strategic *planning* processes to make *strategy,* well more fool them.

And of the second child, what distinguished the positioning school from the design and planning schools was its preference for generic rather than tailored strategy. The design school and planning school believed that strategy should be tailor-made strategy for every situation. Whereas the positioning school believed that a relatively small suite of *generic* strategies — so called 'positions' — could be deduced from case studies and theoretical analysis and matched to particular market and corporate conditions. There are parallels here with the theories of the limited war scholars of the Cold War, such as Schelling. One could argue that, in Vietnam, Johnson and McNamara adopted a (prefabricated limited-war) counter-insurgency strategy to deal with an (assumed) revolutionary insurgency. But in most other respects, the positioning school adopted the design school's main premises.

Let us draw this overview of the Formulation Schools of corporate strategy making to a close, with a point which is fundamental to our quest for strategy making insight. What Mintzberg, Ahlstrand and Lampel convincingly expose is that, when you examine the design, planning and positioning schools to find out how to create strategy, the cupboard seems all but bare.

Proponents of all three schools believe that strategy should be consciously formulated, but all are fairly coy when it comes to how. In the design school, strategy 'emerges' through an unexplained creative process. In the planning school — even assuming one elects to take the rather dubious approach of using a planning system to make strategy — strategy is somehow 'revealed', after an analytical process has cleared away the contextual scrub. And in the positioning school, no creation is necessary, because it has already been done by others: all one needs to do is to take the (consultancy?) caddy's view, reach into the (business school theory?) golf bag, draw the right club and (paying the consultant as he departs?) hey presto. But when it comes to explaining how strategy is created, there is precious little to say. To put it another way, notwithstanding that these strategy formulation schools purport to consciously formulate strategy, none of them can really say how they do it. This illogicality matters less to the strategy formation schools who, to recall, believe that strategy forms in unconscious ways, largely in response to a range of external drivers; and it is to these formation schools that we now turn.

Corporate strategy formation schools

Although Mintzberg, Ahlstrand and Lampel identify seven strategy formation schools, we need concentrate on just two — power and learning — both of which contain much to interest us.

Mintzberg, Ahlstrand and Lampel describe the power school as one which 'characterizes strategy formation as an overt process of influence, emphasizing the use of power and politics to negotiate strategies favourable to particular interests.'[33] The school distinguishes between micro-power used *in* the organization by 'internal actors conflicting with their colleagues, usually out of self-interest' and macro-power used *by* the organization 'acting out of its own self-interest in conflict or cooperation with other organizations.'[34] The power school dismisses the idea that strategists are rational actors. Instead strategy making is about 'bargaining and compromise among conflicting individuals, groups and coalitions ... accordingly it is not possible to formulate, let alone implement, optimal strategies.' This idea is useful. But although there will no doubt be bells ringing for politico-military strategists, we need to interpret it to suit our purposes.

In the politico-military world, micro-power is probably best thought of as internal negotiation and conflict amongst a nation-state's main strategic actors. An example would be the World War II debate in the US over the best Pacific strategy, with General McArthur and Admiral King in opposing (Army and Navy) camps. McArthur advocated an indirect land campaign via the South Eastern Pacific Islands and the Philippines, King a direct maritime campaign across the Pacific. Roosevelt settled for a compromise.

For macro-power, the politico-military parallel is strategy making in coalitions or alliances. For example, in the strategy making debates in 1942, the US and UK agreed on a 'Germany first' strategy. The US was not, though, persuaded by Churchill and Alanbrooke's argument for an *indirect approach* to Germany, via the supposedly soft underbelly of the Mediterranean, but they nevertheless acceded for reasons of alliance unity. By 1943 though, power in the coalition had passed to the Americans and the British necessarily fell into line with the American preference that Normandy take priority over the Mediterranean. In power school parlance, macro-power for Allied strategy making had passed to the Americans.

The sense in the power school analysis is that it is not possible to formulate optimal strategy, because micro-power and macro-power politics prevent this. But this in turn prompts an important question — is there such a thing as optimal strategy?

Taking the micro-power case and internal coalitions; which is better? A theoretically 'optimal' strategy that has little support amongst the team who must execute it? Or a theoretically sub-optimal strategy that has the team's full support? The same question arises for macro power and external coalitions. Which is better? A theoretically optimal strategy that has no support amongst Allies? Or a theoretically sub-optimal strategy to which all Allies are signed up? At the heart of this debate is a question about the function of strategy. Is the role of strategy simply to solve external problems? Or does it also have a role in binding key players? This is a central question and one which we will consider in Part III, when we examine coalition strategy.

The learning school is an equally, if not more, important school to us. Its origins can be traced back to an article in 1959 by Charles Lindblom in which he suggested that:

> Policy is not made once and for all; it is made and re-made endlessly. Policy making is a process of successive approximation to some desired objectives in which what itself is desired continues to change under reconsideration. … A wise policy maker thus consequently expects that his policies will achieve only part of what he hopes and at the

same time will produce unanticipated consequences he would have preferred to avoid. If he proceeds through a succession of incremental changes, he avoids serious lasting mistakes [35]

Mintzberg, Ahlstrand and Lampel set out the school's primary assumption — 'According to this school, strategies emerge as people, sometimes acting individually but more often collectively, come to learn about a situation as well as their organization's capability of dealing with it … Eventually they converge to patterns of behaviour that work.'[36] As we noted earlier, there are clear parallels here with the politico-military experience. The modern military concept of 'mission command' — where the commander issues broad directions to his or her subordinates and then leaves them to act accordingly — is founded on similar thinking. And so too was *blitzkrieg* — recall Geyer's description:

> *Blitzkrieg* … was not new. The core of these operations did not consist of any particular use of new means of warfare, but in a kind of operational opportunism that knew no pre-set and standardized methods, only the fullest possible exploitation of success with all available means in pursuit of the ultimate goal of overthrowing the enemy by breaking the will of its leadership. *Blitzkrieg* lived off the destruction of a systematic approach to military command decisions. It was the opposite of a doctrine. *Blitzkrieg* operations consisted of an avalanche of actions that were sorted out less by design than by success.[37]

Compare this thinking with the learning school's main premises:[38]

- Complex environments preclude deliberate control. Strategy making must above all take the form of a process of learning over time in which, at the limit, formulation and implementation become indistinguishable.

- The leader must learn too.

- The learning proceeds in an emergent fashion.

- The role of leadership thus becomes not to preconceive deliberate strategies, but to manage the process of strategic learning, whereby novel strategies can emerge.

- Accordingly, strategies emerge first as patterns out of the past and only later as plans for the future.

Although Mintzberg, Ahlstrand and Lampel criticise the learning school, they do so a touch half heartedly perhaps because, as they freely admit, they are of the learning school.

I have some sympathy too. This is because I would argue that the learning school essentially codifies much of what successful political leaders and military commanders have been doing for decades. Successful leaders have always taken the time to get out on the ground and talk to people. The obvious reason has been to build morale. But the less obvious but equally important benefit has come from 'smelling the air' and assessing progress, which in turn has allowed leaders to adapt their strategy, in the light of feedback and evidence, so as to maximize their chances of success. In the learning school's terms, leaders have been on the prowl — consciously or sub-consciously — for emergent strategy, so as to refine their thinking.

I suspect that the political and military leaders have not been alone in this respect. For example when Jack Welch says, of his time as CEO of General Electric, that 'it's a job that's close to 75% about people and 25% about the other stuff', I imagine that a free benefit of the 75% of his time spent on people would have been the opportunity to 'smell the air' for the ideas of emergent strategy.[39]

Western militaries have gone even further and developed processes to harvest these ideas. This started with the operational analysis science that grew out of World War II and formally gathered and analysed feedback so as to provide advice on how strategy might be adjusted. And now, in any contemporary operation, most Western militaries have military analysts diligently gathering 'lessons identified' or 'lessons learned' at the tactical and operational levels, with the primary aim of learning.

Notwithstanding these parallels, we must not take the learning school's assumptions at face value because, from a politico-military perspective, at least two of the five premises above are open to criticism.

My first difficulty is with the notion that 'complex environments preclude deliberate control.' War is a complex environment, perhaps the most complex, but that does not preclude a degree of control. Otherwise the idea of one or other side having the initiative would be meaningless. Rather, the premise should surely be that, in complex environments such as war, you should recognize that the degree of control you can exercise will, at best, be limited.

My second difficulty is with the notion that the leader's role is not to 'pre-conceive deliberate strategies but rather to manage the process of strategic learning.' From personal experience, it seems clear that the leader's role is to do both, the balance of emphasis depending on the circumstances.

One final difference between corporate and politico-military strategy needs to be highlighted. As we shall see in Chapter 6, a central idea in politico-military strategy making is that of rational calculation from the outset. As we prepare for and then embark on an operation, we will need a clear understanding of what we are trying to achieve and how we are going to do it. In other words, we will need a formulated strategy of some sort. We will thus not have the luxury of being able to adopt, in corporate strategy jargon, a learning school approach.

History has taught us harsh lessons when we have begun operations and wars without adequately formulated strategy — witness the (learning school?) approaches in World War I and Vietnam. But because we need to begin operations with a rationally formulated strategy, this does not mean that ideas from other corporate schools cannot be woven into our strategy making approach thereafter. And not least because, as we have seen, there are insights in these different schools which read directly across to the politico-military sphere. Furthermore, in the absence of a substantive body of thinking on politico-military strategy making, there are few other modern sources.

This in turn leads us to the important concluding point on all of the corporate schools — namely that there seems logically to be nothing to preclude a philosophy of strategy making that draws routinely from two or more of the schools. This in many senses encapsulates the approach of the last of the corporate schools, the configuration school and is a subject to which we will return in Chapter 10 as we flesh out the main principles of a politico-military school of strategy making.

Conclusion

We have usefully cast our eye over modern theory. We have delved into the world of military doctrine — the language of combat but a sparse field for strategic insight. We have looked too at the similarly sparse field of contemporary politico-military strategy making theory, such as it is, limited to all intents and purposes to Professor Yarger's lonely but important work. And we have also scanned the richer ground of academic thinking on corporate strategy making, to my mind the most fertile of the modern sources.

Not all, nor even a majority, of the corporate theory is relevant to our field. But equally there are ideas which do transfer and bolster our box of insights. And although not all of these transferable ideas are new to the politico-military practitioner, they nevertheless help us codify and better understand our own strategy making experiences and approaches.

In the manner of the last three chapters, let me summarize the insights of modern strategy sources, re-ordering them to suit our purpose:

- Military doctrine, like all theory and aggregated experience, is a useful source of reference but must not be a source of inspiration or lead to indoctrination.

- At the strategic level, you must be clear on what your political objective is and then pursue it relentlessly in the face of competing pressures.

- Only one strategy will be appropriate to a specific situation. However, although your strategy should be rationally conceived and executed, it will not always lead to rational war outcomes, not least because 'the enemy gets a vote.' Therefore, strategies can never be 'fully formulated' but rather are always being fine tuned or refined in response to the results of action.

- We can use the term 'friction' to describe the difference between the ideal strategy and the applied strategy — how it is supposed to work versus how it actually unfolds. As strategy is created and executed, so new information arrives and events occur that cause us — or should cause us — to re-examine and adapt our strategy. And the ability to learn strategically is thus key to achieving strategic success.

- Strategy has a symbiotic relationship with time — a key component of strategic competency is thinking in time. In particular, the ability to maintain a tempo that is higher than your opponent, both in an intellectual and physical sense and

to act within your opponent's decision cycle is a significant
advantage.

• Planning is not strategy. Strategy explains how policy
objectives will be delivered. Plans turn strategy into action.

Herewith the final set of pieces for our jigsaw box. Ordered this
way, the corporate ideas seem to blend well with Yarger's and those
of military doctrine. Nevertheless, as with all these ideas and those
in the preceding chapters, the key is for us to be selective and use
them with judgement.

Let me emphasize this concluding point with a semi-light-hearted
interchange from *Strategy Safari*. Towards the end of the book,
Mintzberg, Ahlstrand and Lampel record a criticism from Gaddis,
a fellow business academic, who is not an advocate of their favoured
learning school:

> [Gaddis] … mentions the Roman general Varro, 'an early
> incrementalist … who "did not need any strategy"' … and
> took his superior force into battle against Hannibal … and
> suffered a devastating defeat. Gaddis concludes (with more
> than a touch of sarcasm): 'Apparently a suitable strategy for
> the superior Roman army failed to "emerge" as the battle
> wore on.'[40]

Mintzberg, Ahlstrand and Lampel take gentle theoretical affront at
Gaddis' ironic critique of the learning school:

> This is hardly a fair test: … strategies do not emerge on
> convenient schedules, let alone in the heat of battle.[41]

Their response perhaps needs re-working — it should surely say
that *learning* strategies do not emerge in the heat of battle. And,
light hearted though the exchange is, it reinforces the need for us
as politico-military strategists to be judicious when drawing strategy

making lessons from other disciplines.

Admiral Spruance entered the Battle of Midway in June 1942 with a clear and well thought though operational strategy. In formulating this strategy he had, in all likelihood, been critically influenced by long and detailed analysis in the Naval War College at Newport Rhode Island in the late 1930s. This analysis had shown unequivocally that, when aircraft carriers were pitted against aircraft carriers, the advantage of a first successful strike would be profound. And this insight surely shaped Spruance's crucial decision to 'bet the farm', launch his carriers' entire striking force and score a great American victory. Had he instead relied on a learning strategy, then US success in the Pacific War may have been delayed by months, if not years.

This is not a criticism of Mintzberg, Ahlstrand and Lampel, nor of the idea of learning strategy, but rather a caution to politico-military strategists about using ideas of corporate strategy and other disciplines. For all the similarities, ultimately we live in a different world. We need to apply rigour in our strategic thinking, but we must do it in a way that is tailored for the matters we have at hand.

As we depart from the world of corporate strategy, it is worth reflecting on one final grand strategic point. It was the wealth that corporate strategy helped create in the great Western democracies that was surely the key determinant in the ultimate defeat of totalitarianism in World War II and the Cold War. Thus, although politico-military strategy may have been the intellectual father of corporate strategy, it has reason to be grateful for its prodigal son's efforts in more ways than one.

And so, armed with the modern insights of Yarger and the corporate strategists and aware of the language of military doctrine, our fishing trip for insights is complete. It is time to start to fit the jigsaw pieces together.

PART III:

THEORY

Chapter 6

Strategy's Context
The Information Transformation: 1991-Future

Major interstate war, including nuclear war, indeed interstate war of any kind, fortunately is not much in favour at present. However, the conditions that have produced these facts are certain to change. When they do, the current literature that proclaims the obsolescence of 'old (regular) war' between states or which finds large scale war obsolete because of the slowly growing likelihood of it having a nuclear dimension or proclaims the mature arrival of war's largely extra-statist 'Fourth Generation', will look more than a little foolish. Alas, it is the fate of optimistic prophets to be perpetually disappointed.

Colin Gray

Introduction

What can we say of the contemporary context in which strategy makers will work, a period that I have termed the *Information Transformation*? Militarily, the case for a technological *Information Transformation*, starting around 1991 and still in progress, rests on the phenomenon of the information revolution, in particular developments such as modern computers, electronic information management, global positioning systems (GPS) and miniaturization. These technologies are having a profound impact on modern warfare and the military context in which strategy makers will work.

Politically, 1991 also marks the end of the Cold War, with an apparent victory for the West in the second defining political confrontation of the *Modern Epoch*. Since then, though, the rise of humanitarian interventions such as those in the Balkans and then 9/11 and the consequences in Afghanistan and Iraq, have set a different tone in international politics. There is as yet little international consensus on the efficacy and morality of using armed force to further political objectives but the lessons of Afghanistan and Iraq will be central to Western thinking and will define the new political context in which strategy makers will work.

Until now, we have been backward looking and reflective, but now we will change to a forward looking and predictive approach. Our purpose is to outline the key military and political characteristics of this new security context and, in a similar approach to Chapters 2, 3 and 4, I will do so first by focusing on key trends in military *means* and political *ends*, in so far as they seem likely to bear on strategy making and then speculate on what might be the defining issues in the coming decades. Detailed prediction is a mug's game, but we can perhaps in sketch out some of the future's structure and thus give some sense of the canvas on which strategy makers will be working.

Military Trends in the Information Transformation

The information revolution has been felt throughout the military. Navies and air forces have led the way and, at the start of the *Information Transformation*, in 1991 solid-state computers were already in general service in ships and aircraft. But the new sophistication has come at significant financial cost. And taken together, these two interlinked yet competing trends — rapid technological development and increasing cost pressure — are now changing the nature of the forces that defined the *Modern Epoch*. This is happening in ways that we do not yet fully understand but that are nevertheless having a profound impact on armed forces and, in particular, on those qualities that defined the forces of the *Modern Epoch* — force complexity, area firepower, importance of mass, limitations of command and intelligence systems.

First, the trend of increasing complexity in armed forces is reversing. Technology and industrial scales of production spawned the *Modern Epoch's* force complexity. But this complexity was expensive and ran counter to the principle of economies of scale. Large proportions of defence budgets were devoted to weapons and platforms tailored for specific roles, so a logical response was to build fewer classes of more adaptable weapons and platforms, 'multi-role systems' in the jargon.

A modern example illustrates the point. Until the mid-1980s, the air groups of US carriers included at least 4 different fast jet types, each generally single or twin role. This limited the weight of effort available for different missions and, as a result, the USN made a conscious decision to develop a multi-role aircraft, the F/A-18 Hornet. Technology now makes this feasible and allows a US carrier to concentrate up to 50 jets on a particular mission, rather than the 12 or at best 24 available with specialized squadrons.

This approach makes good economic sense too, conforming as it does to the economies-of-scale principle — one set of design, development and production costs, spread across one large production run, supported by one logistics chain and one large set of spares. And it also makes good strategic sense, as a hedge against misreading the future. Rather than deciding definitively how many fighters and how many bombers to procure, the USN has 'future proofed' its force structure by buying an aircraft that can do both.

Second, beginning in World War II and reliably from the 1990s, technology has allowed us to guide munitions to their targets. And when the navigational accuracy of Global Positioning Systems (GPS) is integrated with miniaturized computers and sensors, the weapons systems that result have unprecedented precision. The consequence is that there is a reducing need to mass forces when engaging targets.

Third, reliable sharing of real-time information across computer networks now extends to armies as well as navies and air forces.[1] Computers control weapons systems but also manage information, collating Intelligence, surveillance and reconnaissance data so that it can be displayed schematically in real-time. These video representations of tactical situations have replaced pen, paper and manual plotting and now give commanders and subordinates a better spatial feel for tactical situations, thus improving their tactical decision making. Furthermore, the computers producing these pictures are now reliably linked by military internets and information can thus be passed instantaneously between friendly forces.

Thanks to these improved communications, we now work with shared real-time pictures. The principal tactical advantage is that commanders know with greater confidence where friendly forces are, both those under their direct command and those with whom they are cooperating. This development has not cleared the fog of war from the battlefield, nor will it — war's irrational nature will see to that. But it has raised the mist a little and reduced the frequency of 'blue-on-blue' fratricide.

Furthermore, the reach of reconnaissance and surveillance systems is now catching up with the weapons systems. Using a range of optical and radar sensors, deployed in drones and aircraft whose information is transmitted real-time across the network, commanders are increasingly able to 'see' well beyond the visual horizon.

However, computer networks come with their own peculiar problems. The first challenge is simply to manage the sheer volume of available information. The second is to resist the temptation at the higher level to delve into tactical detail that may be just a few mouse clicks or key strokes away. The more complicated medium-term question, for armies, is about their organization. Are military organizations, particularly army structures, based essentially on Napoleonic designs, right for the information era?

This question leads us to a broader strategic issue. Generally speaking, Western armed forces are organized and equipped to fight conventional wars against state opponents. In other words, they are designed for state-on-state war, in the jargon 'symmetric' war. And generally speaking, the technological developments of the *Information Transformation* have improved their conventional fighting capacity. Witness the ease with which the US and her allies defeated the Iraqi conventional forces in 1991 and 2003.

Yet as Iraq and Afghanistan show, the immediate modern challenge for conventional forces is the irregular opponent, be he or she terrorist or insurgent or both. So far, the first important strategic lesson we have learned in the *Information Transformation* is that the usefulness of armed forces designed for conventional warfare is somewhat more variable in these less conventional forms of conflict.

Political Trends in the Information Transformation

What of the political context for strategy makers? Some said that the end of the Cold War would lead to the end of war. Indeed Francis Fukuyama, in his famous book *The End of History and the Last Man*,[2] went on to suggest that we were witnessing, in 1991, the ultimate triumph of liberal democracy. But history has proved Fukuyama and the end-of-war advocates wrong. After the collapse of the USSR, conflicts emerged in former client states, fuelled by previously latent politico-nationalistic tensions. And Western states were prepared to intervene in these and other conflicts. Sometimes this was for national security or national interest. On other occasions the reasons were supposedly more altruistic, for example under the banner of humanitarian intervention. And the state's monopoly of political violence, already under threat in the 1950s and 1960s, was fatally eroded on 9/11. Terrorists' pursuit of political objectives culminated in the tactics of the Twin Towers attacks and the West responded. As a result, we have a geopolitical context as complex as ever.

And yet for all this complexity, I cannot help but feel that future operations will be mounted and (less regularly) future wars fought for political objectives not unlike those of the past. I would be a fool to try and predict the precise nature and form of these future conflicts, but I do think that we can say something about, first, the generic nature of the objectives that political actors will seek to deliver with force and, second, the dominant political factors that might trigger armed conflict in the future.

What can we say about the objectives that political actors might use force to pursue? It would be fruitless to speculate on specific objectives. But I suspect we will be able to categorize the generic objectives by placing them and the operations and wars that result, on a scale of interest, depending on the nature of the political issue at contest. Higher up the scale will be political issues of real gravity, lower down those less weighty. And the nature of the armed conflict that results will be significantly influenced by the place on the scale of interest for the contestants. Let's illustrate the idea with examples.

At the top of the scale of interest would be contests over objectives of the gravest kind, classically those where the territorial integrity of your state or the very survival of your political community is at stake. By definition, such conflicts would be wars of national survival and, although only a fool would rule them out of our future, factors such as globalization seem to make conflicts such as these less probable than in the past, at least in the short-to-medium term.

Next down the scale would be contests to do with national security. Here political objectives would be those to do with maintaining the national values and domestic way of life of your nation-state or your political community. This is how the contemporary NATO operation in Afghanistan is justified. But as the Afghanistan example shows, the problem with the term national security is that it describes a much more subjective idea than national survival. Calculations about how to preserve national security are more complicated and more nuanced. This is particularly so when you are assessing the impact of political developments abroad on your security at home, as 9/11 demonstrates. These calculations get even more difficult when you try to assess the benefits and costs of using armed force overseas to protect your national security at home.[3] Armed force may be but one of a range of levers in such circumstances and generally the wars that result will be wars of choice, rather than of necessity.

Further down the scale would be operations (rarely wars) where your objective is based on issues of national interest, rather than national security. You may, for example, be pursuing a long term foreign policy aim or something that would bear on domestic politics. A modern example is the British operation in Sierra Leone in 2000. Events in Sierra Leone constituted no threat to British national security, but after beginning with an evacuation of EU citizens, Britain calculated that it was in her national interests to intervene further and stabilize the country. Generally, these operations would be discretionary and a likely characteristic would be that the prospects of success were good or the predicted costs of the operation were low or both.

And finally, at the bottom of the scale, would be operations more altruistic, for example those that sought to maintain or pursue international norms and values. A classic historical example was the Royal Navy's operations against the slave trade in the 1800s. And a classic modern example would be any of the humanitarian aid or disaster relief operations of the *Information Transformation*. In such operations, the same calculations on prospects and cost apply as in operations in pursuit of national interest, only more so.

In sum, the higher up the scale of interest, the graver the political issue at stake, the greater the imperative to act and the greater the likelihood of political and national consensus. Whereas the further down the scale, the less grave the issue, the greater the discretion for action and more variable may be the level of political and popular support. We will examine this idea in more detail in Chapter 8, because assessing where an operation might fall on your scale of interest and, as importantly, on your opponent's, should be a critical preliminary step in superior strategy making.

So far so good, but what can we say about the likely utility of force in these different cases? The short answer is that we will only be able to judge the utility on the circumstances of the case. But a key factor will be the perceived *political* utility of force in each case and here the political experiences of our recent operations will influence perceptions. It is too early to make hard predictions, but I would forecast that the conflicts and wars in the Balkans, Somalia, Afghanistan and Iraq will lead to a more politically cautious approach in the West when sanctioning the use of armed force abroad in the future.

What, then, will be the dominant factors that might lead to the use of force in the future? Isolating such factors in the new geopolitical mosaic is fraught with analytic danger but, at first sight, five stand out:

- First is the policy of the United States and of China (the only other credible contender for superpower status in the medium-term).

- Second, as long as oil is the world's primary energy source, the stability of the Arabian Gulf will remain an area of legitimate national interest to those who consume oil.

- Third, extremist Islam, the most potent and frequent source of international terrorism, has not yet run its evolutionary course.

- Fourth, although their internal contradictions will deny them superpower status in the short term, Russia and India are the heavyweights of their regions.

- Fifth, finally and probably the most important in the long term, as the inevitable consequences of global warming play out in the coming decades, the chances of political conflict as a result of resource competition, migration or the search for habitable land may rise.

The list could be much longer. But for factors which might bear on future armed conflict or wars — particularly significant international wars — I would give short odds on one or more of these five being implicated.

Let me speculate further, though and guess which of these issues will be defining in the coming decades. My hunch is that the dominant short-to-medium term threats to the West will arise from terrorism borne of extremist Islam, by al-Qaeda and their affiliates and the dominant medium-to-long term threats will arise from the consequences of global warming. Let's look at each in turn.

The defining short-term issue — Islamic extremists

When America and her NATO allies eventually extract themselves from Afghanistan and Iraq and pause to draw breath, I suspect that they will draw a number of important conclusions. There will, no doubt, be much rumination on techniques and tactics for counter-terrorism, counter-insurgency and nation-building in failing states.

But, as I have written elsewhere,[4] because the Afghanistan and Iraq wars were waged for reasons of national security, there will be a bigger question: how have these interventions improved the West's national security? Are the streets of major Western cities safer as a result of the Afghanistan and Iraq interventions? How do the credit and debit sides of the national security ledger look as a result of these first wars of the third millennium?

On the credit side, as I write (in late 2010) there is a modicum of modern government in Iraq and Western armed forces, lead by the US, are relearning how to do counter-insurgency. Meanwhile, the West's domestic defences against terrorism have become much stronger. But, ironically, perhaps the most important credit entry is one of insight — the West now has a much better understanding of the limits of its power and of the complications of nation-building interventions, particularly in Islamic countries.

On the debit side, the tactical vulnerability of the West's expensive and sophisticated armies to unsophisticated insurgent tactics has been exposed. Strategically, Western forces have been fixed in Afghanistan and Iraq and their ability to act elsewhere in the world has thus been severely constrained. But perhaps the most uncertain, but nevertheless biggest, debit entry is that Western military actions in Muslim lands and the attendant press coverage, have helped extremist Islam's 'recruiting sergeants' and may thus have increased the overall number of potential terrorists.[5] Over a fifth of the World's population follow Islam and the gearing from even a tiny percentage increase in recruitment would be significant. If, through Western actions in Afghanistan and Iraq, just an additional 1% of young Muslim men and women were driven into the psychological arms of al-Qaeda and their affiliates, then the ranks of potential Jihadists would be swelled by over a million.

As the West's leaders step back from the immediate political issues that they face in Afghanistan and Iraq and consider their next steps, my hope is that they will give themselves time to really understand the political context in which al-Qaeda and its affiliates' brand of Islamist extremism exists. We might best summarize this context by saying that the West has found itself an unwitting party to an Islamic civil war of ideas, between modernizers and conservatives. The modernizers believe that the problem is that Islamic nations have failed to keep pace with Western modernization, whereas the conservatives believe the problem to be too much, rather than not enough, Western modernization. In a very real sense, the game being played out in Afghanistan — a corrupt and unpopular government, borne of a Western imposed system of democracy, versus the harsh but fair (in their eyes) and religiously pure Taliban — is a national cameo of this broader international context. We in the West have (largely unwittingly) been drawn in on the side of the modernizers and hence have become a target of al-Qaeda and its jihadists, the military wing of the conservative extremists.[6] We have been drawn into a generational struggle, stretching far beyond the Afghan and Iraq wars.

How will the West operate in this marathon? My guess is that we will seek to extract ourselves from the centre to the sidelines of this civil war. I suspect that we will settle, either consciously or in practice, on a grand strategy not unlike the containment strategy that guided our actions in the Cold War. Having tried open heart surgery — a blend of nation-building and counter-insurgency — in Afghanistan and Iraq, we will probably revert to something less invasive, keyhole surgery perhaps, to root out known terrorists who wish us harm, together with assistance to national immune systems, through training indigenous security forces. Such a strategy is likely to be one where the emphasis is not on 'boots on the ground' but, rather, 'Western boots off the grounds of Islam.' A — perhaps *the* — key feature will be to recognize that it is probably best that the politics of non-Western countries evolve in ways that are inspired by their people and in the grain of their nation's natures, rather than imposed by the West.

Ironically, such a strategy may be forced on the West by fiscal circumstance. Whether one views the interventions in Afghanistan and Iraq in a positive or negative light, it is undeniable that they have been expensive, in both a political and a financial sense. It was calculated in 2008 that the total costs for UK of the Afghan and Iraq Wars by 2010 would be of the order of £20bn. And that, for the US, when the two wars are taken together, only World War II has exceeded their combined financial total.[7]

In an age of austerity, a grand strategy that is less costly, politically and financially, will likely find favour — especially if it proves, in the long run, to be more effective. Such a grand strategy would also have the significant advantage of allowing the West to draw strategic breath and consider the threats associated with global warming that, to my mind, are of much greater concern.

The defining long-term strategic issue — global warming

Although the strong scientific consensus is that global warming is well underway and likely a result of human action, predictions of what will happen next are fraught. From a defence planning point of view, what matters is not to be able to say what will definitively happen, but rather to consider what could plausibly happen.

In his most recent analysis, James Lovelock, the originator of the Gaia theory, suggests that, not only is global warming happening more quickly than we originally believed, but also that it is now beyond our capacity to stop.[8] His thinking rests on the notion of hysterias. This is the idea that some systems are naturally stable and will self-correct back to a natural level when perturbed by some external factor. However, there comes a moment when the force of the perturbation is so strong that it forces the system to a new and different level, around which it will naturally stabilize and self-correct. In Lovelock's view, our climate works in this way. Lovelock believes that, even if there were to be the international consensus for concerted action to reduce our carbon emissions, it is already too late. In his view, the perturbation as a result of carbon emissions has been such that we are now past the moment of self correction and our climate is now heading for a new higher global temperature. And, once it gets there, it will take a significant perturbation in the opposite sense — i.e. a significant reduction on *current* carbon levels — to bring it back to current temperatures. The issue is not whether Lovelock is right, but rather whether his thesis is sufficiently plausible for us to consider it as a contingency. As a one-time ocean scientist and former defence planner, I think it is.

What would be the defence and security implications? Consider the picture painted by Michael Lynas on the impact of a global rise in temperature of 3°C, well within the sensitivity of current global climate modelling scenarios:

> With structural famine gripping much of the subtropics, hundreds of millions of people will have only one choice left other than death for themselves and their families: they will have to pack up their belongings and leave. The resulting population transfers could dwarf those that have historically taken place due to wars or crop failures. Never before has the human population had to leave an entire latitudinal belt across the width of the globe.[9]

The idea of an entire latitudinal belt of people on the move is an apocalyptic view and, for me, on the edges of plausibility. But a commonly quoted, albeit highly speculative, figure for climate change induced migration by 2050 is 200 million people and estimates range out as far as 1 billion.[10] Such, though, are the difficulties of arriving at these estimates that no one can apportion sensible probabilities to them but they nevertheless put the threat of Islamist terrorism into perspective.

What can we say of such a world, with mass migration underway toward the temperate and cool latitudes? An optimistic future would see an international consensus developing for the maximization of the productive economic potential and the creation of living space in the temperate and cool nations, so as to absorb the migrating millions. A pessimistic future would see a hardening of national attitudes in the temperate and cool nations into a defensive sovereign mindset, based on a view that their states simply lack the absorptive capacity and that it is thus every nation for itself. A realistic future probably sees a bit of both.

I suggested earlier that wars of national survival would, because of factors such as globalization, be less probable than in the past, at least in the short-to-medium term. The qualification 'short-to-medium term' was deliberate because, if we are unable to get our political act together and implement collectively the measures needed, both to reduce and mitigate the impact we are currently having on the climate and to prepare for a warmer future, then it seems to me that the chances of wars of national survival featuring in our future are likely to rise. If there was ever an imperative to act on climate change, it is surely this.

This takes me full circle to my original question, the usual problem for defence planners: what to prepare for? Should countries such as Britain prepare their territories as national lifeboats, as James Lovelock suggests? In the short term, the racing certainty is uncertainty, at least on the implications of climate change. Climate modelling is notoriously difficult, but to this must be added the variables of international politics and economics, the security of power, food and resources and the dynamics of migration. So whither armed force and its use in this age of austerity and uncertainty?

Force uses and structures

It seems unlikely to me that we will fall into the classic mistake of preparing for the last war — counter-insurgencies along Afghanistan and Iraq lines — not least because of the expense. But, whilst it is easy to avoid this mistake, it is a lot more difficult to decide what to optimize for. General Rupert Smith argues that future wars will be fought 'amongst the people' and that this will significantly shape the way we think about the future utility of force. But it seems doubtful to me that future wars will be solely those fought amongst the people. It is more likely that war amongst the people will be an occasional fact of operational life, as indeed it routinely was during the *Modern Epoch*.[11]

As Western leaders start to think beyond Afghanistan and Iraq, my guess is that, although some states, particularly the US and the other significant Western powers, will wish to retain the capability to engage in state-on-state operations, this will be for contingency, rather than because they expect to do so routinely. My guess — and it can be no more than that — is that the more frequent use of armed force in the coming decade will be precise counter-terrorist operations and the long term training of indigenous security forces, respectively keyhole surgery and immunotherapy to follow my earlier metaphor. After this, the next most frequent uses will be on those termed, in the modern jargon, stability operations, where the aim is to improve the human security of indigenous populations and those for disaster relief. But in deciding whether to commit to such operations, a key Western calculation will be to do with hands and mangles — there will be little if any appetite, at least for a decade, for prolonged interventions, especially in Muslim lands.

The forces required to execute this form of defence and security policy would need to evolve from those we have now. Western armies will need to become lighter and more flexible, probably optimized for human security operations and, if policy makers agree with my views on climate change, disaster relief but with the capacity to operate across a wide range of roles. In a climate changing world, there will be a renewed interest in a nation's civil defence capacity and we may see a resurgence in national guards and reserves. For this reason and that of cost, Western armies are likely to be smaller than now but with the balance made up by reservists.

The development of air forces and navies, meanwhile, will probably follow a more conventional path. The need to be able to police and command one's own air space will be an enduring defence requirement as will, for maritime nations, the ability to police territorial waters and the large exclusive economic zones offshore. In the short term, when engaging in stability operations, the ability to hold as much of the support to your intervening force out of the countries in which you are intervening, keeping just the minimum in the mangle, will be a significant advantage. There will thus be a premium on the ability to deliver this support — for example, surveillance, firepower and logistics — from the air or the sea or both, which will favour long range air capabilities, together with those deployed from aircraft carriers and amphibious shipping.

Ultimately, if defence planners judge, as I do, that global warming is the gravest long term threat and that Islamist terrorism is, for now, adequately contained then it is for the long term that I suspect — and hope — our armed forces will be optimized and our defence planners will focus. But the compelling advantage of the type of forces I describe is that they seem reasonably appropriate for both contingencies.

Conclusion

The political and military context of today's *Information Transformation* seems to have proved Fukuyama's *The End of History* thesis a little premature.[12] 9/11, the rise of China, Russia's resurgence, India's regional hegemony and questions about Western capitalism; all these things suggest a less certain future. Indeed the more prescient book title has been Colin Gray's *Another Bloody century*. I am not as pessimistic as Gray to believe that 'war is a permanent feature of the human condition.'[13] But I am realistic enough to judge that, on the history of the first 15 years of the *Information Transformation*, together with some of the challenges that face us in the coming decades, the prospects for eternal peace have not yet markedly improved.

Militarily we live in interesting times. Technology and cost pressures — unwitting bedfellows — are turning our armed forces from complex and rigid heterogeneity to simple and flexible homogeneity. Long range precision weapons linked to effective long range sensors and connected by military internets are reducing the need for us to mass for decisive effect. But how relevant are these changes to, for example, counter-insurgency and counter-terrorism? And how will the resulting changes in warfare in the *Information Transformation* challenge strategy makers? How, for example, will the changes play out in 'war amongst the people'?

Politically, we live in interesting times. Popular attitudes toward the use of force are in a state of flux and political trends are difficult to predict. But it will not be an easy future politically. The popular politicization of war and the speed and schizophrenia of the Western free press will see to that. Perhaps the one thing that we can say with some confidence is that, in the short term at least, the contemporary events that will most shape Western political attitudes to the use of armed force will be the lessons we draw from the wars in Afghanistan and Iraq.

The military and political context looks complicated, but will it frame a future in which strategy has no part to play? I doubt it. If armed conflict and war persist as features in international politics, the reverse will be true. Will Clausewitz's thinking be relevant in our modern wars, operations and interventions? Unquestionably yes. Should we try our best to employ armed force in a rational way? From first principles and common sense, the answer seems obvious.

Are there things strategy makers should do differently in this *Information Transformation*? The answer depends on how well you think we have done so far and historically it is still a little too soon to say. Posterity may come to judge some post Cold War operations as successes. Kosovo may be a case in point. But for other operations posterity may judge that we 'could have done better.' If posterity does reach a 'could have done better' judgement on some of these modern operations then, as the (all too predictable) political and media search for culprits begins, the first defendant in the dock should perhaps be the striking lack of new theory on strategy making.

An old Indian proverb says that the best time to plant a tree is 20 years ago — and the second best time is now. My case for our investing in theory for politico-military strategy making — the substance of the remaining chapters — rests on the same logic.

Chapter 7

Making Strategy
Thinking about Thinking

For the strategic mind to work creatively, it needs the stimulus of a good, insightful analysis. In order to conduct a good analysis, it takes a strategic and inquisitive mind to come up with the right questions and phrase them as solution-oriented issues. Analyses done for the sake of vindicating one's own preconceived notions do not lead to creative solutions. Intuition or gut feel alone does not ensure secure business plans. It takes a good balance between the two to come up with successful strategy.

Kenichi Ohmae

Introduction

With the context set out, it is time now to focus on the heart of the matter and begin to piece the collected insights — historical, doctrinal, modern and corporate — into a framework to help us move strategy making on from the 'disorganized, undisciplined intellectual activity' that Admiral Wylie worried about in the 1960s and that I recognize now. I want to try to develop further the body of theory to which he and others — such as Clausewitz, Jomini, Moltke, Corbett, Castex, Beaufre and Brodie — contributed, but not as a recipe for success, rather as a framework and a reference to help discipline thinking and improve judgement.

Our starting point is to recognize that strategy is the product of people's thinking. So when we think about making strategy we are thinking about people thinking.[1] In the Introduction, I said that:

> A key contention, which underpins all of Part II, is that, paradoxical though it may at first appear, the formulation of strategy is an inherently creative activity and as such requires the employment of teams comprised of clever, well-informed and operationally-experienced people — the brightest and the best — who must be given sufficient time, space and opportunity to think and not be rigidly constrained by doctrine or decision making processes and structures or party politics.

Ultimately, the key factor that determines success or failure in strategy is the quality of strategic leaders and strategists. But can we help strategic leaders and strategists with their thinking?

There are two ways we might assist. The first and the subject of this chapter, is simply to raise our collective consciousness of the importance of thinking and the way that we think, when making strategy. The second and the subject of the next chapter, is to introduce devices to help prompt and order our thinking.

Three interrelated ideas help raise our collective consciousness. First, Kenichi Ohmae's corporate insights in *The Mind of the Strategist* will help open our minds to what strategic thinking is and how it contrasts with systems (or analytic) thinking and intuitive thinking.[2] Second, deductions from first principles and personal insight will help us consider how personality and character — in both individual and national senses — play into strategic thinking and strategy making. Third, insights from our historical analysis will help illustrate how successful strategic leaders of the past have gone about their strategic thinking. These insights will, in turn, allow us to give some thought to the question: how can strategic leaders and strategists better prepare for strategy making?

But in all this, it is worth reminding ourselves of an observation of Mintzberg, Ahlstrand and Lampel's:

> We remain far from understanding the complex and creative acts that give rise to strategies. Hence, strategists are largely self-taught: they develop their knowledge structures and thinking processes mainly through direct experience.[3]

As far as I can judge, this observation is equally pertinent to politico-military strategy making. So although raising our collective consciousness of the notion of strategic thinking may seem a rather modest aspiration, it is an important early step in our self-teaching and an important prelude to the harder-edged approach that awaits us in Chapter 8.

Strategic Thinking

What is strategic thinking? In *The Mind of the Strategist,* one of the world's leading management consultants, Kenichi Ohmae, considers strategic thinking in business. He sees strategic thinking as something different in form from both analytic thinking and intuitive thinking. Rather he believes that strategic thinking combines both forms. He describes the pattern of thought of the strategic thinker thus:

> Analysis is the critical starting point of strategic thinking. Faced with problems, trends, events or situations that appear to constitute a harmonious whole or come packaged as a whole by the common sense of the day, the strategic thinker dissects

them into their constituent parts. Then, having discovered the significance of these constituents, he reassembles them in a way calculated to maximize his advantage. ... Besides the habit of analysis, what marks the mind of the strategist is an intellectual elasticity or flexibility that enables him to come up with a realistic response to changing situations, not simply to discriminate with great precision amongst different shades of gray. ... This is always the most effective approach to devising strategies for dealing successfully with opportunities, in the market arena as on the battlefield.[4]

For me, this intermingling of analytical and intuitive thinking codifies how politico-military strategy making feels in practice. There also seems to be some circularity at work. A creative and intuitive mind is needed to ensure that strategic analysis is properly framed. A rigorous and analytic mind is needed to work through the base data for subsequent thinking, but an intuitive mind will help distinguish the wheat from the chaff within the data, in turn providing the ideal stimulus for the strategic mind to work creatively to develop solutions.

History shows parallels with strategic thinking in war. To return to Admiral Spruance's key decision, during the Battle of Midway in 1942, to commit all his carrier aircraft to attack the opposing Japanese carrier force — to bet the (naval) farm so to speak — this is a good example of the analytic and intuitive blend. Spruance would have known well, from theoretical *analysis* of carrier-versus-carrier combat in war-gaming at the Naval War College at Rhode Island in the inter-war years, the disproportionate advantage he would gain by getting his attack in first. But equally he needed to rely on his *intuition* to interpret a mixed and very incomplete operational picture on the day and make the decision to commit.

Now comes a fundamental question: is the capacity for strategic thinking a function of nature or nurture? Is this capacity limited to a minority of gifted individuals or can it be learned? The answer, I suspect, is a bit of both. There is no doubt that the great strategic leaders and thinkers had powerful intellects. But so too did many others who proved unsuccessful, so clearly a powerful intellect is a necessary but not sufficient condition for effective strategic thinking. A handful of other interrelated attributes seem to stand out that are as much those of the strategic thinker as they are of the strategic leader. Vision and judgement seem to feature strongly, combined in Clausewitz's idea of *coup d'œil*, 'a sort of inner eye that vouchsafed the ability to judge strategic as well as tactical situations.'[5] But so too does the capacity to lift one's vision from the day-to-day, together with the self discipline to make time to think and, whereas intellect and vision are likely programmed in from birth, the remainder can be learned and, to some extent, programmed into character and personality, which as we shall see also influences strategy making.

Individual Personality, National Character and Strategic Thinking Styles

A personal anecdote may help introduce the idea of personality and character in strategy making. In the 1990s, I was attached to the staff of Flag Officer Sea Training, a staff whose role was to train ships of the Royal Navy and European nations for war-fighting. Amongst my roles, two were key. The first was to assess the state of a ship on arrival, shape its six week training syllabus, train the ship, monitor progress and oversee the final inspection at the end of the training. The second was to guide, advise and assess the ship's Commanding Officer. After six or so months in the job, I became aware of two things. First was the fascinatingly close relationship between the personality of each Commanding Officer and the atmosphere (or 'collective personality') and performance of the ship. Second was the similarly close relationship between the national character of the different European nations and the approach of their ships' command teams to problem solving. Although these were tactical observations, as we will see shortly in the different thinking styles of Churchill, Alanbrooke, Marshall and Slim, there seems to be a similar relationship at the strategic level. In other words, the personality of the strategic leader and the national character of his or her team play out in the way they make strategy.

An observation from the British historian Andrew Roberts, illustrates the personality point ideally. When Alanbrooke, having gained Marshall's agreement to launch an assault on Sicily, was lobbied by his fellow Chiefs of Staff and most of the UK Planning Staffs with an alternative plan to invade Sardinia (Operation Brimstone) he flatly refused to change his mind:

> It was by sheer force of character, therefore and an implied threat of resignation sooner than go back to Marshall with a change in his proposals, that Sicily was chosen rather than Sardinia. It was a classic case of the influence of personality in strategy making.[6]

The influence of individual personality on strategy making ought not to surprise us. On reflection, we can trace its impact throughout the historical analysis and indeed it helps us to better understand strategic choices of the past.

But it should cause us to think and for two reasons. First, for strategic leaders, an awareness of their own strengths *and* weaknesses will allow them to mitigate the risk of their weaknesses influencing their strategy making. Second, because personality is something that is moulded by experience and training, the right investment in the right people, if they can be identified, at the right stages in their careers will pay dividends in a nation's strategy making capacity decades later.

National character seems to matter too, as these quotes from two soldiers, one German and the other British, demonstrate:

> What was astonishing was the speed with which the Americans adapted to modern warfare. In this they were assisted by their extraordinary sense for the practical and material and by their complete lack of regard for tradition and worthless theories.[7]

> The Americans were analytic. They approached warfare as they approached any other large enterprise; breaking it down to its essentials, cutting out what was superfluous, defining tasks and roles and training of each man as if he was about to take an individual part in some complicated industrial process.[8]

The evidence for national character — in this case American national character — playing into strategy making seems clear. The World War II contrasts in British and American strategy making culture, in part a result of national character, seem to reinforce the point.

For example, the influential US academic, Eliot Cohen has noted that the idea of 'the overall strategic concept' was beloved by American planners, but regarded by Alanbrooke and the British Chiefs of Staff as 'fatuous.'[9] And Alanbrooke *et al* would still be in good company, nationally, if the sense in this ironic quote from an anonymous British diplomat is anything to go by:

> Our skill is in not having a grand strategic concept.[10]

This perhaps reveals an unconscious inclination in the British national character, evident in historical practice, for an approach to policy formulation and strategy making somewhat more *laissez faire* than that of the US.

This influence of individual personality and national strategic culture is clear in the different styles that strategic leaders have adopted when making strategy. For example, some have tended toward analytic thinking and others have been more intuitive. Some have tended to think things through top-down, proceeding from the general to the particular; others have approached bottom-up, proceeding from the particular to the general. And, when interacting with strategy making teams, some have led intellectually from the front, whilst others have allowed their teams to roam freely and engaged intellectually only when a range of alternatives had been devised. The illustrations that follow contrast these alternatives, but also show, unsurprisingly, that there is no single right way to go about strategic thinking.

Analytic or intuitive?

Churchill's and Alanbrooke's different approaches to strategic problem solving — the former more visionary and intuitive, the latter more prosaic and analytic — illustrate their different tendencies on the analytic-or-intuitive axis. Cohen suggests that the essence of Churchill's philosophical approach to the higher direction of war:

> May be found in a pamphlet — and essay, really — about his chief hobby, painting, which he explicitly compared with the art of war. 'It is the same kind of problem as unfolding a long, sustained, interlocked argument. It is a proposition which, whether of few or numberless parts, is commanded by a single unity of conception.' Churchill, a talented amateur painter, brought an artist's perspective to bear on war.[11]

This artist's approach surely placed Churchill on the intuitive wing of strategic-thinking styles — in stark contrast to Alanbrooke. An oft-quoted phrase reveals much about the quite different workings of Alanbrooke's mind:

> [The art of strategy is] to determine the aim, which should be
> political; to derive from that aim a series of military objectives
> to be achieved; to assess these objectives as to the military
> requirements they create and the pre-conditions which the
> achievement of each is likely to necessitate: to measure the
> available and potential resources against the requirements and
> to chart from this process a coherent pattern of priorities and
> a rational course of action.[12]

This phrase is regularly   and wrongly   used in British Military
Doctrine to define strategy. Although Alanbrooke intended to define
the art of strategy, as a re-reading will show, what he unconsciously
did was to describe *his* approach to strategy making. And as such,
he placed himself fairly and squarely on the analytic wing.

Particular-to-the-general or general-to-the-particular?

A second contrast, but this time between Alanbrooke and Marshall,
illustrates the top-down-or-bottom-up axis. And it is Alanbrooke
who (again) unconsciously reveals the issue in his commentary on
Marshall and the US approach to strategy making:

> The American mind likes proceeding from the general to the
> particular, whilst in the problem we have to solve we cannot
> evolve any form of general doctrine until we have carefully
> examined the particular details of each problem.[13]

Although Alanbrooke is consciously criticising Marshall and the
US Chiefs of Staff, again he is unconsciously saying more about his
own strategic problem-solving philosophy and unwittingly placing
himself in the bottom-up school.

Marshall's approach — the general to the particular — was clear in his actions in 1942. As early as the beginning of March, Marshall authorized his planners to 'begin detailed studies for a direct attack on Germany via North West France'.[14] It is clear from this that he was already predisposed to confront the German Army head on. This reflects a number of things: the US Army's (Jominian) concept of war, based on mass and concentration against the decisive point — in Marshall's eyes the German Army — together with a natural American confidence, based on a belief in their ability to raise and train and on their industry's ability to equip, a citizen army able to defeat Germany's. It also shows, more importantly for us, that the US 'strategic concept' in World War II was established very early.

With America and Britain having agreed on a 'Germany first' approach, Marshall, thinking top-down, deduced that it would be necessary first to take on and decisively defeat the German Army. For a modern democracy, time and the length of the war would be a factor, but also US industrial capacity would be a key strength. The simplest way to take on the German Army would be via a direct approach across the English Channel. With this strategic concept established, the Americans could then proceed from the general-to-the-particular and establish the subordinate objectives. This therefore places Marshall in the top-down school.

These contrasting styles may help us understand better the significant differences in strategic thinking between the British and Americans during the World War II on the timing and location of D-Day. Alanbrooke and Marshall were thinking about the same problem — but they were thinking about it in different ways.

Leader-led or team-led analysis?

A third contrast, this time between General Slim in Burma and President Kennedy during the Cuban Missile Crisis, helps illustrate the leader-led-or-team-led axis.

In command of the British 14th Army in Burma, when Slim made strategy, he led from the intellectual front:

> My method of working out such a plan was first to study the possibilities myself and then informally discuss them with my Brigadier General Staff, Major-General Administration and my opposite number in the Air Force. At these discussions we would arrive at the broadest outline of possible alternative courses of action, at least two, more often three or four. ...our team of planners, specially selected but comparatively junior officers, representing not only the general and administrative staffs, but the air staff as well. They would make a preliminary study, giving the practicability or otherwise of each course and its advantages and disadvantages. They were quite at liberty to make new suggestions of their own or to devise permutations and combinations of the originals.[15]

Although command-led, this method also allowed Slim to leverage the thinking of his immediate subordinates and specially selected planners.[16]

The approach is, though, in interesting contrast to that of John F Kennedy's during the Cuban Missile Crisis, an instructive example of strategy making under pressure, albeit no war resulted. In what was an extraordinarily tense period of strategy making, at the start of the crisis JFK set out the political objective, established very broad political guidelines, but then let his team loose intellectually, to propose, examine, develop, refine and present the options. His brother, Robert Kennedy's record of the crisis explains how the President and the dozen or so strong Executive Committee of the National Security Council (EXCOM) developed the strategy:[17]

> [EXCOM] was the group that met, talked, argued and fought together during that crucial period of time. ... by Thursday night [18 October], there was a majority of opinion in our

group for a blockade. ... We explained our recommendations to the President ... However, as people talked and the President raised probing questions, minds and opinions began to change again and not only on small points. The President, not at all satisfied, sent us back to our deliberations. ... Everyone had an equal opportunity to express himself and to be heard directly. It was a tremendously advantageous procedure that does not frequently occur within the executive branch of government ... At 2:30 [on 20 October] we walked up to the Oval Room. The meeting went on until ten minutes after five. ... Bob McNamara presented the arguments for the blockade; others presented the arguments for the military attack. The discussion, for the most part, was able and organized ... The President made his decision that afternoon [20 October] for the blockade.[18]

Although JFK's hands-off strategy making approach was in significant contrast to Slim's, what was common to both, once a number of potential courses of action had been identified was, first, the encouragement that all voices should be heard, even if discordant and second, the willingness of each leader to interact in a questioning but positive way with the strategists. Ultimately, both were successful.

Although we have selected examples to emphasize poles on three theoretical axes, it will come as no surprise that in practice strategy makers instinctively blend the approaches. More importantly, great strategic leaders' successful use of contrasting approaches reinforces the point that there is no single right mode of thought when making strategy.

Preparing for strategic thinking

The concluding question is: are there ways in which strategic leaders and strategists can prepare for strategy making? Naturally, there is not much that one can do to improve raw intellect but, this accepted, on the historical evidence and from first principles, there do seem to be ways in which one can, through preparation, improve strategy making capacity.

A common feature of the great strategic leaders was that not only were they clever, but they also worked hard to expand their intellects. The young Frederick the Great was schooled in the classics and French philosophy and would go on to set out his military thinking in five major treatises.[19] Moltke was multilingual, had a deep interest in the arts and politics and was a successful author. Admiral Spruance, the hero of Midway, had a first class intellect and was deeply interested in non-naval matters. General Slim had, whilst a junior officer, been a highly accomplished author. And of course Churchill was awarded the Nobel Prize for Literature in 1953.

It is no surprise, therefore, that (in stark contrast to my nation's system), in the United States armed forces, the acquisition of higher degrees is seen in a very positive light — the architect of the United States' counter-insurgency doctrine, General Petraeus, for example, holds a PhD from Princeton. A mind self-disciplined by hard thinking is a mind more likely to cope with strategic thinking.

A second and closely related, attribute — which applied to all of the individuals above — was an appetite for history. This seems likely to have helped strategic leaders in two ways. First, history provides catalytic fuel for both the analytic and intuitive thinking needed to create strategy. And second, as Clausewitz believed, the ability to compare and contrast your situation with events past will aid judgement when executing strategy.

The next two attributes are interrelated: the ability to rise above the minutiae of immediate matters and see the strategic wood from the tactical trees; and the self-discipline required to make the time needed for thinking and strategic reflection. The similarity in command philosophy of Admiral Spruance and General Slim, amongst the greatest Western commanders of World War II, reflects these points. Throughout the war, both maintained small staffs and crisp working routines. Slim was in bed by 10 p.m. and, if anyone disturbed him 'for anything short of a real crisis, then he did so at his peril.'[20] Spruance would turn in by 8 p.m., often to read and he too disliked being disturbed for anything other than the most important.[21] As Slim himself noted, 'I had seen too many of my colleagues crack under the immense strain of command in the field not to realize that, if I were to continue, I must have ample leisure in which to think and unbroken sleep.'[22] — a sentiment that Spruance echoed in his own personal practice.

The final quality, that I cannot conclusively attribute to the men above but that I nevertheless suspect they and other great strategic practitioners shared, was that of personal insight. The capacity to know yourself, to understand your personal strengths and weaknesses, together with a conscious intent to capitalize on the former and put protections in place to ensure that the latter do not play negatively into your strategy making. Churchill's choice of Alanbrooke as his Chief of the Imperial General Staff seems to me to reflect this attribute. It is a great credit to Churchill that he had the courage and good sense to appoint an officer such as Alanbrooke who would provide an analytic counterpoint to his master's occasional flights of intuitive fantasy, but also fight this analytic corner relentlessly when he believed he was in the right — as he very often was.

Conclusion

There are, in conclusion, no holy grails here for strategic thinkers, nor was this intended. My purpose was more modest, simply to make us more conscious of the importance of the way we think when strategy making and to lay out some thoughts about how we might better prepare for strategic thinking.

Ohmae's description of strategic thinking as a blend of intuitive and analytic thinking codifies how politico-military strategy making feels in practice. And historical case studies support this view. However, the different thinking styles of the great strategic leaders show that the analytic-intuitive perspective is one of a number. Top-down-bottom-up and command-led-team-led are useful alternative perspectives and of course we need to factor in the play of individual personality and national character into the thinking about-thinking equation.

What are the lessons in all this for the strategy maker? The first is consciousness. We need to be conscious of the impact of factors such as these when we are making strategy. The second is preparation. Although a first class intellect is an essential starting point, other attributes, some of which can be nurtured, are also essential ingredients in the mix: a desire to broaden your mind; an appetite for history; the ability to raise your vision above the detail; the self-discipline to make time for thinking and, last but not least, personal insight to know yourself.

Ultimately, these points seem to reinforce an idea that I set out in the Introduction. This is that, at its heart, strategy making is an inherently creative activity and as such:

> It requires teams of clever, well-informed and operationally-experienced people — the brightest and the best — with sufficient time and space to think. Teams that must not be rigidly constrained by decision making doctrine, processes or structures. That said, in operations and war, creative people often need to organize their thinking with discipline and urgency.

People need to organize their thinking with discipline and urgency because politico-military strategy is about political contest, the battlefield and lives, not the market nor the broader public arena. And with this perspective established, it is now time to turn from the softer issue of thinking about thinking — to the harder issue of thinking about war.

Chapter 8

Making Strategy
Thinking about War

However changed and strange the new conditions of war may be, not only generals but politicians and ordinary citizens, may find there is much to be learned from the past that can be applied to the future and, in their search for it, that some campaigns have more than others foreshadowed the coming pattern of modern war. I believe that ours in Burma was one of those. This may seem a curious claim to make for struggles of comparatively ill-equipped men, groping through jungles. Yet the painters' effect and style do not depend on how many tubes of colour he has, the number of his brushes or the size of his canvas, but on how he blends his colours and handles his brushes against the canvas.

Bill Slim

Introduction

If we are thinking about using armed force for one reason or another, then the obvious but important deduction is that a political contest exists or is potentially in prospect. Why else would armed force be used? In such cases, General Beaufre's previously quoted description of the essence of strategy shows why politico-military strategy differs from other forms:

> It is therefore the art of the dialectic of force or, more precisely,
> art of the dialectic of two opposing wills using force to resolve
> their dispute.[1]

Beaufre's definition may be highly abstract, but he is right to focus on the clash of wills on this plane because it is here that the essence of a war's nature resides. I believe that our ability to understand and shape the clash of wills at this highly abstract level is central to success in strategy making for armed conflict and war.

I thus want, in this chapter, to focus squarely on the issue of contest, the clash of wills, touched on in earlier chapters. First, as a scene setter, I will return to look at strategy's relationship with policy and war and set out the abstract context in which these contests occur and in which modern strategy operates. Second, I will consider at greater length the nature of war and identify the key levels of the contest. Third, I will focus on the key question of any strategic analysis: what is the nature of the political issue at contest? Finally, drawing on insights from Part I and on first principles, I will consider how we might shape the clash of wills. As with the preceding chapter, what follows is not a substitute for hard thinking, but rather a theoretical basis to help us make strategy in a more ordered and rigorous way.

War & Peace — Policy & Strategy

In the *Classical Epoch*, the relationship between war and peace was essentially binary. You were in one state or the other and there was not much in between. The war state was accepted as a perfectly normal feature in the conversations of international politics, in part because the military means to wage war were limited and thus the costs of war were seen as proportionate to the benefits.

The relationship between policy and strategy (as both terms were then defined) had a similar binary feel. Admiral Castex described the 'conventional approach'[2] as one where policy and politicians directed all that should happen up until war commenced, but then gave way to strategy and commanders, standing back from events until the war's outcome was settled. This is a fair analysis of the position in the *Classical Epoch*, but this approach did not persist through the *Industrial Transformation*. As Lincoln's close political oversight of his generals in the US Civil War shows, policy — and politicians — had begun to 'interfere' with strategy making and the conduct of war much earlier.

And, with the new politics **and the** new weapons of the *Industrial Transformation*, the degree of interference would increase. The key catalyst was World War I and its disproportionately high costs, when compared to wars of the past. As the war progressed, political actors rather than military ones sought to limit these costs. And afterwards Western politicians saw that strategy had to become hierarchically subservient to policy — modern war's consequences were too grave for its direction to be left solely to military men.

Writing in the 1930s, with World War I memories still raw, Castex's explanation of the new relationship between policy and strategy gives a clear sense of how thinking had moved on:

> Policy intervenes to orient strategy in specific directions. Such interventions can be positive, that is prescribing actions or negative forbidding specific enterprises. Obviously, political demands are not always the most judicious; their inspiration can be good or bad; they may be lacking in foresight. Frequently policy comes to trespass on the domain of strategy and interferes excessively in the conduct of operations and other matters that do not concern it. Nonetheless, the demands made by policy cannot be neglected or distrustfully dismissed; they have preponderant weight. Consequently,

strategy cannot abstract itself from policy and work in isolation.[3]

In other words, for the Western democracies of the early *Modern Epoch*, the link between policy and strategy was no longer a serial one.

The birth of nuclear weapons concluded the matter. As the superpower arsenals grew and the prospect of mutually assured destruction arrived, absolute war could no longer fulfil a rational political purpose. The overwhelming need for war, strategy and military commanders to become subservient to politics, policy and political masters was beyond doubt. It is interesting to recall, for example, that during the Cuban Missile Crisis, the US Joint Chiefs of Staff unanimously advised on a full scale US invasion of Cuba, notwithstanding its potentially apocalyptic repercussions — JFK, fortunately, was swayed by wiser counsels.

During the Cold War, the binary relationship between war and peace also broke down. Conventional wars, such as the Arab-Israeli and the Indo-Pakistani, were still fought according to conventional ideas. But a range of armed conflicts occurred, sometimes characterized by the military as 'low-intensity' and usually highly political in nature, that seemed to fall somewhere between the classical distinctions of war and peace. Figure 8.1 depicts the flow of these changing relationships between strategy and policy and war and peace.

With time on the horizontal baseline, we see in the *Classical Epoch* the binary relationship — policy directs in peace, but hands over to strategy in war. In the *Industrial Transformation*, the distinction between war and peace begins to break down and, in the second half of the *Modern Epoch*, the notion of war and peace as distinctive political conditions largely disappears, replaced by a spectrum of armed conflicts of different hues and intensities. Policy and politicians direct but tend not to over interfere with strategy and commanders in the *Modern Epoch*, but this too begins to break down in the *Information Transformation* as the actions commissioned by strategy in operations abroad have highly political impacts at home.

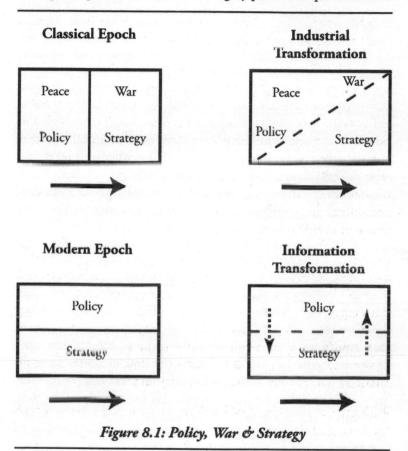

Figure 8.1: Policy, War & Strategy

A key driver for the last of these changes was that, toward the end of the *Modern Epoch*, war gained more popular interest. This was due largely to the revolution in media communications and particularly the arrival of television. Quoting a conversation with a former opponent, Colonel Harry Summers exposes the consequences:

'You know you never defeated us on the battlefield,' said the American colonel. The North Vietnamese colonel pondered on the remark a moment. 'That may be so,' he replied, 'but it is also irrelevant.'[4]

In *On Strategy*, Summers argues that Vietnam was lost primarily because of a failure of US strategy. I agree that this was one of the two key factors. But the other was surely politics. Above all, Vietnam was lost at the political level.

So what? The key point is that in modern war the critical aspects of these contests occur at two levels. The first is what we would have described, in the past, as the 'military-strategic' level. Because we are increasingly deploying civil as well as military power in modern operations, the description 'military-strategic' no longer makes sense. So let us simplify matters and term this level the 'strategic level'. I see this level as the one where the physical components of national power are directed. The second level — and the more important one — is the 'political' level, where the battle of ideas occurs. Thus the analysis to support politico-military strategy making must consider both levels.

In a real sense, these two levels have always been the key ones. However, in the past, decisions at the political level were generally easier in war. For the West, in the defining great wars of national survival of the 20th century, the political issues and choices were straightforward. But as these wars of necessity were replaced by the more modern wars of choice and as, in parallel, war itself became more politicized, then the political considerations became more complex. As we have seen in Afghanistan and Iraq, wars fought for complex reasons of national security, rather than simple reasons of national survival, are difficult politically.

If the critical contests in operations and wars of the future are going to be at the political and strategic levels, then it is here where we need to first focus our thinking when making strategy.

Understanding the Nature of Armed Conflict and War

Clausewitz highlights the importance of understanding the nature of armed conflict or war when he says:

> Wars must vary with the nature of their motives and of the situations which give rise to them. The first, the supreme, the most far-reaching act of judgement that the statesman and the commander have to make is to establish by that test the kind of war on which they are embarking; neither mistaking it for, nor trying to turn it into, something which is alien to its nature. This is the first of all strategic questions and the most comprehensive.[5]

For strategy makers, this is perhaps the most important quote in *On War* so, drawing on the thinking introduced above, let us examine its subtleties. In just 80 or so words, Clausewitz makes four critical observations - let's look at the first.

The political nature of the war will be a consequence of both the political context ('the situations which give rise to them') and the political issue at contest ('the motives').

What compounds the challenge of trying to understand a war's nature is that, as we noted in Chapter 1, its very nature can change over time. The use of armed force is a political act and each act of force contributes to and thus potentially changes, the aggregate nature of the political condition of the conflict. For this reason, in war, strategic actors can never be politically neutral participants or commentators, at least not in Western democracies. All are political actors. This is true even of the journalist. Each comment or popular report contributes to the political debate and therefore influences the political condition and, thus, the underlying nature of the war. As a result, there is a constant interaction between activities and events in the political and strategic dimensions.

Similarly, the military commander who harks back to the 'old days' is a wishful thinker. The days are gone when the political objective was handed down to the military commander and he was then sanctioned to identify the military objective best suited to deliver the political one and pursue it without political interference. Like it or not, military men and women are political actors in modern war. If war is a continuation of politics with the addition of other means then logically it can be no other way. The important point is that military men and women must remain subordinate actors — commanders and advisors — not masters. This is the key to it.

The second of Clausewitz's four observations is that the key judgement on the nature of the war is for 'the statesman *and* the commander' to make (emphasis added). For me, this implies a need for *both* politician and soldier to consider *both* the political and strategic nature of the contest. Third, the statesman and the commander should not mistake the war for something that is 'alien to its nature', that is alien to the nature of the political and strategic contests. Finally, the statesman and the commander should also avoid trying to turn the war into something that is 'alien to its nature.'

These thoughts and Clausewitz's view that to establish the nature of a potential armed conflict or war is 'the most far-reaching act of judgement that the statesman and the commander have to make', should cause us to think and to think hard. History seems to be littered with cases where getting this judgement wrong led to failure on the battlefield — Japan's attack on Pearl Harbour, Germany's offensive against Russia in 1941 and the Argentinian Junta's decision to invade the Falklands in 1982 are but three of many. If, as these cases surely show, the great man is correct, then we need to see how we can improve our chances of getting this first crucial judgement right.

Analysing the Nature of Armed Conflict and War

As we start to consider the nature of a conflict there are different ways to order our analysis, but when thinking deeply about the fundamental issues of strategy it is better to apply Occam's razor and to keep things simple.[6] The starting point is to recognize that, if force is being considered or used, then some form of political contest is either in prospect or underway. Once we have mapped out the political context in which this contest sits, its elemental nature is best analysed through the lenses of the political and strategic dimensions — and understood as a complex struggle in both.

To analyse the nature of the contest in the higher political dimension, we will likely need a longer term focus. We will often focus on less tangible things such as values, political and religious philosophies, perceptions of insecurity, a (sometimes barely conscious) long term view of the world and ultimately ideas. And the means will more often include intangibles such as political capital, national prestige and time.

To analyse the nature of the contest in the lower strategic dimension, we will likely need a shorter term focus. We will often focus on more tangible things such as foreign policy, diplomacy, national power and so on. And the means will more often include tangibles such as blood and treasure.

This is not to say that we should limit our analysis to these two dimensions. To understand the nature of an armed conflict or war, we must reflect widely. But the political and the strategic dimensions should be our starting point because it is here that we will discover the contest's elemental nature.

To understand the nature of the contest, above all we need to be clear about the political issue at stake and about the underlying political and strategic context in which the issue is located. So, having established the political context, the key question is: 'What is the political issue at contest?' In other words, what are we or what will we be, fighting about?

This question has two killer subordinates. Why, how and to what degree does the issue at contest bear on our national interest and national security? And why, how and to what degree does the issue at contest bear on the interests of those who would oppose us?

We need also to consider the means available to us and to our opponents. There is an inevitable tendency to think at the strategic level and of tangible and quantifiable means, for example military forces and to consider the 'balance of power' between the contestants. The intangible and less quantifiable means — such as national will and political capital — are all too often forgotten. But we must not forget the intangibles because they bear critically on the contest at the political level. Or, to put it in a slightly different way, in addition to the 'balance of power', we need also to consider, at the political level, the 'balance of passion.'

In this sense, power, whether hard or soft, is about using (or withholding) tangibles such as military or economic forces. These shape the contest at the strategic level whereas passion is to do with intangibles such as how much you care about the issue, the strength of your national will and the degree of national sacrifice you are willing to make. These shape the contest at the political level. As the French and US found in Vietnam and NATO is now finding in Afghanistan, the power of the supposedly stronger may be as nothing in the face of the passion of the supposedly weaker.

Thinking in this way may give us a more nuanced understanding of the nature of the contest at the political and strategic levels. Different positions are depicted stylistically in Figure 8.2:

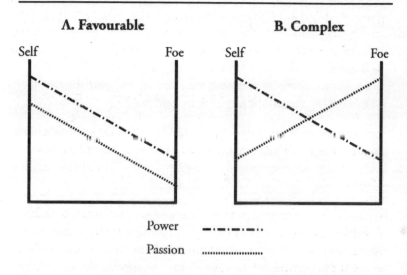

Figure 8.2: Balance of Power – Balance of Passion

The slopes indicate the balance of power and the balance of passion between you and your opponent or opponents.

The balance of power calculation is the easier one, made in the strategic dimension and based on more tangible resources. Note, though, that the calculation must be based on *effective* power, power that is both relevant and employable. Nuclear weapon preponderance is of little use in a counter-insurgency nor is naval superiority in a land-locked country. Neither, for that matter, is power that might deliver a shorter term strategic victory but with the likelihood of longer term political stalemate or defeat.

The balance of passion calculation is the harder one, made in the political dimension and based on more intangible resources. Key factors in the calculation include the relative gravity of the issue at contest, political capital, national will and character and preparedness for sacrifice. Of course, passions can be stirred, but as Clausewitz anticipates:

> If policy is directed only toward minor objectives, the emotions of the masses will be little stirred and they will have to be stimulated rather than held back.[7]

The cause is key. If the early analysis indicates that the contest will be lengthy, the crucial political question — to be answered by political leaders — is whether popular support for the enterprise can be sustained over time and in difficult circumstances.

Figure 8.2 illustrates two potential campaigns. In Case A, with both the balance of power and the balance of passion in our favour, there would be reason for cautious confidence. Whereas in Case B, where power lies with us, but the passion with our opponents, a very sober political discussion would be needed before deciding to proceed, especially if the campaign seemed likely to be lengthy.

Thinking in this way will help us respond to Clausewitz's plea that, first and foremost, we must try to understand the nature of a potential armed conflict or war. But we need to be wary of two traps. The first is the risky assumption that we can accurately gauge power and passion — understanding your own *effective* power is a sophisticated calculation at the best of times and calculating the passion of your opponent even more so. The second is the mistaken assumption that the balances will be fixed through time — they will not, events and unforeseen developments will invariably lead to changes. Pearl Harbour may have tilted the strategic balance of power temporarily in Japan's favour. But the Japanese High Command could not have dreamed up a better way of tilting the political balance of passion catastrophically against Japan than with a surprise attack on a Sunday morning against a fleet at peace in the harbour of a proud, Christian and extremely powerful maritime nation.

In summary, as we begin to create strategy, our analysis needs to focus on the political and strategic dimensions. Above all we should seek to understand the nature of the prospective armed conflict or war. And we need to address central questions. What is the political context? What is the political issue at contest? How does the issue bear on our national interests and security and on those of our opponent? A useful way to think about the resources we might use is through the ideas of 'balance of power' and 'balance of passion'. The analysis that then follows must be wider ranging and will be more complex — but if we address these issues first, it will have firm foundations.

Shaping the Political and Strategic Contests

As we start to think about shaping strategy, we must keep in mind Clausewitz's warning about not trying to turn a war into something that is 'alien to its nature'. We cannot dictate a war's nature. International politics, war's paradoxical logic, its friction, the interaction of chance, rationality and passion, the actions of our opponents and, above all, events are factors that contribute to war as a political condition and are largely beyond our control. The result will rarely be a simple sum of these different factors. So it would be foolish to assume control over the nature of a war. But that does not imply that we do not have some input. As a minimum, we get a vote on the nature of a war simply through the way we choose to act in it. In other words, our strategy will influence a war's nature. We must keep this simple but critical point in our minds as we start to shape strategy.

How should we approach the contest? Recall how Beaufre introduces the idea of contest in his definition of the art of strategy:

> It is therefore the art of the dialectic of force or, more precisely,
> art of the dialectic of two opposing wills using force to resolve
> their dispute.[8]

Mastering the art of the dialectic of force is central to success in politico-military strategy making. Some have used competitive sporting metaphors to show how to shape a dialectical competition — Beaufre favoured fencing, Americans have often been attracted to American football and the British on occasion have chosen cricket. Others, as noted in earlier chapters, propose timeless holy grails. Jomini says we should aim for *decisive mass at the critical point*. Liddell Hart says we should use an *indirect approach*. Contemporary Western military doctrine says we should use *manoeuvre* to disrupt and unbalance our opponent. All these ideas have their place but there is no unique philosopher's stone. Rather, as Admiral Castex suggests:

> To avoid such serious difficulties, one must abjure the illusion
> of invariable principles and remain ever attentive to the
> evolution of strategy and, especially, of its methods.[9]

Thus here it is better for us to identify and examine a range of dialectical techniques, recognising that the appropriateness of each will depend on the unique circumstances of the strategic case.

What follows, therefore, is a menu of strategic techniques for shaping dialectical contests, to be dined on *à la carte*. For each technique there is a polarity involved, for example between the *direct approach* and the Liddell Hart preference for the *indirect approach*. I will say something about the terminology, the technique's underpinning logic, the polarity and its use in history. But throughout, we must see these as useful ideas to help us tailor strategy, not panaceas to guarantee us victory.

To fight or not to fight

It may seem an obvious thing to say but the first question that we must think about before we start to shape strategy for war is to ask whether it really is the only option available. Have we really exhausted all diplomatic alternatives? Have we really thought through the prospects of 'do nothing'? Have we really tried to investigate the unintended consequences of conflict? Even when we have satisfied ourselves about these questions, this will not be the last time to consider them — we will need to return to them regularly, right up until hostilities commence and then keep thinking about them throughout the conflict.

Attack & defence

Attack and defence — offence and defence in modern parlance — is the most fundamental of the polarities and the place to start. Without attack and defence there would be no conflict, no war. Clausewitz's explanation of defence having a passive purpose, *preservation*, whilst attack has a positive one, *conquest*, still works well.[10] We must thus consider, at the outset, the question: are we or will we be, on the offensive or defensive?

Again though, as with other terms, war and peace for example, the binary relationship between attack and defence has become more complex, not least because you may be in different postures at different levels. For example, a strategic offensive or strategic defensive may be combined with a tactical offensive or tactical defensive, leading to four possible combinations. Using Summers' analysis of Vietnam, we can see how critical it is to understand precisely which of these postures you are in:

> Our so-called strategic offensive in the South was never more than a tactical offensive, since we were unable to carry the war to the enemy's main force — the North Vietnamese Army

— and instead expended our energies against a secondary
force — North Vietnam's guerrilla screen.[11]

In Summers' view, this was a fatal error because when South Vietnam
fell in 1975, it was not as a result of the tactical offensive of the
secondary force of Viet Cong guerrillas. South Vietnam fell to the
main force, a conventional North Vietnamese Army, comprising
four corps, undefeated by the US.

Surely though, the key level in Vietnam was the political, rather
than the strategic or tactical? Because of failures in US strategy and
increasing US domestic opposition to the war, by the late 1960s the
position at the political level was in the balance. The Tet Offensive in
January 1968 was a tactical defeat for North Vietnam, but provoked
a political crisis for President Johnson and, from then on until the
US withdrawal in 1972, he and his successor, Nixon, were on the
political defensive and never regained the initiative.

So, simple though it may at first appear, the question of whether
we are on the offensive or defensive has lost none of its relevance.
Because it needs to be thought about at the political as well as the
strategic level, it will be a difficult question to fathom in practice.
Who, for example, is on the political offensive in the US's Global
War on Terror? Nevertheless, the answer to the question provides
a good test for strategy. If a strategy does not make clear what our
posture will be at the political and strategic levels, we will have cause
to question the strategy.

Attrition & manoeuvre

Although not new, the ideas of attritional and manoeuvre warfare,
are in vogue. Or at least the idea of manoeuvre warfare is in vogue
in Western military thought.

The doctrine of manoeuvre originated in Napoleonic times. The

French theorist Guibert was a leading advocate, calling for a war of movement, which would 'throw [an] enemy into consternation, stun him, give him no chance to breathe, force him to fight or to retreat continuously before him.'[12] This idea presciently anticipated modern 'manoeuvre' warfare. The concept was refined in the writings of thinkers such as Liddell Hart and Fuller and the practice of German generals such as Rommel and Guderian. It is based on ideas of mass, tempo, defeating enemy forces in detail, dislocating the sinews of enemy power and ultimately disrupting him psychologically. As with all doctrinal ideas, the definition has and continues to evolve over time, but this modern version gives a good sense of where we now are:

> Manoeuvre warfare is a war-fighting philosophy that seeks to defeat the enemy by shattering his moral and physical cohesion — his ability to fight as an effective, co-ordinated whole — rather than by destroying him physically through incremental attrition.[13]

The German campaign in France in 1940 is the classic example of manoeuvre warfare in practice.

Attritional warfare is not advocated in Western military doctrine in the same way as manoeuvre, but is nevertheless needed in our toolbox of strategic techniques. It is about wearing down an enemy's strength through the destruction of his forces and war materiel and is defined along these lines:

> Attrition warfare [is] a style of warfare characterized by the application of substantial combat power that reduces an enemy's ability to fight through loss of personnel and equipment. Essentially it aims at the physical destruction of the enemy.[14]

It is not pretty, but neither is war. And history shows that it has its place. Slim gives an excellent sense of the concept when he describes the second phase of the Imphal-Kohima battle as 'attrition' — 'as week after week in man-to-man, hand-to-hand fighting, each strove to wear down the other's strength and break his will.'[15]

One clue to understanding the Western militaries' preference for manoeuvre over attrition lies in the Cold War and the prospect of operations on the Central Front in Europe. British Military Doctrine of this period said:

> War will invariably be a combination of both manoeuvre and attrition and stages in between. ... Though manoeuvre is the more difficult art to acquire and requires the greater investment in training and equipment, it provides for greater flexibility. It also enables a small force to engage a larger one with some chance of success instead of being forced into a battle of attrition that it could not sustain.[16]

The last sentence contains the clue, offering the West the possibility that a smaller NATO land force could hold its own against a larger USSR one by adopting this style of warfare.

But there will be times when a manoeuvre style of warfare will be inappropriate. It is hard, for example, to think how the idea could have been applied in the Battle of the Atlantic or the Battle of Britain. And there does not appear to be much logic in adopting the doctrine of manoeuvre in modern counter-insurgencies, where the insurgents' strategy is generally based on strategic patience and outlasting the invaders politically.

The authors of British Military Doctrine are not alone in making the obvious but important point that there is a place in strategic design for both ideas. Professor Gray suggests that:

> As a general rule, powerful countries or 'causes-in-arms' that would like to be countries, cannot be manoeuvred into defeat.

There is a perpetual dialectic or dialogue between attrition and manoeuvre, defence and offence and fire and movement.[17]

I balk at general rules in strategy — France, a powerful military country, was defeated by German manoeuvre warfare in 1940 — but there is nevertheless much truth in what Gray says. In armed conflict and war, both approaches will likely be needed. The fine judgement is to get the balance right.

Sequential & cumulative

The idea of sequential and cumulative approaches was introduced by Admiral Wylie. The notion is simply that war can, in his view, take two patterns:

A series of discrete steps or actions, with each one of this series of actions growing naturally out of and dependent on, the one that preceded it. The total pattern of all the discrete or separate actions makes up, serially, the entire sequence of the war. If at any stage of the war one of these actions had happened differently, then the remainder of the sequence would have had a different pattern. The sequence would have been interrupted and altered. ... But there is another way to prosecute a war. There is a type of warfare in which the entire pattern is made up of a collection of lesser actions, but these lesser or individual actions are not sequentially interdependent. Each individual one is more than a single statistic, an isolated plus or minus, in arriving at the final result. ... They are not incompatible strategies, they are not mutually exclusive. Quite the opposite. In practice they are usually interdependent in their strategic result.[18]

Wylie summarizes the ideas well.

The point about a cumulative approach is that the impact of the individual actions is less perceptible than in a sequential one; that is until the sum of the actions leads to a culminating point of success. Examples of the cumulative approach are the Battle of the Atlantic, the Battle of Britain and the US submarine campaign against the Japanese merchant fleet, the first two defensive, the last offensive. But cumulative strategies are not the sole preserve of navies and air forces. Guerrilla campaigns and their counter-insurgency responses also illustrate the idea in action.

There are indeed similarities and overlaps between the Sequential-Cumulative and Manoeuvre-Attrition polarities, but there are contrasts too. For example, the focus of attrition tends classically to be grinding down an enemy force but the cumulative approach could have a very different purpose. The primary cumulative purpose of the Battle of the Atlantic was to secure Britain's sea lines of communications but the secondary attritional consequence was to draw significant German naval and economic resources into a battle in which they would expend significant national strength.

Direct & indirect

I have criticized Liddell Hart for his unswerving advocacy of an *indirect approach* but it is not the idea that I have difficulty with, rather his view that it can be used to explain most of the strategic successes of history. The idea has much merit and Liddell Hart's phraseology best captures the thinking:

> During this survey one impression became increasingly strong — that, throughout the ages, effective results in war have rarely been attained unless the approach has had such indirectness as to ensure the opponent's unreadiness to meet it. The indirectness has usually been physical and always psychological. In strategy, the longest way round is often the shortest way home. More and more clearly has the lesson

emerged that a direct approach to one's mental object or physical objective, along the 'line of natural expectation' for the opponent, tends to produce negative results. ... In most campaigns the dislocation of the enemy's psychological and physical balance has been the vital prelude to a successful attempt at his overthrow.[19]

But Edward Luttwak would no doubt raise the equally pertinent riposte, based on the paradoxical logic of war, that the most *indirect approach* may, for that very reason, seem likely to a wise enemy to be the most likely direction of approach. And so it goes.

The idea of the *indirect approach* as holy grail falls at the twin hurdles of logic and historical counter-example. First, you may have no alternative to a *direct approach*. When considering how to keep Britain resupplied during World War II, what plausible alternative was there to the *direct approach* of convoys across the Atlantic? Second, if you judge that you have a preponderance of power, then you may actively seek the confrontation or battle that a *direct approach* may deliver. This, ultimately, was the point of the disagreement between the US and the British on the invasion of France. The British saw the opportunity for an *indirect approach* via the 'soft underbelly' of the Mediterranean, the Americans the necessity to take on and decisively defeat the German Army via a *direct approach* into France. In a way, both were right, but the Americans more so. As such, the D-Day landings could be viewed as an example of a *tactical indirect approach*, in the unexpected location of Normandy, to support a *strategic direct approach* of defeating the German Army.

Symmetrical & asymmetrical

It would be remiss not to include in our toolbox a modern favourite, the dialectic of the 'symmetric' and 'asymmetric'. The thinking is based on the contrasts in the way in which 'conventional forces' (such as armies, navies and air forces) and 'unconventional forces' (such as guerrillas, insurgents and terrorists) fight wars. A symmetric contest is between forces of a similar nature. An asymmetric contest is between forces of different natures, for example between a conventional army and a terrorist group. But although the symmetric-asymmetric terminology is new, the idea is not.

Rather it reflects an approach used by weaker actors against stronger ones for centuries. It is to do with the idea of a weaker actor confronting a stronger in a contest of the weaker's choosing, on ground — physical or psychological — where the stronger's strengths are difficult to deploy.

Asymmetry concerns more than just the physical capabilities of the forces involved. An asymmetric opponent may choose, for example, to act outside the laws of armed conflict and ignore ideas such as proportionality in the use of force. And he or she may choose deliberately to target civilian populations for political effect, through acts of political terrorism. And although supposedly weaker, asymmetric opponents are often deeply inspired by their political cause and the *balance of passion* is often in their favour.

This leads us to the key point about asymmetry. It is in the political dimension that the key acts of such contests play out. And so, when contemplating a contest with an opponent who may adopt an asymmetric approach, it is in the political dimension that the important early analysis must take place. It is analysis in the political dimension that will give statesmen and commanders the best chance of understanding the nature of an asymmetric war on which they may or may not want to embark. And it is this analysis in the political dimension that will critically inform, first, a decision to engage and, second, the strategy adopted once such a decision has been taken.

Dialectics combined

The different dialectics are not mutually exclusive and indeed successful strategic leaders combine them instinctively. Taking the contemporary case of counter-insurgency, you may choose, for example, to adopt a strategy that seeks, as its political objective, to improve security through *cumulative* gains and support it with *attritional* military operations to wear down those who would undermine security. Ultimately, the choice of combination depends on the unique circumstances of the case and is the real stuff of strategy making.

Above all, it is critical to keep clear in our minds the ideas that underpin these abstract terms and not 'over-generalize' them, nor use them to explain each success of every past war. Proponents of the modern school of *manoeuvre warfare* are as guilty as Liddell Hart in this respect, all too often explaining past successes in their own *manoeuvrist* terms. For example, Lyman suggests that Slim's Burma campaigns are classic examples of the manoeuvrist approach — which is curious, given that Slim makes not one mention of 'manoeuvre' in his final reflective chapter of *Defeat into Victory*.[20] Indeed, I suspect the suggestion would have left Slim mildly perplexed, not least because the doctrine to which he avowedly subscribed was different:

> Many years ago, as a cadet hoping someday to be an officer, I was poring over the 'Principles of War', listed in the old Field Service Regulations, when the Sergeant-Major came upon me. He surveyed me with kindly amusement. 'Don't bother your head about all them things, me lad', he said. 'There's only one principle of war and that's this. Hit the other fellow, as quick as you can and as hard as you can, where it hurts him most, when he ain't lookin'!' As a recruit, I earned that great man's reproof often enough; now as an old soldier, I would hope to receive his commendation. I think I might, for we of the

Fourteenth Army held to his Principle of War.[21]

This quote also shows that our list is not comprehensive — as a minimum, we could add the idea of 'Hit the other fellow as quick as you can'.

Conclusion

Ultimately, politico-military strategy is about contests and struggle, so this chapter's dialectical focus is key. I believe that our ability to understand and shape the clash of wills at the higher abstract levels is central to success in strategy making for armed conflict and war. So, whilst many modern writers have examined different forms and types of modern warfare — counter-insurgency, asymmetric warfare, manoeuvre warfare and so on — I have preferred to keep our focus up at these higher levels.

Our examination of strategy's relationship with policy, armed conflict and war, shows that the context in which modern strategy operates is, for a range of reasons, more political than ever before. And, for this and other reasons, the key levels are the political and the strategic. If we can understand the contest at these levels, then we stand a better chance of understanding the true nature of an armed conflict or war. And if we understand the true nature of an armed conflict or war, we stand a better chance of being able to shape our strategy for success.

The list of dialectics — Offence-Defence, Manoeuvre-Attrition, Sequential-Cumulative, Direct-Indirect, Symmetric-Asymmetric — is a source of reference as we think about shaping our strategy. And although the ideas above have classically been used to shape contests at the strategic level, the interesting challenge is to work out how to apply them to shape contests at the political level. But there are no holy grails here. Nor, given the complexity of the human condition, particularly the human condition in war, is a holy grail ever likely to emerge. But the ideas are a start, catalysts for strategic leaders to dine on *à la carte* as they start to devise strategy for the contest at hand.

That said, the chapter also shows there are no easy answers. Indeed, I started with the caution that we should avoid the mistake of thinking that there is anything here that can replace clear hard-headed thinking in strategy. The ideas are prompts — not substitutes — for strategic thinking but it nevertheless seems to me that they provide an intellectual starting point for thinking about strategy. Having set out these ideas to help prompt our thinking, we are now in a position to consider how we might order our thinking, in other words to consider how we can turn thinking into strategy — strategy for action.

Chapter 9

Strategy for Action
Frameworks for Thinking

War is a pulsation of violence, variable in strength and therefore variable in the speed with which it explodes and discharges its energy. War moves on its goals with varying speeds; but it always lasts long enough for influence to be exerted on the goal and for its own course to be changed one way or another — long enough, in other words, to remain subject to the action of a superior intelligence.

Carl von Clausewitz

Introduction

In this concluding chapter of Part III, we step beyond the devices of the earlier chapters designed to help *prompt* our thinking when strategy making and instead consider more practical theoretical frameworks to help us *order* our thinking.

First, I want to consider a key question; one to which very little thought has been given. What are the characteristics of superior strategy? Or, more simply, what does good strategy look like?

Second, drawing on Western military doctrine, I want to introduce the idea of the *Strategic Estimate*. The 'Commander's Estimate' is a set of structured questions used by a commander and his staff to add rigour to the command team's thinking when confronted with an operational or tactical situation. It has always seemed to me that, although designed for the operational and tactical levels, there is no reason why it should not be adapted for the strategic level.

Third, drawing on historical insights and corporate theory — particularly Mintzberg's ideas of deliberate, emergent and realized strategy — I want to introduce a framework to help organize ideas and thinking when creating and executing strategy and then adapt strategy in light of experience gained as it is turned into action.

Fourth, building on our analysis in Chapter 1 on the nature of war and the role of strategy, I will set out a framework to help us understand the different ways we need to think about strategy and war during the different stages of strategy making. This analysis draws on insights from historical and political science schools and links them with the idea of rationality. The simple thought is that we may need to be prepared to think differently in the creative and executive stages of strategy making.

What Does Good Strategy Look Like?

So far, our only tests for superior strategy — effectiveness, efficiency and endurability — are tests after the fact. Note also that the first of these tests is relative rather than absolute — effectiveness is measured in comparison to your opponent's performance and a strategy can only be judged in relation to the situation for which it is designed. Nevertheless, if our objective in strategy making is to produce good strategy, then it helps to have a view of what good strategy looks like.

A personal experience may help highlight the importance of the issue. In late 2007, having worked out what a comprehensive counter-insurgency strategy for Afghanistan might look like (through the simple approach of drafting one), one of the early responses, by a senior UN official, to one of my briefing slides was: 'This is useful because it gives us a sense of what good strategy looks like.' The first presentation was dated 4 December 2007 and, for interest, Figure 9.1 shows the slide that prompted the remark:

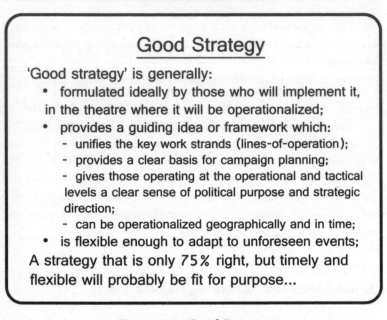

Figure 9.1: Good Strategy

Sketched out before I had started the major research for this book, I missed at least one key characteristic. Good strategy should include a clear statement of the overarching political objective. And there is another important criticism. My use of the word 'good' in 'good strategy' is loose. The first test of strategic performance is of relative effectiveness which can only be judged with reference to your opponent's performance. So a better term is 'superior strategy.' But on reflection the slide was not a bad start.

A second important insight on superior strategy comes from General Slim, in his record of the Burma campaign:

> The principles on which I planned all the operations were:
>
> i.   The ultimate intention must be an offensive one.
>
> ii. The main idea on which the plan was based must be simple.
>
> iii. That idea must be held in view throughout and everything else must give way to it.
>
> iv. The plan must have in it an element of surprise.[1]

Operating as he was at the operational rather than the strategic level and in a conventional war, Slim was not burdened by politics and policy in the way that we tend to be nowadays, but these principles nevertheless have an enduring quality.

A third equally important insight comes from our introductory analysis in Chapter 1. Here we identified strategy's three faces: upwards, as servant, to our policy; sideways to our opponent; downwards and directorially, to our agents and instruments. And we noted too that a real strategy was inherently organic — the cohered thinking, ideas and decisions of men and women, laid down in a communicable form which, in broad terms, answers the critical question: 'How are we going to do this?' So from first principles, superior strategy must surely answer the 'how' question, but from the perspective of all three faces:

- Policy — it should set out the policy objective, identify any policy constraints on action and indicate broadly what resources have been allocated.

- Dialectical — it should describe the nature of the political contest and explain how we intend to fight (if we have to), with an underpinning rationale.

- Command — it should provide sufficient guidance to strategic planners, civil leaders, operational commanders and others, to make the strategy actionable.

Drawing on these thoughts, on Slim's principles and on the characteristics of successful strategy in recent history, we can blend the insights into a register of common characteristics for superior strategy:

- First, the political objective is clearly described and there is a strong sense of political purpose.

- Second, the nature of the political contest is explained, as is the way we will confront our opponents if this proves necessary.

- Third, the strategy includes an element of surprise and seeks to gain and maintain the initiative.

- Fourth, the strategy has at its heart either a single big idea or a coherent and linked collection of smaller ideas, with a clear underpinning rationale.[2]

- Fifth, the strategy provides guidance on timings and priorities and can thus be a basis for campaign planning.

- Sixth, the totality is generally quite simple or at least capable of explanation in simple terms.

- Seventh, the strategy must have the capacity to bind the key players and the instruments of power.[3]

- Eighth and last but not least, the strategy must be practical — it must be 'doable' in the available time and space.

This is not an exhaustive list, more a starting point for debate. It is, though, an important starting point because, unless we know what superior strategy looks like, it is difficult to see how we can begin to create it other than through good fortune — which is no way to go to war.

The Commander's Estimate

In the British military and its Western contemporaries, when embarking on a new phase of a campaign or undertaking a tactical mission or action, a standard way to think the matter through is to use the 'Commander's Estimate'. The term will be second nature to military readers and the estimate is no more than a set of questions that provide a structure for operational problem solving.

Like all such devices, the estimate can be misemployed. As with doctrine, it is an aid to thinking, not a replacement. It is thus only as good as the user. Nevertheless, it has a reliable real world track record and, if employed intelligently, can be used to advantage. It is a familiar way of doing business for military members of strategy making teams and its generic approach is immediately understood by military personnel when co-opted into tactical or operational problem-solving. The questions bring rigour to the thinking and the structure reduces the risk that key factors will be missed. In addition, the written record of the analysis is a useful reference material, as events take shape and changes of strategy and plan become necessary.

It has always seemed to me that the same approach could be used at the strategic level and, in what follows, we will transfer the logic of the military estimate to the strategic level, to provide a structure for strategic analysis and strategy making. In the transfer, we will dispense with some of the tactical questions, given the higher level nature of the issues. The questions are not arbitrary but, with one exception, deduced from the insights of earlier chapters or from first principles or both. Whereas the ideas in Chapters 7 and 8 help prompt our thinking when creating strategy, these provide an overall structure for this analysis. They help us get our thinking into the right ball park and put us into a position to then create strategy in a more ordered way using the analytic tools and strategic techniques of earlier chapters.

The Strategic Estimate

To introduce the idea, I lay out the estimate in bare form to give a sense of the logic flow and then discuss each question in detail:

1. What is the overarching political context?

2. What is the political issue (or issues) at contest?

3. What is the political objective and why?

4. What are the resources available?

5. What courses of action could we adopt?

6. What course of action should we adopt?

7. What should be the spirit of our approach?

Whilst there is a deliberate logic in the sequence, in practice the questions simply help structure an iterative analysis and debate. Although the questions may seem simple, there are important and complex issues underlying most if not all.

What the astute reader will immediately note is the political focus of the early questions. This is to help ensure that we apply the same degree of rigour to shaping the political objective as we do to devising the politico-military strategy to deliver it.

1.   *What is the overarching political context?*

The thought that we need to understand the political context for an operation or campaign seems such an obvious thing to say. But on how many occasions have we fallen at this first hurdle or suffered setbacks, by failing to complete a satisfactory preliminary analysis? Such analysis should occur on at least three levels: national; regional; international. The failures in Suez and Vietnam can be laid, to a significant extent, at the door of failures of political analysis at all three levels.

The Russian analysis in Afghanistan is another example. The Soviet General Staff's reconnaissance in late 1979 failed to note that Afghanistan was involved in a civil war and that a *coup de main* would only seize control of the central government, not the countryside. Given that the people had always taken up arms against invaders, it was predictable that they would do so again:

> Unlike the Communist guerrilla movements in China and Vietnam, the Mujahedeen guerrillas were not trying to force a new ideology and government on their land. Rather, they were fighting to defend their families, their *Qawm* and their religion against a hostile, atheistic ideology, an alien value system and oppressive central government and a foreign invader. Individual groups, unconnected to national or international political organisations, spontaneously defended their community values and their traditional way of life.[4]

There is, incidentally, an uncanny resonance between these remarks and the situation the US and NATO face in modern Afghanistan. To avoid this type of mistake, we must be able to visualize the political context through the different cultural eyes of each of the key political actors. As such, the analysis needs to be political in the broadest sense of the word.

We may examine, for example, anthropological, religious, ideological, historical, linguistic and economic factors. But there is no template to say what we should and should not take into account. From personal experience, a list longer than ten or so key factors is as likely as not to confuse matters. A key strength in the strategic leader is the judgement to recognize those factors critical to the operation and the willingness to set to one side the remainder.

Furthermore, the political context is not static. Our political analysis needs constantly to refine the picture. We need to clarify early areas of uncertainty but also to forecast and be ready to respond to events. The modern military approach to information management often uses the term 'recognized picture'. The 'recognized air picture', for example, fuses real-time spatial information from many different inputs, from radars, air traffic controllers, visual reports and so on. In our political analysis, we should aspire to something similar. Because the use of armed force is a political act — more so now than ever before — those who direct such acts, be they politicians, diplomats or military men, need to have the best view possible of the political context, the 'recognized political picture' for want of a better term.

I do not underestimate the challenge of developing a recognized political picture, but without it we will be prone to repeating the mistakes that led to Suez, Vietnam and the Soviet experience in Afghanistan. Ultimately, political calculations prior to an intervention need as much, if not more, rigour as the strategic calculations to create strategy and guide the use of force. Otherwise strategy will be built on weak foundations.

2.   What is the political issue (or issues) at contest?

If the use of force is being considered, then some form of political contest is either in prospect or underway, hence: 'What is the political issue (or issues) at contest?' Yet a question that seems so obvious is all too often by-passed. As I noted in Chapter 8, the question has two killer partners. Why, how and to what degree does the issue at contest bear on our national interest and national security? And why, how and to what degree does the issue bear on the interests of those who might oppose us?

There are other related questions. Why are we considering a military contest? What are the alternatives? What is the impact of 'do nothing'? Do we know enough about the issue or issues to make an informed decision? George Kennan's testimony to the Senate Foreign Relations Committee on 16 February 1966 exposes the underlying need for the analysis:

> If we were not already involved as we are today in Vietnam, I would know of no reason why we should wish to become so involved and I could think of several reasons why we should wish not to. Vietnam is not a region of major military, industrial importance. It is difficult to believe that any decisive developments of the world situation would be determined in normal circumstances by what happens on that territory. If it were not for the considerations of prestige that arise precisely out of our present involvement, even a situation in which South Vietnam was controlled exclusively by the Viet Cong, while regrettable and no doubt morally unwarranted, would not in my opinion, present dangers enough to justify our direct military involvement. ... From a long term standpoint, therefore and on principle, I think our military involvement in Vietnam has to be recognized as unfortunate, as something we would not choose deliberately, if the choice were ours all over again today.[5]

These words need no further explanation. If one were to imagine a fantasy world where a Kennan's Russian twin had been invited to speak to the Politburo in mid-1980, soon after the Soviet General

Staff had advised that the war in Afghanistan was unwinnable, then I suspect the message would have been very similar.

We must never underestimate the importance for problem solving of grappling with, narrowing and finally delineating the issue or issues at contest. In the quote that follows Kenachi Ohmae is talking about corporate strategy making, but his logic works equally well in our world and illustrates the point perfectly:

> Solution-oriented questions can be formulated only if the critical issue is localized and grasped accurately in the first place. A clear common understanding of the nature of a problem that has already been localized provides a critical pressure to come up with creative solutions. When problems are poorly defined or vaguely comprehended, one's creative mind does not work sharply. The greater one's tolerance for lukewarm solutions, half measures and what the British used to call muddling through, the more loosely the issue is likely to be defined. For this reason, isolating the crucial points of the problem — in other words, determining the critical issue — is most important to the discovery of the solution.[6]

This is not to say that it is easy to isolate the issue at contest but it is worth the effort, for the very reasons that Ohmae lists. Moreover, if it proves impossible to isolate the issue, then this should warn us to tread carefully before committing ourselves to a strategy and expending resources, possibly treasure but particularly blood, in a vague pursuit.

3.   *What is the political objective and why?*

Question 2 leads naturally to Question 3. What should be our political objective? And how does it relate to the issue at contest? What do we want to achieve and why?

Defining the political objective is often as challenging as devising a strategy to deliver it. This is especially the case in a fast moving situation. In a crisis, when the use of military force is being contemplated, there is a not unreasonable desire in military commanders that the political objective be clearly defined. But this is not always possible. Because the task of defining the political objective is often difficult, the answer may simply take time to work through. But there may also be a political desire to retain political freedom of manoeuvre and to avoid an overly prescriptive position, at least initially. Military commanders and civil servants must understand these political realities. Equally, political masters must understand that political freedom of manoeuvre comes at a price.

The absence of a clearly defined political objective significantly increases the difficulty of strategy making. Indeed, such a deficiency may critically prejudice the chances of success and ultimately lead to military failure — whose historical bedfellow is usually political failure in one form or another. It is thus essential to have a shared understanding of each other's position and the contrasting political and military risks that both parties bear.

But once an operation or campaign has begun, there can be no excuse for not having clearly defined the political objective. Recounting his retreat from Burma, Slim explains the consequences of failing to do so:

> We needed from the highest national authority a clear directive of what was to be our purpose in Burma. ... No such directive was ever received. In the comparatively subordinate position of a corps commander, immersed in the hour-to-hour business of a fluctuating battle, I could not know what pressures were being exerted on the local higher command, but it was painfully obvious that the lack of a definite, realistic

directive from above made it impossible for our immediate commanders to define our object with the clarity essential. Whoever was responsible, there was no doubt that we had been weakened basically by this lack of clear object.[7]

Summers exposes the same problem in Vietnam:

Brigadier General Douglas Kinnard found in a 1974 survey of Army generals who had commanded in Vietnam, 'almost 70% of the Army generals who managed the war were uncertain of their objectives.' Kinnard goes on to say that this 'mirrors a deep-seated strategic failure: the inability of policy makers to frame tangible, obtainable goals.'[8]

In a narrow sense, Kinnard is right to blame policy makers for the failure. But the quote also begs questions. Were senior military officers in the USA aware of the uncertainty amongst their subordinates in the field? If not, why not? If so, was this uncertainty explained to political masters? But ultimately, when all is said and done, it is not difficult to see why, without a clear understanding of the desired political objective, strategy making in Vietnam would have been difficult.

The message is plain. If our subordinates do not know what the overarching objective is and how it is to be delivered, then the prospects of our success will be reduced.

4.   What are the resources available?

The next question, too, is more subtle than it appears. What are the resources available? What *means* do we have to achieve the objective? It is all too easy to think in terms of forces — military and civil — and diplomatic instruments, such as economic aid, of 'blood and treasure' in its broadest sense. But as already discussed, we forget, all too often, that we may need to expend at least three other, less tangible, resources — time, political capital and national prestige. Let's consider these in more detail.

Time is the imponderable, particularly in the interventions, be they for humanitarian or harder edged reasons. We see this in the counter-insurgencies that have evolved in Afghanistan and Iraq. The paradox is that in interventions such as these, the received wisdom is that there is a need for strategic patience: 'These things take time.' And yet time is all too often in short supply and for two reasons. First, the introduction of armed forces of foreign nations in the sovereign territory is akin to introducing foreign tissue into the human body and the longer that they're present then, generally, the higher the chance of an adverse reaction. Second, because the wars that can result will most likely be wars of choice, rather than wars of necessity, the domestic consensus of the intervening nations will be less certain. Politicians and populaces will be much more sensitive to casualties and more likely to weary of the mission. The result is that the time that these modern interventions need is often time that is not available. This is one of the reasons why we are likely to see fewer, rather than more, such operations in the near future.

Political capital and national prestige are also at stake. Iraq provides a clear example of how these costs can accrue. George Bush and Tony Blair both squandered large amounts of political capital domestically, as a result of the action. In parallel, Britain's failures in Basra also led to significant loss of national prestige, both in the Gulf and further afield. Her actions in Afghanistan have not, so far, done much to restore this. As we think in these sober terms — of costs in time, domestic political capital, international prestige, treasure and blood — then we may decide to reflect more deeply on Question 2. What is the political issue at contest? Why, how and to what degree does the issue bear on our national security and national interests and those of potential opponents?

It is useful, also, to consider the cost benefit question. What price are we prepared to pay in pursuit of our political objective? What will be the benefits if it is achieved? Do we have to fight to achieve them? Here too, we often fail to think things through:

> [There is a conception that] ought to be utterly commonplace in strategic discourse or related national policy decisions but that seems on the contrary to be often neglected or omitted. It is the conception simply of reasonable price and of it being applied to strategy and national policy — the idea that some ends or objectives are worth paying a good deal for and others are not. The latter includes ends that are no doubt desirable but which are worth attempting to achieve only if the price can *with confidence* be kept relatively low. Can it really be that such a simple and obvious question is often neglected and overlooked? The answer, most decidedly, is yes.[9]

Cost-benefit calculations such as these should critically inform a decision for action. So too should an idea of the chances of our success and the risks of failure. And to address these latter issues, we need an idea of the strategies that we could use to deliver the political objective.

5.   *What courses of action could we adopt?*

With this question, we now enter the narrower realm of strategy creation. The word 'could' in the question is to prompt us to consider different ways of achieving the objective and draws on Slim's approach, which has lost none of its relevance — recall our earlier quote:

> My method of working out such a plan was first to study the possibilities myself and then informally discuss them with my Brigadier General Staff, Major-General Administration and my opposite number in the Air Force. At these discussions

we would arrive at the broadest outline of possible alternative courses of action, at least two, more often three or four.[10]

Recall too that, during the Cuban Missile Crisis, JFK's crisis strategy team initially assessed five different courses of action.

As well as devising three, four or more courses of action with the political objective and allocated resources fixed, we might also wish to consider options where these are varied. In other words, we may wish to see what would happen if we varied the *ends* or the *means*, as well as the *ways*. For example, how would we do things differently if the political aspiration was more modest? Alternatively, what would we do with additional resources? And how would these adjustments bear on our chances of success? And last but not least, what about 'do nothing'?

As we refine and then narrow down courses of action, two of the most important checks are political feasibility and logistic feasibility. The political feasibility of a course of action can only be tested through regular political engagement in the strategy making process. Whereas outline planning is a useful way to test the logistic feasibility of a course of action and indeed it is here that strategic planning comes into its own as a servant of strategy making. Slim's method is instructive. Having identified three or four broad courses of action, he would pass these to:

> our team of planners, specially selected but comparatively junior officers, representing not only the general and administrative staffs, but the air staff as well. They would make a preliminary study, giving the practicability or otherwise of each course and its advantages and disadvantages. They were quite at liberty to make new suggestions of their own or to devise permutations and combinations of the originals. The results of the planners' examination were put up to me as a short paper, largely in tabular form and from it I decided on

the main features of the plan to be followed.[11]

The great advantage of this approach is that the Commander's imprint is on the work at the outset. But equally he is able to draw on the skills and insights of a bright and talented staff with the expectation that the whole will be greater than the sum of the parts.[12]

6.   What course of action should we adopt?

The question 'how should we do this?' does two things. First, it gets the strategists off the fence and forces them to make a reasoned recommendation for a particular course of action. Second, it prompts a decision. A decision will be based on many factors, but ultimately there is no substitute for good judgement. Four tests, based on common sense and military experience, stand out:

- 'Action on' — in the event of a likely strategic event X occurring, what would be our action?

- 'What if' — what would we do if an unlikely strategic event Y occurred?

- 'Plan B' — if the whole scheme appeared to be failing, do we have a fallback?

- 'Enemy action' — what is our opponent's likely response to the strategy and should this cause us to make changes?

Applying these tests, individually and collectively, to the different courses of action will enable us to gain a better understanding of their individual strengths and weaknesses. For example, if strategic event X occurred, how would we handle this under course of action 1, 2, 3 or 4? What would the fall back be for course of action 1, 2, 3 or 4? Is one course of action a feasible fall back for another, in the event of the chosen course of action failing? All this will help us to narrow down the options and reach a decision.

As we think about the last of the tests, Slim, in a tantalising insight, exposes a critical issue for us to think about when considering the possible response of an enemy to a particular course of action:

> [Having selected a particular course of action] I usually discussed with the intelligence officer whom I had selected to represent the Japanese command at my HQ ... what the enemy's reactions to this plan were likely to be. I was, of course, kept daily in the picture of the Japanese actions, intentions and dispositions, as far as we know or could surmise them, but I intentionally waited until I had selected my plan before considering the enemy response to it, as I intended him to *conform to me, not me to him* (emphasis added).[13]

The italicized statement of intent is crystal clear and reflects the uniquely competitive nature of politico-military strategy. And it also allows me to reiterate a key point: the superior strategy is the one that captures and then retains the initiative.

7. *What should be the spirit of our approach?*

On the face of it, this final question has less logical foundation than its predecessors but it nevertheless feels important. I trace the idea back to a conversation I had with an MoD colleague whilst we were formulating British defence policy. As we were concluding the work, he made the point to me that we needed to ensure that the policy we had drafted was interpreted in the spirit in which we had written it. It is worth returning again to Slim, to get a sense of a similar idea in action:

> I suppose dozens of operation orders have gone out in my name, but I never, throughout the war, actually wrote one myself. I always had someone who could do that far better than I could. One part of the order I did, however, draft myself — the intention. It is usually the shortest of paragraphs,

but it is always the most important, because it states — or it should — just what the commander intends to achieve. It is the overriding expression of will by which everything in the order and every action by every commander and soldier in the army must be dominated. It should, therefore, be worded by the commander himself.[14]

There seem to be two thoughts embedded in this quote, one conscious, the other subconscious. The conscious thought is in the term 'just what the commander intends to achieve'. Interpreting this using our terminology, Slim is explaining how important it is for the commander personally to set out the objective and the strategy to deliver it. But there is also something subtle in the words 'overriding expression of will'. In this personally penned expression will be an indelible imprint of the commander's character, personality and will reflecting the spirit with which he or she aims to approach the mission.

In sum, the questions of the *Strategic Estimate* can never be a panacea. Nevertheless, they provide a structure for decision making based on a process that has a successful track record at the operational and tactical levels. The next question is how should we order and organize the ideas that emerge as we work through them and then turn them into strategy and the strategy into action? The characteristics of superior strategy, discussed earlier in the chapter, provide a framework for ordering the ideas but we will need to refer to earlier chapters when we think about creating strategy for action.

Strategy for Action — a Framework for Execution

I examined, in Chapter 5, the schools of corporate strategy making and their similarities and contrasts with politico-military strategy making. Of particular interest were the ideas of Mintzberg, represented in the diagram reproduced in Figure 9.2, about deliberate, unrealized and emergent strategy.

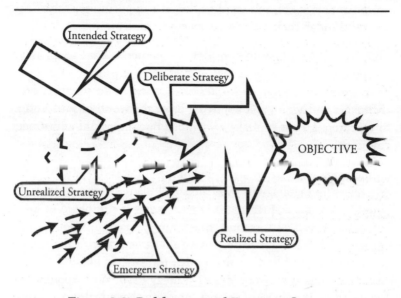

Figure 9.2: Deliberate and Emergent Strategy

To recall the logic flow, you start in the top left hand corner by creating a strategy, your *intended strategy*. As you execute this strategy, some parts — your *deliberate strategy* — succeed and others — your *unrealized strategy* — fail. But as you execute the strategy, you also find, in the bottom left hand corner, that other approaches — your *emergent strategy* — also succeed in the field, notwithstanding that they were not part of the intended strategy. Put simply, you create and execute a strategy, retain the parts that work, discard the parts that don't and adopt new ideas from the field. We saw that these corporate ideas resonated in our world. Moltke's axiom, for example, that no plan survives contact with the enemy sat comfortably alongside the idea of *unrealized strategy*. And the base assumption of the doctrine of *blitzkrieg* was that the *intended strategy* represented only the broadest guidance and that it would be for front line commanders to see, seize and exploit the opportunities, that is to devise through their actions the *emergent strategy*.

The issue I want now to consider is whether we can adapt these corporate ideas to help us better manage the process of creating politico-military strategy for action. I want to do this by taking Mintzberg's diagram and adjusting it for the world of war. And as a first step, I want to make a nuanced but important adjustment to his thinking.

Mintzberg uses the term 'strategies' in the plural and represents these 'strategies' in the diagram with the small black arrows. As such, he implicitly assumes, first, that higher strategy is composed of lower or sub-strategies and, second, that strategy making is not the sole province of the senior team. I have no difficulty with the second assumption. But I find the first more problematic, because it seems to me to weaken the very idea of strategy itself. With apologies to Swift, there is a sense of 'bigger strategies have little ones, upon their backs to bite them and little ones have littler ones still and so on *ad infinitum*.'

For me, viewing strategy as simply the sum of sub-strategies loses the sense communicated by Slim here: 'The *main idea* on which the plan was based must be simple ... That idea must be held in view throughout and everything else must give way to it (emphasis added).'[15] It also risks muddying the relationship between strategy and planning — recall Dick Yarger's thoughts:

> Strategy is not planning. ... Planning makes strategy actionable. ... it partakes of a different mindset. It relies on a high degree of certainty ... Planning is essentially linear and deterministic, focusing heavily on first-order cause and effect. ... The planning process works because the lower the level, the

more limited the scope and complexity and the shorter the timeline. ... [Whereas] strategy lays down what is important and to be achieved, sets the parameters for the necessary actions and prescribes what the state is willing to allocate in terms of resources. ... It bounds planning. ... The planner is Newtonian or scientific in his approach; the strategist is more 'fuzzy' [although both] share the paradigm of ends, ways and means.[16]

This is an important distinction because it too takes us away from the view of a strategy being a simple sum of sub-strategies. And it takes us away from the question 'What are our strategies?' Instead, it takes us toward the question 'What is our strategy?' And it takes us toward Churchill's 'unity of conception', Slim's 'main idea' and the American Chiefs of Staff's 'strategic concept'.

However, if one thinks of the small arrows in Mintzberg's diagram not as 'strategies', but instead as the 'ideas, judgements and decisions' that comprise a strategy, then the diagram takes on a slightly different sense. With this adjustment, the notions of intended, deliberate, unrealized, emergent and realized strategy (not strategies) take on a clearer sense.

As such, the corporate ideas of Mintzberg are useful not because they codify the politico-military experience but rather because we can adapt them to codify the experience. Figure 9.3 seeks, stylistically, to do just that and explain theoretically how politico-military strategy making proceeds over time.

Taking first *strategy in creation*, the diagram depicts the early creative stage of strategy making. The large well-defined arrow to the top left represents the created strategy. And the smaller component arrows inside the large arrow represent the *ideas, judgements and decisions* which make up the strategy. But also included is the Moltkean idea that 'no plan survives contact with the enemy'; we will need to make changes to our strategy. The large empty arrow in the bottom left simply represents conceptual space where the ideas, judgements and decisions can emerge, as learned in the field.

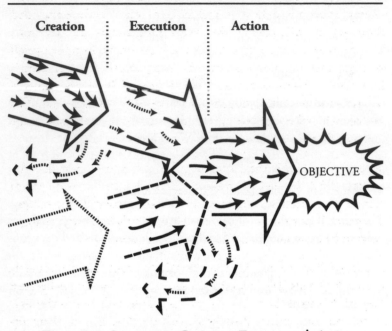

Figure 9.3: Strategy in Creation, Execution & Action

How might this conceptual space work in practice? It might be through the provision of a reserve to the commander. Or it might be an agreement on a *blitzkrieg* doctrine that allows front line commanders the freedom to decide how best to proceed, working in the grain of the higher commander's intent. This is similar to what we nowadays now call 'mission command' but what would, in corporate thinking, be the sort of approach advocated by the learning school.[17] In a sense, what we are talking about is a more conscious form of flexibility.

In *strategy in execution*, some of the ideas, judgements and decisions of *strategy in creation* fail — for example, due to contact with the enemy, 'friction' and the irrational reality of war — and are discarded. Similarly, as anticipated, other ideas, judgements and decisions emerge in practice, are seen to work and are drawn into the overall strategy, integrated and promoted. The process of integration is important and is more than a simple addition of the new elements to the mix. The new ideas, judgements and decisions must be identified and consciously integrated with the survivors of the original strategy and together reworked into a broadly coherent whole.

Strategy for action is the result. But this is not to suggest that the result is final. Instead what the stylisation represents is a cyclical system with creation, execution and action constantly interacting. The point is not that strategy changes but rather that the changes need to be consciously and coherently managed.

Politico-military strategy is about struggle and contest and, ultimately, the battle of wills. The first mistake is to discard ideas simply because they do not work first time. Some need to be adhered to through thick and thin, others dispensed with quickly. And if 'them up there' are to avoid the accusation of 'always changing their minds' there needs to be some sense of consistency. Getting these particular judgements right — working out what works and what does not, what needs to be retained and pushed through and what must be discarded — is the one of the greatest challenges for the political leaders and strategic commanders. Theory is unlikely to help. Rather, in making judgements such as these, it is experience and, perhaps, a knowledge of history that will help most, reflective rather than prescriptive thinking. Which in turn leads us to the second of my two frameworks.

Strategy for Action — a Thinking Framework

How should we think when we are creating strategy for action? The likely answer is in different ways, at least if we are to be successful.

In the conceptual stage, when we are creating strategy, we will be thinking in the rational place of the strategic drawing board. But when executing strategy and in the mire of operations, we will be working in the irrational place of the political condition that is war. Figure 9.4 gives a stylistic sense of the simple idea that we may need to adapt the way we think in these two different places. The central arrow is intended to represent linear time from the creation of strategy for a campaign through the execution of that strategy to the operational actions that result. In practice, feedback loops operate throughout, but the key point is that the further right you move along the arrow, then the less rational the world becomes.

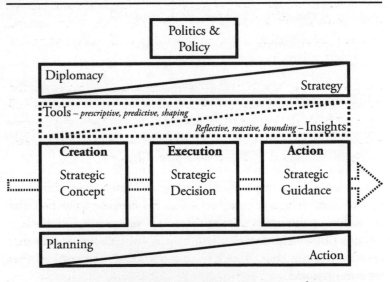

Figure 9.4: Strategy in Creation, Execution & Action

To the left, in the rational world of strategy creation, we will tend to rely more on rational thinking *tools* — prescriptive, predictive and shaping — that we can (very) loosely group under the heading of a *political science* or Jominian school of strategy making. Whereas to the right, we will tend to rely more on *insights and judgements* gleaned from unfolding events — reflective, reactive, bounding — which we might (again very) loosely group under the heading of a *historical* or Clausewitzian school of strategy making.

This is how the prescriptive thinking of the political science school interacts with the reflective thinking of the historical school. The overall sense will be of shovelling rationality onto the conveyor belt at the concept tail of the arrow. But accepting that, notwithstanding our best efforts, we will be faced in return with a flow of results and events some of which will be those we had hoped for but others will be unexpected and seemingly irrational. The irrational results and events will be an inevitable consequence of war's irrational nature, so we must simply accept, try to make sense of and then respond to them, by shovelling in more rationality to the concept end of the conveyor belt.

The key is to keep your nerve when the results are not entirely as the strategy intended because the likelihood is that your opponent will be faced with the same problem. Indeed if you have shaped your strategy well, the enemy will be confronted by dilemmas, paradoxes and irrationalities that will be even worse than yours.

Such a flow — rational inputs leading to a confusing mixture of rational and irrational outputs — is the nature of the political condition of armed conflict and war, epitomized in Clausewitz's notions of friction, chance and passion; Moltke's observation that no plan survives contact with the enemy; and Luttwak's idea that for every rational action, there is a paradoxical and often unforeseen, result. These are the strategic facts of life. The secret is to cope better in this world than your opponent — and this is where superior strategy helps.

Conclusion

We opened this chapter by asking and answering the key practical question: what does superior strategy look like? Ultimately a strategy can only be judged against the situation for which it is designed, so the characteristics that we identified to start with are for guidance and not principles for rigid application. But they at least give us a sense of the form we should be aiming for when making strategy.

We then introduced frameworks to help us order our strategy making. We have used a mixture of disciplines to develop these frameworks. The *Strategic Estimate* is a development of the Commander's Estimate of military doctrine. Although the *Strategic Estimate* is no more than a set of structured questions, the questions have robust rational roots in theory and the estimate process has a proven track record in military practice.

The action framework is a development of the thinking in the learning school of corporate strategy. The corporate ideas are useful; not because they codify military experience but rather because they help us think about how such experience could be codified. Perhaps the key idea in our codification is the deliberate assumption that, because 'no plan survives contact' and because of war's irrationality, a created strategy will never work precisely as conceived — there is thus a need to create conceptual space within the strategy for the adaptations that will be needed for success.

'Conceptual space' is not a mandate for constant change in strategy, whose impacts can be catastrophic lower down the command chain. Rather it is to do with the preparedness to change in response to unforeseen developments or new opportunities — 'learning experiences' in the corporate jargon. The great skill of the commander is to distinguish between those moments when a strategy needs to be pursued in the face of great difficulty and those where change is necessary. No amount of theory will help with this critical judgement.

The thinking framework draws from the political science and historical schools, Jominian and Clausewitzian if you like, and links them through the idea of rationality. As we proceed with strategy making, we need to tune the way we think. A prescriptive strategy making process should be able to create a rational strategy to deliver a political objective. But, because of war's irrationality, the rational strategy will not always lead to rational results. And when we are faced irrational results, the teachings of Clausewitz and others, come into play. A study of the lessons of history will help improve our strategic judgement and the reflective Clausewitzian mindset will help us take the unexpected in our stride and adapt. The two modes of thought are not mutually exclusive, quite the reverse. They are highly complementary and the trick is to get the balance of emphasis right.

Let us conclude with an historical illustration. It seems doubtful that, when they began the Tet Offensive In 1968, North Vietnam's high command would have anticipated the magnitude of the tactical reverse they would suffer, including the loss of 100,000 fighting men. But as Summers observes:

> Tet 68 was a resounding [tactical] failure for the North Vietnamese. But we also saw that it was a strategic success against our center of gravity — American public opinion and the American political leadership.[18]

Reacting to that success, including the impact that the offensive had on the United States and South Vietnam alliance, the North Vietnamese strategic leaders recognized that:

Now all they had to do was wait us out. Although they committed regular troops in the South to make up for the Viet Cong losses, they did not mass them but used them as an economy of force on the tactical defensive. ... the North Vietnamese evidently believed that by the spring of 1972 their strategy had succeeded. They believed that the United States was no longer capable of supporting South Vietnam.[19]

Their analysis of the unexpected nature of the strategic success that resulted from their tactical reverse caused them consciously to adjust their strategy. And in following through this adjusted strategy, they were ultimately successful.

This leads me to the key concluding point to keep in mind as we order our thinking. Above all, strategic performance is relative. It is easy to be overwhelmed psychologically by the setbacks and reverses, the unanticipated events and the unexpected outcomes that are the stuff of strategy and war. But this is to lose sight of the likelihood that your opponent will be faced with the same flow of phenomena. And, if you have shaped your strategy well, then keeping your nerve and seeing it through has as much a part to play in its success as being alert to the irrational.

PART IV:

PRACTICE

Chapter 10

Strategy Making & Institutions
A Politico-Military School

Because Nazi Germany was an autocracy, Hitler was able to impose a grand strategy on his generals that few at the beginning, but many by the middle and almost all by the end, thought suicidal ... By complete contrast, the strategies of the Western Allies had to be exhaustively argued through the Planning Staff, General Staff, Chiefs of Staff and then combined Chiefs of Staff levels, before they were even capable of being placed before politicians, where they were debated in microscopic detail all over again.

Andrew Roberts

Introduction

The theoretical tools and frameworks of Part III are all very well but how do we turn the theory into practice? Here, in Part IV, I will address this question and consider the practical issues that confound us as we create strategy for action.

I will start by drawing on Part II's historical and corporate insights and on first principles and personal experience, to propose, in this short chapter, some design premises for a *politico-military school* of strategy making. In so doing, I have two inter-related objectives. First,

I want to codify some of the important premises — conscious and unconscious — of our current strategy making processes. Second, I want to propose other premises that could improve our strategy making.

The result is not, though, a blueprint for an idealized strategy making process. Rather I want to stimulate the thinking of, first, those leaders who are wondering how they might improve their own processes and, second, those citizens who want to better understand their national processes and, perhaps, influence the improvement. The very act of codifying your strategy making process is an essential first step on the road to recovery and, if nothing else, these premises provide a point of reference for such an exercise.

To begin the analysis, we will return to corporate strategy and conclude some unfinished business by reviewing the last of the corporate strategy making schools, the *configuration school*.

A Configuration School of Corporate Strategy Making

In Chapter 5, we focused on three of Mintzberg, Ahlstrand and Lampel's ten corporate strategy making schools, the design, power and learning schools. We noted, in these, the similarities to and contrasts with politico-military strategy making.

Not all corporate thinking is relevant and there are also important philosophical differences. Corporate strategy tends to focus, for example, on the health and prosperity of the whole corporation. In our world, this is akin to the survival and prosperity of the whole nation-state and the realm of high politics and so called grand strategy. In contrast, politico-military strategy tends to focus on individual campaigns and operations. In the business world, this is akin to specific corporate initiatives. More fundamentally, in our world, we use strategy to achieve political objectives in the face of organized violence. But accepting these differences, we found useful insights in the different corporate schools. Some can help codify politico-military experience; others, selectively applied, may help improve the way we make strategy.

We did not, though, examine the last of the corporate strategy making schools, the *configuration school*. This is because the central idea in the configuration school is an ideal introduction to a *politico-military school* of strategy making.

The configuration school's central idea is that the strategy making approaches of the other nine corporate strategy schools are not mutually exclusive but can be integrated. The configuration school proposes that the different approaches should be integrated in time, based on a business life cycle. For example, at an early stage when a company is starting up, an entrepreneurial school or learning school strategy making approach might be best. Whereas once the company has grown and matured and has a clearer sense of purpose and direction, then a design school approach might be more appropriate. It seems to me that this idea has mileage in our world. As we incorporate configuration school thinking into the politico-military strategy making world, we can adapt and improve it in two ways.

First, there seems to be no reason why we need restrict ourselves to integrating different schools' approaches only by sequencing them in time. There seems to be no reason why we should not take a wholly eclectic view and dine *à la carte* on the schools' ideas, integrating them within politico-military campaign phases, if you like vertically *in* time, as well as horizontally *over* time. Second, the way in which we select the ideas should be guided by which of the schools' ideas seems most appropriate for a particular phase of a campaign. These adaptations move us from *configuration over time* to *integration in time*. But they also seem to me to help codify what is already existing generic politico-military way of strategy making. Therefore, I have chosen the term *politico-military school* to describe what follows.[1]

This question is: which premises from which school might a *politico-military school* draw upon? To help answer this, we need to remind ourselves of the key features of the corporate schools. The design school's key idea is that strategy making should be 'a deliberate process of conscious thought.'[2] This ties with a central idea in the *politico-military school* philosophy, founded on long historical experience, of the essential need for rational calculation at the start of a campaign. The power school reminds us that there are the power relationships between strategy makers which impact on strategy making, particularly in coalitions as we shall see in Chapter 11. And in the learning school, the central idea is 'strategy making must above all take the form of a process of learning over time.'[3] This too ties with another central idea in the *politico-military school* philosophy of the essential need to learn and adapt over a campaign.

A Politico-Military School of Strategy Making

Dining *à la carte* on the corporate schools' premises, but also drawing on the theoretical ideas and historical insights of earlier chapters, let us set out the premises for a *politico-military strategy making school*. The aim is to help codify, better understand and ultimately improve strategy making processes in a modern liberal democracy.

To give a sense of how the premises interlink, I list them first for overview and then examine each individually:

- At the outset of a campaign, we should create strategy using rational deliberation and calculation.

- Although we should take account of history, doctrine and other analytic sources, each strategy should be uniquely tailored for the specific issue at hand.

- Strategic leaders should oversee strategy creation and there should be early and continuing political engagement in the process.

- Responsibility for creating strategy need not lie with a single strategic leader but may reside with teams of strategic leaders and thinkers. These teams should be tailored to suit the situation and, ideally, include the leaders who will execute the strategy in the field.

- Strategy should be created in the most appropriate place, which need not be a national capital. Rather it should be based on the location of the best knowledge and people to support the strategy making, taking account of environmental, cultural and internal/external power factors.

- In its early stages, the creative process should produce three to four courses of action to: give political choice; test alternative thinking; and act as a source of fallback options, should the chosen course of action fail.

- Strategies created in the initial process need not be 'full blown' but rather will be better conceived with the possibility that, soon after implementation, they will need to be adapted as plan meets reality.

- Leaders should champion and communicate the strategy. But they should also champion learning, ensure that feedback mechanisms exist and anticipate the need for early strategic review.

- The political objective should be always kept central during strategy creation and used as the key reference point for measuring progress during strategy execution. But it should also be periodically reviewed, at high level, to ensure it is still valid.

- Those who lead the strategy making process should be alert to changing strategic circumstances and prepared to adapt the strategy making process if necessary.

Some tenets are logically deduced from one or other school or from history, but others draw on personal experience or seem clear from first principles. The list is not definitive but rather a 'first go' for others to add to, subtract from or adjust. On this basis, let us examine the premises individually and flesh out the thinking within each.

At the outset of a campaign, we should create strategy using rational deliberation and calculation.

It is clear that, at the outset of a campaign, we need an initial strategy based on rational calculation. There are three (overlapping) reasons. First, how can a decision to deploy armed force for political purposes be 'rational' without some form of deliberation and calculation? Second, if we do not have a sense of our likely strategy, how can we predict the costs, benefits and risks of our intended actions to thus inform a decision to proceed? Third, how else can we decide on the type and scale of forces needed and on what else will we base our operational and logistic plans that are essential to deploy these forces? It is for all these reasons that we need a starting strategy and it is difficult to see why we would want to devise this using anything other than a process of rational calculation.

Although we should take account of history, doctrine and other analytic sources, each strategy should be uniquely tailored for the specific issue at hand.

We must avoid the trap of thinking that we can use stock solutions to solve strategic problems. This idea has failed too often. In World War I, the generic French strategy of the offence failed. In Vietnam, two stock strategies were used. The first was based on an academic theory of limited counter-revolutionary war. The second was based on UK counter-insurgency experience in Malaya. Both failed. In Northern Ireland, an initial counter-insurgency strategy based on the UK's colonial experience failed. And it would be a modern day mistake to assume that a counter-insurgency strategy that worked in Iraq could be transferred without adjustment to Afghanistan.

This is not to say that we need not understand and, where appropriate, draw on ideas from strategies past. Of course we should. This is essential for superior strategy making. But the historical evidence argues overwhelmingly that an individual strategy needs to be uniquely tailored for the circumstances of the case.[4]

Strategic leaders should oversee strategy creation and there should be early and continuing political engagement in the process.

As we have seen, two common historical features in superior strategy making appear to be, first, that political leaders were closely engaged from the outset and, second, there was a strong sense of political ownership at the highest level. Indeed, some of the greatest strategists were political leaders — Lincoln, Roosevelt, Churchill, Mao Tse Tung. And some of the best strategy making was undertaken by strong politico-military combinations, Bismarck-Moltke, Churchill-Alanbrooke, Roosevelt-Marshall, Lyttelton-Templer. We seem, though, to have lost sight of this lesson in the *Information Transformation.*

I always found it surprising, whilst working as the UK Chief of Defence Staff's Personal Staff Officer,[5] how little dedicated time was given by the UK's political leaders to strategy in Afghanistan and Iraq. I cannot recall, for example, a single occasion in 2005 and 2006 when the Prime Minister, Foreign Secretary, Development Secretary, Defence Secretary and Chancellor sat down with the Chiefs of Staff to discuss strategy for both campaigns and Britain's role in each. At the time I thought this was curious. Now with the benefit of my research, I see it as an important factor in explaining the problems that Britain has encountered in both operations.

With the increasing politicization of modern war, this premise has greater weight than ever before and not just for reasons of oversight. If we accept the argument in Chapter 8 that the two key dimensions of strategy are the political and the strategic, then political engagement is essential because of the expertise that politicians bring to the party. Who, after all, will have more experience and understanding of the political level of a contest than the politician?

Responsibility for creating strategy need not lie with a single strategic leader but may reside with teams of strategic leaders and thinkers. These teams should be tailored to suit the situation and, ideally, include the leaders who will execute the strategy in the field.

The era of the strategist-genius, such as Frederick the Great, probably passed away during the *Industrial Transformation* as the scope of war increased beyond the capacity of a single mind. Strategy making needs now to be a team affair and not just for reasons of scope. The cultural complexity of many modern situations argues for drawing in experts with local knowledge.

Where possible, there are significant advantages of including, in the strategy making team, the leaders who will execute the strategy in the field or their representatives. If the executors have been involved in the creative process, they are more likely to buy-in to the strategy and execute it aggressively. More subtly, the collaborative process of strategy making will help build, between the key strategic actors, the personal relationships so important for effective execution. It follows that where one is operating in concert with indigenous leaders and their forces — as has been the case in Afghanistan and Iraq — then they too must be incorporated in the strategy making. This can and should lead to a virtuous cross-fertilization of local knowledge and technical know-how.

Strategy should be created in the most appropriate place, which need not be a national capital. Rather it should be based on the location of the best knowledge and people to support the strategy making, taking account of environmental, cultural and internal/ external power factors.

It is important to think through where best to make strategy. Strategy makers need access to the best knowledge. And it may seem an obvious thing to say, but the best knowledge is usually found in the region where an operation occurs, not the national capitals that are providing the troops for the operation.

It is a conceit — often unconscious, but hopelessly mistaken — to assume that those in Washington, London, Paris or Berlin will always know best. The reality is that it is more often the men and women on the spot, who are not separated by thousands of miles from the action, who will know best.

An observation of Herbert Simon, the American polymath, reinforces the point about the problems of decision making from distance:

> There is an additional objection to centralization that goes beyond those already considered. It has been assumed thus far that, given ample time, the superior could make more accurate

decisions than the subordinate. This will be true, however, only if the information upon which the decision is to be based is equally accessible to both. When decisions must be made against a dead line or when the organization is characterized by geographical dispersion, this may be far from the case. The 'facts of the case' may be directly present to the subordinate, but highly difficult to communicate to the superior. The insulation of the higher levels of the administrative hierarchy from the world of fact known at first hand by lower levels is a familiar administrative phenomenon.[6]

Two reasons surely underpinned the success of Britain's strategy in Malaya. First, the Colonial Office Minister, Sir Oliver Lyttelton, believed that the man on the spot, General Templer, was the best placed to devise, decide upon and execute the strategy. Second, Lyttelton backed Templer and firmly resisted continued attempts at interference from others, in Whitehall and the national press — who of course thought they knew better, notwithstanding that they were over 6,500 miles from the campaign.

In its early stages, the creative process should produce three to four courses of action to: test alternative thinking; give political choice; and act as a source of fallback options, should the chosen course of action fail.

We introduced in Chapter 9 the idea that, when creating strategy, we should devise more than one possible course of action before reaching a decision. This was the approach used by General Slim in Burma and by JFK's strategy makers during the Cuban Missile Crisis. As well as being an important factor in their successes, the idea has a strong basis in first principles.

Working through three or four courses of action will allow us to test alternative approaches. It will also give politicians choice. For example, we might want, when creating a strategy, to see what impact there would be in varying the *ends* and *means*, that is the political objective sought and the national resources committed. Would a more modest political objective reduce the risk of failure? Or would an increase in resources significantly improve chances of success?

Should the chosen strategy ultimately prove unsuccessful, then we may be able to switch to one of the alternatives. On this point, it is instructive to examine Slim's key decision in the Irrawaddy River battle. As evidence emerged that his offensive strategy against the Japanese would not work, Slim changed tack:

> My problem was now to cross the river first and defeat [the Japanese] afterwards — a much harder one that to defeat them then cross. My staff and I, before preparing our original plan, had naturally studied several alternatives. Amongst them was a project to pass a considerable force up the Gangaw Valley to seize a bridgehead over the Irrawaddy near Pakokku and then, striking east, appear south of Mandalay. This idea I had discarded because I was sure the Japanese would remain north of Mandalay and I should require 4 Corps there if I were to defeat their main force. The route to Pakokku was long and most difficult, but, after some hard thinking, I reverted to this scheme in modified form.[7]

As we noted earlier, Slim would go on to defeat decisively General Heitarō Kimura, considered one of the most brilliant officers of the Japanese Army.

Strategies created in the initial process need not be 'full blown' but rather will be better conceived with the possibility that, soon after implementation, they will need to be adapted as plan meets reality.

The premise that an initial strategy need not be 'full blown' is, again, based on historical experience. If you accept Moltke's military truism that 'no plan survives contact with the enemy', then there is surely no point in trying to devise a 'full blown' strategy — because the circumstances for which it is devised will change when it is executed. The classic way that successful military organizations have dealt with this problem is to use a command philosophy epitomized in *blitzkrieg* or, in the modern jargon, 'mission command'. This philosophy assumes that, once action begins, the commander at the front will have the best view of what needs to be done and should be empowered to act accordingly.

The premise's general assumption is that a conscious strategy should initially guide action but that it is almost inevitable that this strategy will need to be adapted in the light of action. Indeed, this likelihood should be built into the very fabric of the initial strategy. As well as acting as the guide for early action, the initial strategy acts as a reference for front line commanders as they seek to identify the 'learning ideas' that will best help achieve the higher objective.

Leaders should champion and communicate the strategy. But they should also champion learning, ensure that feedback mechanisms exist and anticipate the need for early strategic review.

This premise flows from the preceding premise, but also from first principles. It is about leadership and learning. It is a key principle of leadership that the leader must explain what he or she wants to be done and why. This applies as much at the strategic level, as any other. Slim, again, provides us with an example of the idea in action. Once he had made a decision on his strategy for a particular phase, he would travel forward to his subordinate HQs to communicate it:

> The next step was to take the operation order myself to the subordinate commanders who were to act on it. On principle, in the field, it is better to go forward to them, than to call them back; to give their orders at their headquarters rather

than your own. This applies whether you command a platoon or an army group.[8]

And the idea of championing learning flows from the previous premise and the need to be able to adapt a strategy in the light of operational experience. We can only do this if we consciously gather and act on field lessons. More specifically, it is very often in the early phases of a campaign that we will need to make most changes to the strategy — this is why leaders should anticipate the need for an early strategic review.

This premise is, in many senses, the politico-military equivalent of the corporate *learning school* approach. But the idea significantly predates the *learning school*. Throughout the 20th century, Western militaries have worked hard to learn from operations. They have used, in the jargon, formal 'lessons learned' or 'lessons identified' processes that seek to analyse the operational lessons and respond rapidly, with improved equipment, doctrine and training and, when necessary, adapted strategy. Indeed the ability to learn more quickly than your opponent has often been a key characteristic of success in war.

The political objective should be always kept central during strategy creation and used as the key reference point for measuring progress during strategy execution. But it should also be periodically reviewed, at high level, to ensure it is still valid.

We have seen in Chapters 1 and 9 that a clearly defined political objective is an essential ingredient for effective strategy making and also a key attribute of superior strategy. We have also seen that the lack of a clear political objective has led to confusion and historical failure, for example in Vietnam. This premise falls out of that thinking. It also mirrors the first military principle of war, 'the selection and maintenance of the aim':

> In the conduct of war as a whole and in every military operation, it is essential to select and define the aim clearly. … The purpose having been defined, it is also fundamentally important that the aim be sustained and that the application of force is matched to the desired endstate. Plans must be continually checked against the purpose of the campaign or operation to ensure they are kept in harmony and that the aim remains valid.[9]

Although I have argued consistently against the universal applicability of principles such as these, this one perhaps comes closest to deserving the status. In short, although it is easy to be distracted by other issues, it is essential that we keep clear in our mind what we are trying to achieve, both when we are creating strategy and when we are executing it. And, as strategy is executed, the political objective must be the key reference for measuring progress and for judging the adequacy or otherwise, of the strategy.

We must also regularly review the validity of the political objective, because sometimes political objectives evolve during a campaign. A change in our political objective may require a change in our strategy and must, as a minimum, prompt a strategic review.

Those who lead the strategy making process should be alert to changing strategic circumstances and prepared to adapt the strategy making process if necessary.

Circumstances change during a campaign and this premise is based on the deduction that a strategy making process that is right for one phase of the campaign may not be right for another. A case in point is the contemporary campaign in Afghanistan. Over time, responsibility for the security operation has been was transferred from a small American-led 'coalition-of-the-willing' to a large security alliance operation under NATO. The number of international actors involved has thus increased. And the primary military HQ has moved from US Central Command HQ in Florida, to the Supreme Allied Commander Europe HQ in Belgium. Therefore, the strategy making processes ought logically to have been reviewed and adapted to reflect these changes. Given the novel nature of this operation for NATO, the alliance's own strategy making processes ought also to have been reviewed. 'Ought' is, I'm afraid, the operative word in both observations.

Conclusion

Some might say that there is no need to add yet another strategy making school to the ten identified by Mintzberg, Ahlstrand and Lampel. However, the plain fact is that the *politico-military school* already exists and does not conform to any of the corporate models. Some of its premises have been mirrored in the corporate world, but the majority have not and are founded on insights gained decades, in some cases centuries, before the corporate schools existed.[10]

I do not pretend that the list of premises is definitive. Nor do the individual premises help us with the creative act of strategy making. But they do provide us with a practical structure for a rational strategy making process. It would be a mistake, though, to try to put more flesh on the process bone. To do this, we would need to know the political and strategic cultures of the nation-states or security alliances involved. An ideal strategy making process for a parliamentary democracy might be different from that for a presidential republic or a multi-national security alliance. What is offered here is, thus, less a design charter for a nation's strategy making process and more a catalyst for thinking.

The fact that we have largely failed, until now, to codify these premises is a symptom of the lack of rigour in the way we think about the art and science of politico-military strategy making. Another symptom is evident in the concern that I share with Admiral Wylie in this repeated quote:

> What I do decry is that strategy, which so clearly affects the course of society, is such a disorganized, undisciplined, intellectual activity.[11]

Improvements in our processes would not, of themselves, lead to better strategy. But they would help turn our strategy making into a more organized, a more disciplined and a more intellectual activity — which, intuitively, is not a bad place to start on the road to superior strategy making.

Such a codification would, though, need to take into account the fact that most modern operations require the use of a nation's hard and soft power, combining political, diplomatic and economic levers as well as military ones. Most modern operations are also conducted in international coalitions. Individually each case brings complications, collectively the complications increase geometrically. So it is to strategy making in coalitions — internal, external or both — that we now turn.

Chapter 11

Strategy Making in Coalition
Internal & International

The evidence suggests that neither the Americans nor the British started [World War II] with a strategic blueprint. The patterns they fashioned for victory were molded by circumstances, necessity, trial and error and comprised amongst themselves and with their allies in the changing context of the war. Each strategic case reflected the national traditions, interests, geography, resources and the predilections of its political and military leaders — an amalgam molded on the anvil of necessity.

Maurice Matloff

Introduction

Strategy making in coalitions is complex and frustrating but also the norm. Coalitions can take a number of forms, but we will consider two here, internal and international. Internal coalitions are taken as internal to a country and comprised of different government agencies. Whereas international coalitions are comprised of different nations cooperating together, usually for reasons of national self interest.

Internal coalitions of different government agencies are needed in operations where we wish to use a range of state levers of which armed force is only one. In such cases, our strategy will need inputs from a range of different actors most particularly diplomats and development aid specialists as well as politicians and military officers. We sometimes think of such operations as something new but in reality they are as old as war itself. Throughout the history of international relations, states have routinely combined the instruments of so-called soft power, such as diplomacy and development aid, with those of so-called hard power, most obviously military force.

Similarly, we sometimes think of operations in international coalitions as something new but they too have featured throughout history. Operating in international coalition was the norm, rather than the exception, in the 19th and 20th centuries and the same is true, so far, for the 21st. Therefore, complex and frustrating though coalitions may be, we must understand the implications of making strategy in a coalition context. To do this we will look first at general considerations when working in coalitions and then focus on issues specific to the two different forms of coalition.

Coalition Principles

Internal and international coalitions bring additional challenges to the process of strategy making. This is particularly so when they coexist; when international coalitions deploy hard and soft power simultaneously. Strategy making in such cases is difficult, not least because of the organizational complexity caused by the large number of agencies involved. Furthermore, the national agencies have different organizational cultures depending on their aims and make up. Layered on top of this are the different national cultures of the international coalition partners. In such circumstances, effective strategy making is all the more important because the creation and execution of a shared strategy is a – I would argue *the* – key means of pulling together the many different strands of effort.

This does not mean that we need to look for new insights to add to those of earlier chapters. There are, though, some additional factors to consider before setting out on a coalition enterprise. First, the different partners' thinking on the political context and political issue at contest needs to be shared so that negotiations start with a common analysis of the problem. Second, there needs to be, as far as is possible, a full and frank discussion of the different partners' motives. How does the issue bear on each partner's interests, be they institutional or national? And what, ultimately, are they seeking to get out of their engagement?

Although it is advantageous if coalition partners share the same objective, it is not always the case that they do and it is not the end of the world if they don't. Strategies can be crafted to deliver more than one objective but only if these different objectives are clear.

Related to the issue of motives is that of choice and here there is usually a difference between internal and international coalitions. In the former, the institutions involved will usually have been instructed to operate together by their governments — and have no choice but to participate. Whereas, for international coalitions, countries are likely to join because they calculate it to be in their national interest and they are likely to leave, too, when they perceive this is no longer the case, as was the case with Spain's departure from the Iraq coalition in 2004 and Holland's from the Afghanistan coalition in 2010.

Finally, there are more subtle issues. How will the institutional cultures of the different organisations and the national cultures of the different allied nations mix? Critically, will it be possible to build the strong coalition relationships that are central to effective strategy making? If you accept that power matters in strategy making — the more power you have, the more say you get — then the thinking of the power school of corporate strategy will have relevance here, too.

When using the tools we have looked at in previous chapters, the first point to recall is that we are still in the business of rational strategy making. Thus, when beginning a strategic analysis, the starting point must be to consider how to solve the problem at hand, not how to keep the different internal and international partners sweet. The analysis should proceed thus. What is the best strategy to deal with the issue at hand? Then, how might we adjust this strategy to accommodate the particular interests of different partners, internal or international? And not the other way round. With these thoughts in mind, we turn to consider internal coalitions.

Internal Coalitions

Although the need to use a range of state instruments has been brought back into our consciousness as a result of Afghanistan and Iraq, blending hard and soft power is not a new idea. The Malayan Emergency and the Vietnam and Soviet-Afghan wars are 20th century examples and, indeed, the British used both forms to build and run their Empire throughout the 18th and 19th Centuries. In contemporary operations, as in the past, the degree to which we utilise the different levers of national power will depend on the circumstances of the case. But, as Afghanistan and Iraq demonstrate, at the extreme we may need to use the full range of those available to us. Modern operations such as these, intricate and challenging mixtures of state-building[1] and counter-insurgency, have been termed 'Three Block Wars'[2] in the US and 'complex emergencies' in the UK. But, despite the complexity, the approaches we have devised in earlier chapters should still be relevant. Indeed, if used intelligently, they should help us to deal with the complexity. Furthermore, if we can employ these tools effectively in such challenging circumstances, then we will improve the chances of success in future operations.

Strategic leaders and strategy making teams will, though, need to reflect widely, not least on three key questions. First, what should be the balance between hard and soft power? Second, what should be the balance between actions that seek to stabilize situations in the short term and, in particular, provide adequate levels of human security, and actions that promote economic and political development and lead to state-building success in the medium-to-long term? Third, how much time do we have? Because of the nature of Western politics and Western electoral cycles, there is often a political desire for quick results. Yet the evidence of history suggests that, in such operations, a key factor in achieving strategic success is a recognition of the possible need for a long haul so that the slower acting levers of development can have effect.

To blend hard and soft power into successful strategies in such circumstances, we need internal teams — internal coalitions — with the right balance of expertise. Because of their different training, experiences, organizational cultures and underlying philosophies, these different specialists have different outlooks. They often think, for example, in different timescales. A key strategy making challenge in internal coalitions is to manage the cultural differences of the different team members but some institutional characteristics seem to transcend national boundaries. In practice, there can be no substitute for the strategic leader getting to know and understand his or her individual team members but it will help to have a preliminary sense of the cultures from which they emanate. So herewith a brief canter, based largely on personal experience, through the generic cultures of the diplomatic, development and defence institutions and their people.

Diplomats' great professional strengths lie in political analysis, political reporting and the management of diplomatic relations. In contrast to their military colleagues, the professional training that diplomats receive is surprisingly small, indeed vanishingly so on military matters or strategy.[3] There is often an interesting tendency, when in problem-solving mode, to think in the short term. Sir John Coles, one of Britain's foremost diplomats, implicitly acknowledges this when he quotes an anonymous senior British diplomat: 'Our skill is in *not* having a grand strategic concept.'[4] Although Western diplomats will have operated throughout the world, not all nor even a majority will have been exposed to armed conflict or war. Finally, although diplomats have great political vision and first class reporting skill, they often have very little leadership experience. Most diplomatic embassies have far fewer people than the platoons or small ships that junior army and naval officers command in their formative years. The number of people in, for example, the top two or three UK embassies in the world is no more than in an army company, commanded at the relatively junior rank of major. In campaigns where significant military and development resources are deployed, we need to be sure that the ambassador in the field really is the best person to both lead the national effort and advise foreign governments on strategic leadership and national governance.

The development professional is a different animal from the diplomat and proud of it. Because they routinely deploy to poor and insecure countries, they tend to have more experience of conflict than their diplomatic colleagues. Their professional strengths lie in team-building, economic and development analysis and planning. The general objective of international development is usually poverty reduction, so the natural inclination is to think long-term. This is for the very good reason that long-term development solutions represent best long-term value. There tends to be a corresponding distrust of short-term schemes, development elastoplasts so to speak. The body of academic development literature is large and in a sense corresponds to the body of military doctrine. There is no shortage of 'development strategy' in the development community. For example, the Afghan National Development Strategy is based on a 'standard' Poverty Reduction Strategy Paper (PRSP) that:

describes a country's macroeconomic, structural and social policies and programs to promote growth and reduce poverty, as well as associated external financing needs. PRSPs are prepared by governments through a participatory process involving civil society and development partners, including the World Bank and the International Monetary Fund.[5]

However, as this case shows, the development world is as prone to the mistake of adopting stock solutions as the military world. I was interested to discover, for example, that one of the 'standard' PRSP assumptions that underpinned the Afghan National Development Strategy shaped in 2005 was that there was no significant conflict in progress.[6]

Finally, the key skills of the soldier or the marine — it is generally soldiers or marines, as opposed to sailors or airmen, who have most field experience in these modern campaigns — are leadership, an action philosophy, a short-to-medium term planning outlook and a desire to get things done. Most have extensive operational experience, borne on post Cold War deployments to the Balkans, Afghanistan and Iraq. All are very well versed in their core professional areas but usually have little, if any, training in diplomacy or development. Of course, ultimately, all may be required to conduct offensive military operations, dominate the ground and if necessary close with, engage and defeat the enemy — a mindset that needs to be a touch de-tuneable, in order to integrate harmoniously with the other softer skilled members of the internal coalition's strategy making team.

Of course, there will also be other professions added to the mix. In Afghanistan, for example, as well as working routinely with diplomats and development professionals, I engaged with policemen, prison officers, lawyers, customs officers, economists and communications experts, to name but a few. On reflection, it is not surprising that when people from these and other such different cultures were thrown together in the early days of Afghanistan and Iraq, they took time to get to know each other's ways. This is not a criticism, simply a statement of fact. But, because each discipline brings vital skills and experiences to the table, some understanding of each other's cultures, professional jargon and outlooks is an important prelude to effective strategy making. I am not implying that the cultures need to change, quite the reverse. The different perspectives are healthy and, amongst other things, help reduce the risk of 'group think'. Indeed, when added together it is quite likely that, if the team is well led, the whole will be much greater than the sum of the parts. But, when we decide to blend soft and hard power, a period of getting to know each other and each other's business, will help improve the chances of success.

As we start to think about a post-Afghanistan, post-Iraq future, a key question for policy makers in foreign offices, defence ministries and development agencies will be how often do we envisage blending the levers of hard and soft power in operations in the future? If the answer is 'often', then we need to have soft power levers that are ready to deploy and employ in conflict situations. It is a generally accepted criticism of the Afghanistan and Iraq campaigns that the lack of soft power experts, ready to deploy to areas of conflict and with the infrastructure to operate side-by-side with military actors, was a critical weakness in the early years. If we think, therefore, that we will deploy soft power into future conflicts, we need to invest to ensure that we have civilian professionals who are readily deployable to and employable in, the challenging conflict situations to which we may wish to send them. Accepting the costs, such an investment could deliver benefits out of all proportion to those needed to fund the hard power of the classic military formation.

International Coalitions

International coalitions are nothing new, nor are the challenges associated with them — Castex illustrates the dilemmas:

> In coalition warfare, policy also has a vital internal role. A coalition is not an idyll, a cloudless marriage of devoted partners, but a transitory assembly of nations brought together by temporarily shared interests on some points but still disagreeing on others. Conflicts spring up within coalitions, causing anything from minor dislocation to complete disintegration, the latter a catastrophe that destroys strategy as well. Policy alone can guard against these dangers, avoid them, minimize discord, level differences and maintain cohesion. In coalitions, policy sees open before it an internal field — inter-allied policy — in addition to the external area. Both kinds of policy aid and support strategy.[7]

Just so. Although Castex is using the term policy in a foreign policy or diplomacy sense, his early 20th century description still captures the atmospherics of coalitions in the early 21st century.

Given these problems and the problems that have been apparent within the NATO coalition in Afghanistan, why should we continue to operate in coalitions in the future? The answer is twofold. First, at the strategic level, individual coalition members may be able to bring capabilities, in quantity or quality, to the table that improve the overall chances of success. Second, at the political level, coalition members can bring something less physically tangible but on occasion more important, international legitimacy — which may, of course, be a key advantage in the contest of wills at the political level.

International coalitions can be categorized in two ways. The first is by form. The classic distinction is between *ad hoc* 'coalitions of the willing' or formal coalitions in a treaty-based security alliance, such as NATO. The US-led coalition in Iraq is an example of the former and the current NATO operation in Afghanistan of the latter. The second categorization is based on whether or not one of the coalition members is the host government of the state in whose territory the operation takes place — Malaya and Vietnam are good examples. These two different categories can coexist and there is thus a range of different combinations, each with different challenges. But strategy is strategy and again there is no logical reason why we should not apply our earlier insights when strategy making in coalitions. The key, when so doing, is to understand a little bit about the specific nature of the challenge in each of the cases.

Coalitions with allies

What makes strategy making more complex in coalitions is that there will likely be different national views amongst the coalition members in three interlinked related areas.

The first is that of political analysis and in particular, the answers to early questions of the Strategic Estimate. What is the political context? What is the political issue at contest, why is it important to us and how much do we care about it? What is the political objective? Second and related, is the answer to Clausewitz's crucial question, highlighted previously but repeated for convenience:

> The first, the supreme, the most far-reaching act of judgement that the statesman and the commander have to make is to establish by that test the kind of war on which they are embarking; neither mistaking it for, nor trying to turn it into, something which is alien to its nature. This is the first of all strategic questions and the most comprehensive.[8]

Do the different nations' statesmen and commanders share a common view of the nature of the war? Third, it is inevitable that there will be different views on how best to solve the matter. For example, nations with a cultural propensity to use hard power may prefer a quite different strategy to those that favour soft.

Prior to an operation, these areas need to be discussed by the partners — these preliminary discussions will provide, among other things, an essential litmus test for judging the likely cohesion of the coalition. In a multi-national alliance, it would be extraordinary if we found unanimity of view on all issues. This is not only most unlikely but it is also not essential. Two things matter more. First, are our views on the desired political objective sufficiently convergent that we can craft a strategy to deliver it? Second, will the strategy be adequate for the task at hand and are we all prepared to sign up to it? For reasons already hinted at, these are areas for subtle calculation.

The question is what design principle should guide the strategy makers? In theory, we should devise a strategy optimized to deliver the coalition's political objective or objectives and this is certainly how we should begin our thinking. But in practice, we may find ourselves opting for a strategy that ensures the cohesion of the alliance. Put another way, we may default to a strategy that is coalition-optimized rather than mission-optimized. There may be important political reasons for designing a coalition-optimized strategy, but the ultimate test is success. A coalition-optimized strategy may deliver success in a more costly and less timely way than a mission-optimized strategy but these extra costs may be worth bearing for reasons of alliance politics.

Equally, the compromises needed in a coalition-optimized strategy may critically prejudice its chances of delivering success. If so, the dominant coalition partners will need to take a long, cold, sober look at the value of having all coalition partners on board. Failures in coalition operations are doubly costly. Not only will the political objectives not be achieved, but also coalition relationships will likely be damaged, often significantly so.

Let's bring these ideas together with a modern example. In Afghanistan in 2007, the insurgency was confined to the Pashtun provinces of the South and East regions, reflecting the Taliban's Pashtun lineage and language. The traffic light system on the UN access maps showed green for the regions of the West and North, indicating that it was safe for UN personnel to operate there. The lack of fighting in the North and West was not, though, due to the presence of NATO forces because the forces deployed were too small to have any real security effect. In the West, for example, although there were over two thousand Italian, Spanish and Romanian troops based at the Regional HQ at Herat, a large proportion was manning the regional HQ or providing logistics and air support and only three rifle companies, roughly six hundred in total, were available to be deployed on the ground. Furthermore, each of these rifle companies was on four month rotations, so at any moment, one was either just arriving or departing. In effect, therefore, the Italian regional commander had just four hundred effective troops to cover his area of responsibility, an area that amounted to half the size of Italy.

Clearly this force was not there for security but rather for political reasons. Being in the West allowed the Italians, Spanish and Romanians to participate in the mission yet avoid the hard fighting of the South and East. The same was true of the Germans in the North. There was, though, a very strong argument for NATO to withdraw from the North and West, for three reasons. First, the most likely reason that the insurgency would spread north was the 'magnet' of Western forces — remove this magnet and there would be a better chance of containing the insurgency in the South and East. Second, handing over security to the Afghans in the North and West could be presented as a totemic demonstration of strategic progress. Third and finally, withdrawal would undermine a key Taliban message: 'The Westerners will not leave and must be ejected.' In developing a mission-optimized strategy, one would thus have looked very closely at this particular option. But, because of concerns about the cohesion and unity of the NATO alliance, it was very rarely discussed. We were thus, by default, in a coalition-optimized mode of thinking. Of course the irony is that, if NATO were to fail in Afghanistan then the alliance would be damaged and badly so. In this case, we may come to the judgement, on reflection, that a coalition-optimized strategy had little to commend it.

In security alliances such as NATO, there are also key issues downstream for strategy creation. The first is how the mission is directed politically once we begin to execute a strategy. This is not an easy subject, as the case of Afghanistan shows. Here there are a number of key players engaged — the UN, World Bank, IMF and so on — who bear no formal allegiance to the key security player, NATO, but who are primary providers of soft power and who thus have a central role to play in campaign success. Although historical experience suggests that political direction is best vested in either an empowered individual or a single organization, this approach is not always agreeable to all players and may not be feasible.

Equally important is the question of the best command structure to execute the strategy. Should this be based on the extant formal alliance model, such as the UN's or NATO's? Or should it be specifically adapted to deliver the strategy? Should form follow function? Both approaches have merits but, as a general rule, there is much to commend the idea of form following function. No two campaigns are the same and, taking NATO's Afghanistan command structure as an example, it is by no means clear — at least not to me — that a command structure designed to defend European territory in a conventional NATO-Warsaw Pact war is best for a complex out-of-area operation such as that in Afghanistan.

On both issues, we need to keep clear the risks we may bear if, for reasons of alliance politics, we favour a coalition-optimized strategy over a mission-optimized strategy. If, for example, a lack of clear political direction or the use of a dated Cold War command structure is going to significantly prejudice campaign success, then nations and alliances need to take a long hard look, individually and collectively and decide whether the risks and consequent costs are worth bearing, individually or collectively.

But for all these difficulties, coalitions can work and work well. As we saw in Chapter 4, sustaining the US and British coalition throughout World War II was tough and time consuming. Strategy making took place in eighteen major conferences, starting in Washington in December 1941 - January 1942 and finishing in Potsdam in July 1945. Andrew Roberts notes of Roosevelt, Churchill, Marshall and Alanbrooke, 'Their decisions were produced through hard-fought interaction using logical debate and compromise, over many months of constant and unimaginable stress.'[9] It was hard going, but as the result showed, it was worth it and, in my view, it remains the exemplar for coalition strategy making.

Coalitions with hosts

Very often a key political actor in a coalition may be the government of the territory where an operation is taking place. The current positions in Afghanistan and Iraq illustrate the case. If the host government is legitimate — and it is difficult to think why we would want to act in support of one that was not — then clearly its strategic leaders should be key — indeed probably *the key* — actors in our strategy making.

This being the case, then the three areas we identified as key in early coalition discussions with allies — the first three questions of the Strategic Estimate, Clausewitz's question on the nature of the war and the general approach to solving the problem — are just as relevant, indeed probably more so. So too is the decision about whether we devise a strategy that is mission-optimized or, in this case, host-coalition-optimized.

This question is particularly important when you are operating with a host government that, although legitimate, lacks institutional capacity and, thus, effectiveness. The classic dilemma occurs when the coalition rather than the host holds the bulk of the effective power. This leads to a key question: should the coalition take the lead role by creating and executing the strategy, or should it take the supporting role, mentoring and assisting the host government as it creates and executes the strategy? There is no stock answer to this question. Sometimes, for reasons of political expediency, there is pressure on coalition nations to take the lead role, in theory to get the job done quickly. But, often, the best answer is to take the supporting role. By accepting responsibility of the lead role, the host government enhances its political legitimacy and, with coalition assistance, is likely to build institutional capacity more quickly and more deeply. All other things being equal, this should improve the prospects of success in the medium-to-long term.

A final question to think through is what posture should we adopt when faced with those who oppose the partnership of coalition and host? Here the most interesting contemporary approach is that used by the NATO-UN coalition in the Kosovo operation. The key thought is:

> Until peace has become viable, the requirements of the peace process will need to be given top priority by all in the mission. A passive, fragmented or incoherent approach only undermines the process of transformation and prolongs the international presence. Thus, the primacy of the peace process should be the overarching guidance for all civilian and military peace implementation efforts. In Kosovo this guidance was expressed as a paramount mission directive: *we support those who support the peace process and actively oppose those who obstruct it.*[10] (emphasis added).

The idea in the last sentence helped coalition forces — civil and military — work out how to take sides. But, more importantly, the idea can perhaps be used more generally, both as an approach in the field for state-building adventures and humanitarian interventions of the future and also as a key test in our preliminary political analysis.

As we consider future operations, particularly interventions, the idea suggests key questions. Are we prepared to support those who support the peace process? And are we prepared to actively oppose those who obstruct it? If there is a 'no' to either question, then this may be the time to question the wisdom of our engagement. And, if there is a 'no' to either question from an ally, this may be the time to question their value to the mission. Furthermore, debates about whether or not a coalition should favour national leader A over leader B or national party C over D, lose their relevance if our position is simply to support the peace process. There may perhaps be an antidote here to the occasional (but generally unhelpful) inclination of Western powers to act as king-makers.

Conclusion

Coalitions undoubtedly complicate strategy making. However, these complications do not have to and indeed must not prevent effective strategy making. Coalitions are the norm and to be effective they need effective strategy. For this reason we must surely learn — or relearn, reflecting on Allied strategy making success in World War II — how to create and execute strategy in coalitions.

In the complexity of the coalition situation, superior strategy becomes even more important as a guide for the strategic actors. Some may conclude that, because of the complexity and the coalition pressures, it is just all too difficult and instead that 'muddling through' is the answer? Perhaps. But without a shared strategy, 'muddling through' will be multiplied across the different nations and then multiplied again across their foreign affairs, defence and development departments. Without an agreed strategy, national contingents will inevitably and necessarily refer back to national capitals for direction that, when given, will be based on distant and incomplete appreciations of the position on the ground and will often be shaped by other factors based on domestic politics. This will be 'muddling through' to the power ten and we will have to pin our chances of success on the hope that the herd of internal and international coalition actors heads blindly but broadly in the right strategic direction.

Effective strategy making seems the better way and, even if it is mind-numbingly difficult and we do not always get it right, surely we should try? Surely we owe it to our agents of strategy — military and civil — who stoically risk their lives in the call of duty? Surely we owe it to the host populations of the territories where our coalitions act and whose destinies are so often caught up in the success or otherwise of our actions. Surely these actions are better guided by rational strategy rather than the blind and random progress of the herd? This is not to suggest that we will always be successful in coalition strategy making but, even if our attempts at strategy making in coalition do not in practice improve our prospects of success, it would be beyond conscience not to try.

Chapter 12

Strategy Making in Time
Contests & Culminations

If a losing battle can be caught before its conclusion and turned into a success, the initial loss not only disappears from the record, but becomes the basis for a greater victory. For on closely examining the tactical progress of an engagement it becomes obvious that, up to its very end, the results of each of the subsidiary engagements are only suspended verdicts, which not only may be revoked by the final outcome, but may be turned into their very opposites.

Carl von Clausewitz

Introduction

Until now, we have discussed general politico-military strategy making but said little about how we would make strategy in different postures during a campaign or at different stages of a campaign. This is not to suggest that we need necessarily to employ completely different approaches from those that we have developed so far. As we will see, the ideas and logic we have developed so far retain their relevance but there will be nuanced differences in how they are applied in different campaign postures and at different campaign stages.

We need, first, to consider strategy making when we are in a reactive or responsive, rather than a deliberate, decision making posture. And we need, second, to consider strategy making where a campaign appears to be approaching a culminating moment, ideally in our favour but perhaps not. What links these two different scenarios is that, as well as being common occurrences in operations and wars past, each has associated and identifiable strategy making risks that can be mitigated if leaders and strategists are conscious of them.

Contests in Time

For modern democracies, the more discretionary nature of contemporary operations — wars of choice as opposed to wars of necessity — means that there will often be a period of time for deliberate strategic calculation. A modern example is the approach to the invasion of Iraq in 2003 where it is clear, from publicly available material, that US preparations began over a year beforehand. The key point is that this time gives the opportunity for measured calculation and some objectivity given that you may not yet have committed to the operation. In this situation it should be easier to maintain a rational footing in the strategic analysis and strategy making. In such circumstances, we can describe ourselves as being in a *deliberate* strategy making posture.

There are other situations, where events are moving so quickly or unexpectedly that you are making strategy on the hoof. Examples include the British position after the Argentinian invasion of the Falklands and the rapidly unfolding situation in Afghanistan after 9/11. This may also be the case during a campaign where a wholly unexpected strategic event takes you off guard. The Tet Offensive in Vietnam is a case in point. In these cases, it will be less easy to maintain a rational footing, particularly with political rhetoric and popular debate swirling around and the accompanying press pressure to 'do something'. But even though more difficult, it is nevertheless highly desirable to keep your rational footing. This is because, in strategy, early mistakes can have catastrophic effects that may take years to correct. In such fluid circumstances, we can describe ourselves as being in a *reactive* strategy making posture.

There is also a third set of circumstances during a campaign where one is responding, perhaps simply with a periodic campaign review, perhaps to emerging unexpected developments or perhaps because things are not proceeding as intended. The last of these positions is often the most complex because usually, at the heart of the matter, lie three difficult questions. Have we got the strategy wrong? And, if so, how do we need to adjust it? Or, is the strategy right? Perhaps we simply need to redouble our efforts to deliver success. Answers to these questions require finely tuned strategic judgement and accurate supporting analysis. In such circumstances, we can describe ourselves as being in a *responsive* strategy making posture.

In practice, the differences between these three postures — deliberate, reactive and responsive — will be less well defined than described here. But it is nevertheless important to have some sense of the posture you are in given the different risks of miscalculation in each. And, whichever posture — or combination of postures — the key principle is that, because your task is strategy making, the ideas introduced earlier do not lose their relevance. The trick is to get the decision making tempo right and to use the right balance of tools and techniques to suit the circumstances of the case and meet the criteria of rational strategy making.

Reactive strategy making

The primary risk in reactive strategy making is rash miscalculation and the key way to mitigate the risk is to be acutely conscious of it and to keep your options open — the former is usually easier than the latter. Consciousness can be maintained by asking, periodically, the question, 'What are the possible unintended consequences of our posited course of action?' Keeping your options open can be more difficult, especially in defensive situations. If you are attacked, there may be no other rational option than to defend. Equally, though, if events allow you to adopt a flexible posture as the situation clarifies, this will be to your advantage.

If the key risk in reactive strategy making is miscalculation then, as the crisis begins, the three key questions concern the political contest, the political objective and time. First, what is the nature of the political issue at contest? Second, what should be our political objective and why? If, as is often the case, we are unable immediately to hone down the political objective, what does the spectrum of possible objectives that we might want to achieve look like? And are there strategies that would allow us to pursue some or all of the objectives in this spectrum and thus to keep our options open, before we firm up on a precise objective. Third, how much time do we have before a decision is needed? Can we buy more time? Should we buy more time? The Falklands War provides us with a useful modern case study of the reactive strategy making problems and provides some insights for the strategic leader in the reactive strategy making posture.

Notwithstanding some prescient warnings, most vividly those in early 1982 from Captain Nick Barker of HMS Endurance, the invasion of Falkland Islands by the Argentinians on 2 April came as a shock to the British Government and to most of Whitehall officialdom. As the UK's options were gloomily mulled over in the Prime Minister's rooms in the Houses of Parliament, the desired political objective may not have been clear initially.

However, a first element was evident in the advice to Margaret Thatcher from the First Sea Lord, Admiral Sir Henry Leach, who offered the perfectly proper military view to the Prime Minister that the islands *could* be retaken but also the wholly political view that they *should* be retaken because 'if we don't do that, in a few months we will be living in a different country whose word will count for little.' In other words, the recovery of national prestige and reputation was a first key component of the political objective. Like it or not, the political survival of the (then increasingly unpopular) Conservative administration would have been a tacit second component. And a third would have been to do with international precedent and countering the use of unilateral and unsanctioned aggression to solve international disputes. In hindsight it is clear that these three components essentially comprised the overall political objective and that the strategic objective of re-taking the islands would deliver all three.

In the short term, as these issues were being refined, the decision to prepare and send a task force achieved three things. First, it gave the Prime Minister something with which to go to the House of Commons and the nation the next day (and, for the time being, secured the Conservative Government). Second, it sent a strong public notice of intent to the Argentinian Government — as well as shocking the Junta psychologically and, no doubt, prompting a dawning recognition of their grievous miscalculation. Third, it laid open the possibility of a military option at some stage in the future, but did not commit Britain to it. Or did it?

Militarily, turning the Task Force back would have been the simplest of strategic matters, requiring just one signal from the Fleet Headquarters at Northwood. But politically? Key was the domestic contexts for both governments. The political survival of each administration would be critically influenced by the result of the military contest, a factor that Thatcher and the Argentinian President, Leopoldo Galtieri, would have known only too well. And then there was the character of Margaret Thatcher who was not known for backing down. With these issues at contest and no

Argentinian withdrawal, I have always doubted that the recall of the Task Force was a plausible political option. Therefore, with the sailing of the Task Force on 5 April, Britain, probably unconsciously, committed herself to war.

Turning from political objective to the time available, the latitude was quickly clear for simple military-strategic reasons. It would take three weeks for the lead combat elements of the Task Force, including the aircraft carriers, to reach the Falklands. It would take a further two to three weeks before the amphibious and land components arrived. And, by early July, the South Atlantic winter weather conditions would be much as to critically preclude operations at sea and ashore. So by early April the key timelines of a practical campaign were obvious. Diplomatic negotiations could continue until late April and potentially until mid-May (and indeed continued in practice until 1 June). But thereafter the landings would need to begin as soon as the amphibious forces arrived off the Falklands and, to avoid a land stalemate, the islands would need to be retaken by the end of June.

Thereafter, Britain's military strategy did not pan out exactly as expected. In particular, neither the Argentine Navy nor the Argentine Air Force engaged in the contest that the commander of the Task Force, Admiral Woodward, wanted. No plan survives contact with the enemy.

Sea control was established sooner than expected when the sinking of the Argentine cruiser, ARA General Belgrano, caused the Argentine Navy to retire to home waters. But the air superiority contest came with the landings, rather than before them and was fought out in the skies above and around San Carlos. With the Argentine Air Force pitted against the ship-borne missile defences of the Royal Navy and, more importantly, the Sea Harriers of the Fleet Air Arm, the battle for air superiority between 21 and 26 May was, with hindsight, the most important of the campaign. Once won, the freedom of action that it gave British forces did not make the result a foregone conclusion. But it did weight it preponderantly in their favour. It was not a perfect military strategy nor did it play out as expected. As with all strategy, it is not absolute performance that matters, but performance relative to that of your opponent. At the end of the day, the three tests of effectiveness, efficiency and endurability were met — the islands were retaken, losses were fewer than predicted and the result endured.

Ultimately, this example illustrates that, notwithstanding the fast moving nature of a crisis, when in a reactive strategy making posture there is no reason why we should not use the tools and techniques we have developed in Part II. To employ them successfully, we need to keep at least three points in mind. First, we need to apply them selectively and with judgment. Second, we need to be acutely conscious of the increased risk of miscalculation in fast moving strategic situations — and thus, as far as is possible, weave in strategic flexibility as we shape our possible strategies. Third, we need urgently to work out the influence of time, both in a constraining and shaping way, on our decision making processes.

Responsive strategy making

What will tend to distinguish a responsive strategy making posture from a reactive strategy making posture is that time pressure will be less critical. This is particularly so in the context of an ongoing campaign. There are unexpected events that do not press you on time but nevertheless cause you to think about your strategy. Or it may be a perception or dawning recognition that the strategy is not working. Or it may be simply be that you are undertaking a routine periodic campaign review or a planned 'first look' soon after action has started. Notwithstanding that there is more time, the position is often no easier than in the reactive one and, indeed, sometimes more complex. This is because usually the central question is whether or not the strategy is working and if not, why not.

There may be a number of reasons why a strategy is not working, but five stand out:

- First, one or more of the assumptions on which the strategy's underpinning analysis was based is incorrect.

- Second, the assumptions are correct, but the strategy that has been devised is weak or inadequate.

- Third, there have been problems — either unforeseen or unrecognized — executing the strategy.

- Fourth, the strategy has not been given time to deliver.

- Fifth, there is a combination of two or more of the first four factors.

In coalition operations, a further possibility is that there may be more than one strategy operating and that these differing approaches are in conflict. Because of the possibility that the strategy has not been given sufficient time, we need to be open minded and not start with the assumption that the strategy is failing or has failed.

As we review the strategy, we can bring into play, in a selective way, all of the tools and techniques developed earlier. And the five possible reasons for strategy not working as intended provide a useful framework for the analysis. If the strategy was originally devised using the tools and techniques proposed in earlier chapters, then the power of the rational approach can be leveraged, because the written record of, for example, the Strategic Estimate, provides immediate and invaluable reference material for the review. The other essential source of reference for the strategic leader and strategist is the front line. Commanders working at the tactical level will not have all the answers but their insights will still be invaluable. From my own personal experience, these insights are best obtained through discussion with front line units *in situ* and selective debriefing of those who have had a moment to reflect after their operational tours. But, ultimately, the insights available to us in a review, the central question of whether the strategy is flawed or just needs more time may have no easy answer. Two historical examples demonstrate the alternative positions.

In Malaya, on taking over as High Commissioner in early 1952 after the murder of his predecessor, General Templer reviewed the strategy in place (the so-called Briggs Plan). Although he identified areas for refinement, he generally accepted the strategy as sound and set about vigorously executing it. The key improvement was perhaps to recruit and employ Sir Arthur Young, Metropolitan Police Commissioner, to rejuvenate and refocus the civilian police training programmes. Meanwhile, in London, Sir Oliver Lyttelton, the Colonial Office Minister, resolutely defended Templer from those in Whitehall and the British press who wanted to change the strategy. When Templer departed in 1954, the campaign was well on the way to a successful conclusion. A case, surely, of a sound strategy that, with some refinement, essentially required political will, effective leadership and strategic patience to see it through.

In Iraq in 2007, the US faced the alternate position. After the post-invasion setbacks of 2004 and 2005, the US strategy was to build up and then conduct a phased security handover to the Iraqi Armed Forces. However, security was rapidly deteriorating and Iraqi forces were struggling to maintain control in key areas, most particularly the so-called Sunni Triangle. In the eyes of a number of influential US strategic thinkers, the strategy was failing and failing badly. Inspired by retired General Jack Keane, former Vice Chief of the US General Staff and drawing on key analyses by the American Enterprise Institute and General Petraeus at Fort

Leavenworth and guided by the feedback of General Odierno in the field, these thinkers reviewed the strategy. They questioned US counter-insurgency doctrine, particularly in the light of tactical successes by Colonel H.R. McMaster in Tal Afar in 2005 which showed, above all, the need to stay on after operations to clear out insurgents so as to provide reassurance to the local populace.

These ideas were, in turn, developed into the strategy that envisaged a surge in US troop numbers so as to support a new approach encapsulated in the expression 'clear, hold, build' — clear out the insurgents, hold onto the areas that you have won, then build within them security, local capacity and, above all, hope. With Bush won over to the idea and Rumsfeld and other key figures replaced, the 'surge' played out in 2008. After hard fighting, security incidents fell dramatically and the conditions created allowed significant political progress. This is not to say that Iraq post-surge was and is a talismanic success — the damage done by inept strategy making in, first, the run up to the intervention and, then, the early post-war period was always likely to be impossible to repair properly not least because so much of that precious strategic resource, time, had been squandered. But, by critically analysing the strategy, acknowledging that it was failing and then decisively changing to a new strategy, the US were able to avoid defeat and gain some strategic breathing space.

Notwithstanding these insights and illustrations, it would be a mistake to leave the impression that there is some holy grail for answering the perennially difficult question, is the strategy wrong or is there some other problem? There is no substitute for superior judgement. That said, a rigorous and organized analysis of the context, issues and key factors will significantly support, and the study of history and the thinking and practice of the great strategic thinkers and parishioners will significantly inform, that judgement.

Culminations in Contests

We turn now from strategy making in terms of time or posture to strategy making in terms of the ultimate outcome; that is victory and success or defeat and failure. Clausewitz's words concerning decision in battle illuminate the issue and deserve close scrutiny:

> Even if the course of battle is not predetermined, it is in the nature of things that it consists of a slowly shifting balance, which starts early, but, as we have said, is not easily detectable. As time goes on, it gathers momentum and becomes more obvious. ... But whether the equilibrium remains undisturbed for some time or whether it swings to one side, rights itself and then swings to the other, it is certain that a commander usually knows that he is losing the battle before he orders a retreat.[1]

Although Clausewitz was writing in the early 1800s and about battle, rather than campaigns and war, these words resonate still. They could be used to describe the flow of events in, for example, the Allied campaigns against the two major Axis powers in World War II, the later wars of the Cold War and more contemporary developments in Afghanistan and Iraq.

Keeping these examples in the front of our minds, let us focus on what Clausewitz describes as the culminating point:

> It is not possible in every war for the victor to overthrow his enemy completely. Often even victory has a culminating point. This has been amply demonstrated by experience. ... the matter is particularly important in military theory and forms the keystone for most plans of campaigns, ... This culminating point in victory is bound to recur in every future war in which the destruction of the enemy cannot be the military aim and this will presumably be true of most

wars. The natural goal of campaign plans, therefore, is the turning point at which attack becomes defence. If one were to go beyond that point, it would not merely be a useless effort which could not add to success. It would in fact be a damaging one, which could lead to a reaction and experience goes to show that such reactions usually have completely disproportionate effects.[2]

The last sentence warns the potential victor of the risk of overreaching himself. But before this, there is a potential ambiguity in what Clausewitz means by 'a culminating point in victory'. The phrase could be interpreted as the point at which it becomes obvious that, from the successes you have achieved and the momentum you have gained, the campaign is largely won. Or alternatively, it could be interpreted as the point at which your forces are exerting their maximum leverage, where further expenditure will not deliver proportionately the same level of benefit. Both ideas are of interest, the first being about overall success and the second about economy in the use of force. Clausewitz importantly warns us of the risks in either case. But the key point is that we must judge culmination against the bench mark of the overarching political and military objectives we have set ourselves. In other words, we must judge against what it is we are trying to achieve, rather than a more arbitrary notion such as 'victory.'

Objective culmination

We will use the term *objective culmination* for the moment when the prospect of success becomes clear. The two associated but contrasting risks will be well known to military readers. The first is the potential for efforts to relax, leading to a loss of momentum and, potentially, even a reversal. Leadership is the key to avoiding this trap. And General Templer's approach in the later stages of the Malayan Emergency is an illustration of this in practice. He refused to countenance precipitate use of words such as victory and his 'don't relax' attitude was crystal clear — 'I'll shoot the bastard who says this Emergency is over!'[3] As we reflect on Afghanistan, I suspect we may reach the conclusion that, in 2005, we fell into precisely the trap that Templer astutely avoided in 1954.

The second risk is the opposite of the first: that of momentum taking you beyond your objective whether political, military or both. Here the position is more complex and the advantages and disadvantages of choosing to keep going can only be judged on the circumstances of the case. The key point is that if you do decide to press on for a more ambitious political or military objective than you had originally sought, you should do so consciously and not simply let yourself be taken there by momentum.

An important component in decision making in such circumstances will be a review of the *Strategic Estimate*, concentrating in particular on the early questions. What is the political context? Is the political issue still the same or have events changed it? What is the case for stopping when the original political objective is achieved? And what is the case for using the momentum and pressing on for a more ambitious political objective? And what should this new objective be?

An obvious case study is the First Gulf War and the US decision to stop after 100 hours of the land campaign, with the Iraqi forces ejected from Kuwait. Were George Bush Senior and his Chairman of the Joint Chiefs of Staff, Colin Powell, correct to stop at the point of objective culmination, with the original objective achieved? Or should they, as Margaret Thatcher believed, have pushed on into Iraq and toppled Saddam's regime by defeating his army?

With his prior roles as World War II naval aviator, congressman, US Ambassador to the UN, Director of Central Intelligence and Vice President it would have been difficult to find a more broadly experienced President than George Bush Senior. Bush had been a congressman during, and Powell had seen active service in, the Vietnam War. And in both minds would have been the Beirut bombing, less than eight years earlier in 1983, resulting in the deaths of 241 US servicemen in an unpopular peacekeeping operation beset by unclear political objectives. It is, therefore, not surprising that both would have been wary of pushing beyond their objective of liberating Kuwait on into Iraq. The 100 hours had led to a famous victory, at low strategic cost and there was reason to assume that Saddam would, in any event, fall. Whereas to push on would have incurred twin political risks of strategic quagmire and loss of coalition support that had, until then, been strong. Impossible to say, now, whether they were right or wrong but with, at the time of writing, US forces well into the seventh year of the Second Gulf War and only now disengaging, posterity seems to favour George Bush Senior's decision.

Leverage culmination

We will use the term *leverage culmination* for the moment where your deployed power has achieved its maximum leverage. This position will lead to quite different calculations, because here the issue is not how to manage and exploit victory but how to manage and mitigate against stalemate or reverse. When thinking this position through, we will need to answer a number of interlinked questions. First, notwithstanding that we are losing momentum, have we sufficient to achieve our objective? Second, if not, could we and should we invest additional resources to achieve that objective? Third, if sufficient resources are not available or will not make a difference, could we and should we adjust our objective to something less ambitious? Fourth, if so, what should that more modest objective be? Fifth and finally, would that changed objective require a changed strategy to deliver it? The key point about the second, third and fourth questions is that any changes that result will be changes of policy and must be politically sanctioned.

Although there are a number of case studies in history to represent this situation, in modern Afghanistan we can see the situation being played out in real time. The early Afghanistan campaign had, for the Americans and their coalition allies, been a singular success. But as Iraq loomed, the US took their eye off the Afghan ball, as too did key Coalition allies including the British.

Critically, they missed two key points. First, the Taliban had been deposed, but not defeated and they were regrouping. Second, with their Ghilzai Pashtun lineage, it would be in the Pashtun provinces of Southern and Eastern Afghanistan that they would seek to return to the contest. The calm and stability that the British, for example, had experienced in Mazar-e-Sharif in the Northern Alliance areas was, thus, not a good indicator of what NATO forces might expect as they moved south to the Pashtun provinces of Kandahar, Helmand, Uruzgan and Zabul.[4] By late 2006, NATO forces had become engaged in a counter-insurgency that included fighting as intense as anything since World War II.

In early 2009, with the momentum shifting to the Taliban and a general reluctance amongst NATO Allies to commit more troops, President Obama and his advisors considered the five key questions. Of these two were of particular importance. Should the objective be a democratically governed and secure Afghanistan or something more modest? And should additional resources be deployed? The result was a new and less ambitious objective — disrupt, dismantle and defeat al-Qaeda and its safe havens[5] — together with a decision to surge more troops and focus on training the Afghan National Security Forces and providing security for the Afghan people, using the 'clear, hold, build' doctrine. As I write, the position is in the balance, not least as a result of our having squandered, again, that precious strategic resource, time — and only time will tell whether the new strategy will be successful.

Opponent culmination

The discussion above assumes that we (or an allied force) are the 'culminating party'. But it would be remiss for us not to pause and reflect on the issue of being faced with an opponent's culmination and the prospect of our failure or defeat. This is naturally not something I want to spend huge amounts of time on. But nevertheless knowing when — and how — to cut one's losses is as challenging a question as any. A sobering example is the Soviet-Afghan War where the Soviet General Staff had, after just eight months, deduced the war could not be won and advised their political masters of this — and yet the war carried on for a further eight years with the loss of nearly 15,000 Soviet personnel and over a million Afghan lives.

In the losing situation the key questions are, what is the actual status of the contest? And what is the overall trajectory of the campaign? In making this assessment, we must be neither overly optimistic nor pessimistic but sober and hard headed. The next question to consider is, why are we failing? Is it to do with ways, means or ends? Or is it a mixture of all three? Was the political objective too ambitious? Were the resources allocated too meagre? Was the strategy selected too weak? Or was it some or all of these things? There then needs to be a hard-headed discussion about the importance of the objective. Is it of sufficient gravity that we need to make changes, for example invest additional resources, to correct the problems identified? Finally, if the objective is not of sufficient merit for us to bear additional costs, the only question left is when and how to disengage.

The Vietnam and the Soviet-Afghan wars illustrate the dilemmas that strategic leaders face in these circumstances and are examples where the decision was left too late. To this end, Kennedy's withdrawal from the Bay of Pigs is instructive — as Brodie observes:

> 'it was not actually United States' prestige that suffered at the Bay of Pigs so much as Kennedy's and he knew that, too. ...

In any case, at the moment of decision, Kennedy knew that whatever prestige loss he would suffer at the Bay of Pigs did not warrant actions more injurious to the good name either of the United States or himself. He therefore was able to end the operation and cut his losses.'⁶

The key point is that, in the discussions to support difficult decisions such as these, the insights of the earlier chapters are as pertinent in the negative case as they are in the positive. Ultimately it's all about rational, not emotional, calculation. At the sobering moment when it becomes clear that failure is a possibility, the chances of success through greater investment must be balanced against the impact that a greater defeat would have later on. It must be remembered that if you invest additional resources and still lose, the defeat will be even more galling and significant.

Conclusion

Although we have moved from ideas of general strategy making that assumed a deliberate strategy making posture to strategy making in different postures and at different stages of a campaign, the discussion is still largely generic. This is because the general thinking can — and should — be applied to most campaigns, operations and wars, but with nuanced differences.

We cannot prescribe for every possible situation. A *reactive* strategy making approach may be needed in a range of situations other than that of being caught off balance by an unexpected attack or unanticipated international crisis; for example, unanticipated success, either in time or scale and working out how best to exploit it. Whereas in long campaigns, *responsive* strategy making becomes one of the strategic leader's core skills. But it will always be difficult when, in dogged circumstances, you are addressing the knotty question of whether a change in strategy is needed or simply more shoulder to the wheel.

On *culminating points*, Clausewitz's prediction that his thinking would hold good in future wars has, so far, proved accurate. Here, the antidote to being blown off track is, as in most other areas of strategy, to keep a very clear idea of what your objective is and how you intend to achieve it. And, as far as you are able, to judge events against these two overlapping guides. But it is not easy. And it is particularly difficult when faced with the prospect of an opponent's culmination, that is our defeat — as both Cold War superpowers discovered in different ways in Vietnam and Afghanistan.

In all this, the underpinning safety net, if there is such a thing, is that of rationality. When you are faced with passion, events, friction, chance and the blizzard of information flowing into your calculations from the incoming conveyor belt of war's irrationality, the answer will be to respond by loading rationality, judgement and strategic intuition onto your outgoing conveyor belt of strategy making and stick it out as best you can.

Changes in strategy need to be thought through and not undertaken lightly. It is often easy to forget, in the lofty towers of Washington, London, Paris or Berlin, the impact on administrative and logistics plans and, worse, morale that result from too many changes of strategy. By way of illustration, in a Remembrance Day conversation, some years ago, a Royal Marine veteran of the Suez operation recalled to me how the UK's maritime forces had been subject to continual changes of plan, turning East, then West, then East, up and down the Mediterranean. Eventually, the decision to commence hostilities was made. His particular Commando[7] was soon on the beach and on the receiving end of determined and accurate defensive fire from Egyptian forces. When the first supporting landing craft arrived at his beach, he felt some relief with the prospect of armour in support.

Sadly, the first tracked vehicle disgorged from the belly of the ship into the fire zone was not the hoped for tank, but rather a mobile cookery — such was the operational and logistic impact of political indecision. [8]

PART V:

REFLECTIONS

Chapter 13

Strategy Making Improved
Philosophy, Policy, Process & People

There is more work to be done, a great deal of it, before we can force order into situations inherently disorderly, before we can better predict the unpredictable and before we can apply equivalent experience to situations inherently novel in the vast social and technological revolutions of our time.

J.C. Wylie

Introduction

In this, our penultimate Chapter, I want to pick up the gauntlet and make some suggestions about how we in the West could improve the way we make strategy.

Four issues — or shortfalls — are worth examining, four 'P's. The first is the philosophy of strategy making, that is our general approach to strategy making, underpinned by theory and informed by practice. The second is policy and the relationship between policy as master and strategy as servant. The key issue here is the place of broader foreign policy in strategy making. The third concerns the processes that we use for strategy making. The fourth, final and most important, is people. This includes the question of how strategic leaders and strategists are identified, selected, nurtured and promoted and how strategy making teams are created.

Although I live in a modern, liberal democracy, my observations and criticisms are not aimed at a particular nation-state, form of governance or political philosophy. The shortfalls are, I sense, more generic than this. Some parts of my commentary will be relevant for some nations and institutions and other parts for others. Although I offer thoughts on how we might address these shortfalls, my aim is not to problem solve but rather to prompt a debate. I may be wrong. The shortfalls I sense may not exist. But, given the international gravity of strategy making, it feels right to at least raise the issues.

Philosophy

The first fundamental problem in our strategy making appears to be a loss of understanding of what strategy is or should be. This is something that I have attempted to address in Part III and indeed throughout the book. The lack of a body of academic material to support strategic leaders and strategy making is also curious. Professor Strachan has written on his views on the lost meaning of the word 'strategy', exposing some of the issues, but in my practical experience the problem is worse than these important academic reflections suggest — some clues may help illustrate its true nature.

The first clue is the one that Hew Strachan identifies — because of the word's overly liberal use in contemporary affairs, strategy's meaning has been thoroughly and unhelpfully diluted.[1]

The second clue is the lack of modern theory to guide the strategy makers. Professor Colin Gray's list of great theorists of the 20th century is interesting — in descending order: Wylie, Luttwak, Brodie, Liddell Hart, Castex, Custance and Boyd — because only one, Edward Luttwak, is living today. My own 20th century list, again in descending order, is: Beaufre, Brodie, Corbett, Wylie, Yarger, and

Liddell Hart. Similarly, just one, Yarger, is alive today. At a time when the international issues that strategy deals with are so remorselessly studied in the academic and think tank communities, the lack of living figures on either list is surprising. And, notwithstanding Professor Gray's explanation of strategy's sheer complexity, this lack of modern thinking is surely not because the subject is too hard?[2]

The third clue is the lack of modern military writers and writing on general strategy — a point also made by Bernard Brodie in 1973 and Harry Summers in 1982.[3] It is not that there has been a general shortage of military thinking or writing — in some of the more fashionable areas of doctrine and warfare, such as counter-insurgency, there have been huge amounts. But there has been nothing of a seminal nature by serving military writers on general strategy. Even more startling is the lack of senior military writers, given that strategy is a senior preserve. During the 20th century, General Beaufre was the only military author of 4 star rank to write on strategy and Rear Admiral Wylie the only 2 star.

The fourth clue is the difficulty in getting hold of many of the great texts of strategy. For example, Wylie and Beaufre's classics are both out of print, as is one of Brodie's two major works.[4]

Fifth and not unsurprisingly given the first four points, is the lack of training on the subject of strategy making. I was interested to find that the two lectures that I gave on the theory and practice of strategy making to the Royal College of Defence Studies, in 2008, were the first ever in the syllabus.

Finally and probably a result of all the earlier reasons, is the loss of senior understanding of the importance of strategy. It is illuminating, for example, to recall as I did in the Introduction that, in Afghanistan at the time of my departure in December 2007, with the campaign in its sixth year, there was no single, shared, coalition strategy — agreed between the Government of Afghanistan, NATO, the UN and the other international key actors — with which to confront and defeat the Taliban insurgency.

Why have we lost our philosophy of strategy making? There is no need for us to dwell for long on the reasons but perhaps the reader will indulge me in some light and speculative diagnosis, based entirely on military gut instinct.

Things probably began to go wrong for politico-military strategy when nuclear weapons arrived. The pressing need to get to grips with these tools of Armageddon necessarily acted as a magnet for much if not most of the intellectual effort. Nuclear strategy drew in a range of civilian theorists from across the academic disciplines. And, whilst military men occasionally contributed to the thinking, they were generally in the minority. Furthermore, they were no better placed than the theorists because, like the theorists, they had, thankfully, no actual experience of nuclear war fighting.

Over time, Cold War thinking on strategy came to be dominated by civilians, some academics, others political advisors, often both. The nuclear risk also radically changed the context in which strategy makers were working. Limited war theory was developed to guide the use of conventional force in a nuclear world. But much of its thinking was based on academic assumptions, occasionally ill conceived and generally unleavened by military experience.

Strategy might have been able to cope with these developments but the next blow probably came from an unexpected source; the corporate strategy theorists. After World War II, the corporate sector looked acquisitively at the military war-fighting experience, war's competitive context and the role of doctrine and strategy in the Allied success. As military men demobilized into industry and as the ideas in the early works of the great corporate strategists such as Michael Porter radiated out from the business schools, corporate strategy took off as a discipline. And, as *Strategy Safari*'s ten corporate strategy schools show, it took off with a vengeance. Because it offered a route — or was perceived to offer a route — to competitive advantage and, thus, to profit.

What happened next? The corporate schools evolved the ideas in ways that suited the corporate context but these ideas were then subjected to the flighty winds of business theory fashion. And then came the killer blow, as these windblown ideas wafted back, virus-like, through the public sector into the politico-military world.

The infection may have caught hold in two ways. The first may have been the direct injection of corporate thinking into policy and strategy in the McNamara Pentagon. And the second may have been via the viral agency of management consultancy. In the British form this would have probably have begun with a general political intuition that business practice was best practice. Public service efficiency and effectiveness could only be enhanced through the adoption of business methods. Enter, stage right, the management consultants, offering back to us the residue of the ideas that the corporate theorists had stolen from us in the first place — and charging a pretty price for the privilege.

Thus the destruction of the original idea of strategy was complete. And in its place, a term that came to mean everything and anything to everyone and anyone, from the 'learning strategy' for the primary school toddler through to the 'containment strategy' of the Cold War that shaped the fate of nations.

Although the analysis is light and speculative, it does contain a simple but important thought. Ideas and theory impact on practice. And if the speculation is remotely close to the mark, it shows that this impact is not always positive.

But returning to the central issue, if, as the earlier clues seem to confirm, we have lost our philosophy of strategy making, how can we recover it? There are a number of ways.

First, we could improve the body of academic theory on the subject. When I first ventured into the world of modern strategic studies, as part of a doctoral reconnaissance, I was surprised by the lack of modern thinking on strategy making. Take, as illustration, an excellent, introductory strategic studies text, authored by some of the field's most distinguished academics, *Strategy in the Contemporary World*.[5] There are useful insights dotted around its 372 substantive pages but there is no single chapter nor single section nor even single page that discusses how strategy is made. This is not a criticism, simply an example and not atypical. I would be very wary of unleashing an academic avalanche on the subject but a little more thinking would be useful.

Second, we could re-energize discussions between leaders, practitioners and theorists to help advance our understanding of the art of strategy making. All three have much to bring to the table. An important step would be to encourage successful leaders and practitioners — political, military and diplomatic — to reflect and write on their experiences. In this respect, Slim's *Defeat Into Victory* is a model of its kind not least because of its compelling frankness and the lack of hubris. The writing of Churchill, Alanbrooke and, latterly, Rupert Smith are also rich veins of insight. Without honest reflections from the field, our academic colleagues will always have a difficult time of it.

Third, we could improve the way we train leaders and practitioners. Some readers may have been surprised that strategy making was not, until very recently, taught at the Royal College of Defence Studies. But without a body of theory, what would we have taught? And if there is a lack of training of military officers in strategy making, it is a racing certainty that matters are even worse in all the other practitioner communities.

I hope that this book will be a modest contribution to all three of these 'lines of operation'. More importantly, I hope that it will be followed, soon, by other offerings.

Policy

An altogether more difficult subject is that of foreign policy including in its hard edged form, grand strategy. Why does foreign policy matter for strategy makers?

Although he is writing in the 1930s, Admiral Castex's explanation of the questions that should frame foreign policy helps set the scene:

> What are France's interests? What is the best direction in which to focus French Effort? How should we pursue our historic development and the work of our predecessors? Where should we struggle for profit, to improve the current position? Where, on the other hand, should we resist to conserve what we have? Whence are the most dangerous threats to come? To what attacks are we particularly exposed? What should we do to meet our needs, be they positive or negative, expansionist or conservative? What specific plans flow from these needs? What are the appropriate political, military, maritime, colonial economic, moral, etc., plans for our situation?[6]

Castex is unsure whether the French government addresses these questions: 'Not being privy to the secrets of the gods, I do not know. I only hope that this is how they act, because such an approach is necessary to produce a plan of war or a plan of action worthy of the name.'[7] The last point is key. From history, first principles and personal experience, it important that we have a higher foreign policy to refer to when we are making strategy.

We can refine Castex's thinking. If we are considering a military operation in a region, then our thinking will be on a firmer footing if placed in the context of our regional foreign policy. In particular, this will allow us to ensure that any political objective that we seek to deliver using military action contributes to the broader regional design. Without regional policy the only way to work out our political objectives in a crisis will be to 'muddle through.'

Sometimes 'muddling through' may be the best and only option. There may be no other alternative. But all things being equal, where there is a higher foreign policy to draw on, it will be easier to derive and design coherent political objectives for military operations. And if we can refer to a regional policy then, when we are in concurrent operations, it will be easier, first, to ensure that the objectives for each are mutually supporting and, second, to decide on the priorities when resources are stretched. After one of my first lectures at Royal College of Defence Studies on strategy making, a very senior retired British diplomat took me aside afterwards and said: 'You know, I must apologize because I never realized how important our foreign policy was to you in the military.'

That said, in a complex, globalized, interdependent world, foreign policy making is not easy. Far from it. It is complicated and challenging and it may be that the British approach of 'not having a grand strategic concept' is, in the long run, best. This is not an ironic comment but entirely serious. The proposition needs, though, to be consciously tested.

One of Britain's most senior retired diplomats, Sir John Coles, takes a different view and believes that we could do better in foreign policy. I too tend to this view, albeit less from a narrow UK perspective, more from a broader, Western one. A clue for me is that the body of theory on diplomacy and foreign policy making is even more meagre than that for strategy making. Yet, having been a policy planner as well as a strategy maker, I can attest that the problems are remarkably similar for both.

Furthermore, if we want to do other than 'muddle through', there are insights out there for us. For example, a logical starting point for shaping foreign policy lies in the answers to the questions that Castex sets out in the quotation above. Similarly, the US diplomat, George Kennan's thinking shows how we would go about identifying the fundamental objectives of foreign policy:

> Our foreign policy, in short, is only a means to an end. And that end must consist of whatever we consider to be the general objects of American society. ... If we look closely at other sovereign entities, in history as in our own time, I think we will see that each of them has had some overall purpose, going beyond just the routine chores of government. ... So far as I can ascertain, our forefathers believed that such progress and improvement as might conceivably be brought about in the condition of human beings would be most apt to ensure if men were left as free as possible to pursue their own self-interest and happiness, each in his own way. ... [I]n the handling of our relations with other nations what could be done to promote the accomplishment of these objects? The first and obvious answer was: that one ought to protect the physical intactness of our national life from any military or political intrusion ... Secondly, one could see to it that insofar as the activities of our citizens in pursuit of the private interests spilled over beyond our borders and into the outside world, the best possible arrangements were made to promote and protect them.[8]

I have quoted Kennan at length here not just for the content, although for me his analysis has an iridescent and enduring quality. Rather I want to demonstrate the simple but compelling deductive logic that he uses to arrive at the key two objects of US foreign policy.

It will be for foreign policy specialists — practitioners and theorists — to consider whether this logic could be applied in contemporary foreign policy making. Instead I want to leave the reader with the observation that, without higher foreign policy, the strategy maker's task will always be more difficult.

Processes

Although strategic leaders and strategists incline to ideas rather than processes, processes seem nevertheless to matter in strategy making. We have already examined, in Chapter 10, the key premises on which a politico-military school of strategy making would rest. These premises provide a template for institutions to examine their processes. So, rather than second guess such examinations and, noting that many Western foreign, defence and security ministries are understandably fixated on Afghanistan, I want to focus here on what I judge are the priority areas.

Three questions are useful in kicking off an analysis of one's processes. Where is our strategy made? Who makes it? How do they make it? If you find these questions difficult to answer or if you are given opposing answers by different institutions, this is good reason to examine your processes more closely. Two priority areas seem likely to drive any redesign.

First, if you accept the insights of earlier chapters, then the amount you need to adjust your processes depends on the capacity of the current ones to accommodate these ideas. It also depends on your view on the related issue of whether form should follow function. Should your decision making processes be optimized to deliver sound policy and superior strategy? Without being privy to a particular nation's processes, on the question of whether form should follow function, generally I believe it should. The process's key design principle should be effective strategy making and the process's key output should be superior strategy.

Second, it is important to consider the other key issue: how often you think you will work in coalitions, particularly international coalitions. Although it may be relatively straightforward to design a national strategy making process tailored to the thinking of earlier chapters, this may not help much with strategy making in an international coalition. This is because what matters in coalition operations is not your national strategy — an overused but particularly meaningless idea when acting in coalition — but rather the coalition strategy. And, unless you are a superpower, it is unlikely that a coalition strategy will be devised in your own national capital using your own national processes.

Indeed the only national capital that has much to commend it as a strategy making location is that of the host nation on whose territory an expeditionary operation is taking place. In expeditionary operations, the national capitals of the nations who are deploying forces and the higher command HQs of security alliances such as NATO are routinely thousands of miles distant from the campaign. In such cases, strategy making is better undertaken in-region — this is the only place where we have reliable and regular access to the essential ingredients of superior strategy making: the political atmospherics, the strategic insights and the leaders and commanders who will execute the strategy.

This is not to exclude distant national capitals from the strategy making process. Indeed, within coalition operations, three things are better considered from the perspective of the national capital of a coalition partner. First, key preliminary questions are best thought through at the seat of government for each partner. What will our national objectives be? And what resources are we prepared to commit to the coalition to achieve them? Second, there will need to be discussions with possible coalition colleagues, including on the key issue of what the overarching coalition objective should be. Third, the capital will be the best place to view the operation in its broader regional and international perspective, to identify where it sits within the nation's hierarchy of competing policy objectives and decide on its priority for resources. But, once the operation is underway, it would be rare for the national capital to be the best place for strategy making. In short, national capitals are the best place to decide on national policy and coalition policy but, once the operation is underway, coalition strategy making is best done in the country or region of interest.

Ultimately the adjustments you make to your strategy making processes will depend on a range of factors but these two will be key. In theory, each may pull you in a slightly different direction, given that for an optimized national process you need form to follow strategy making function but, as a coalition contributor, you need process flexibility so that you can deploy your strategic thinking horsepower forward to the strategy making locations and the coalition operations. In practice, this ought not to be an issue if the process is responsible and flexible. Ultimately, strategy is made by people and no changes to your process can substitute for the right people. But, if you have the right people working within the right processes, your chances of success will likely be better.

People

The issue of people is a perfect place to conclude this final substantive chapter. No amount of philosophy or policy or process will be successful without the right people and the right combinations of the right people. In strategy making, people matter above all else. Castex has one reason and Liddell Hart another:

Strategy is, at least for the most part, an art. One sees the intervention of individuality, of personality, in a word, of the psychological and moral factors, which play no role in science.[9]

There is a defect in the system if the instrument is superior to the artist.[10]

Actually, Liddell Hart is analysing the US Civil War and the relationship between the strategic leaders and the armies they commanded but the comment works as well for modern strategic leaders and the decision making processes they use.

Individuals

But are the 'right people' for strategy making the product of nature or nurture? We touched briefly on this in Chapter 7 but an observation from the cognitive school of corporate strategy helps frame the question for a slightly longer examination:

Cognitive psychology has yet to address adequately the question of prime interest to strategic management, especially how concepts form in the mind of a strategist.[11]

It follows that, if we do not yet fully understand the creative mind, then we will find creativity in strategy makers difficult, if not impossible, to nurture. And it further follows that, for now, successful strategic leaders and effective strategists will more likely be products of nature. Nations and institutions that wish to be successful need thus to be able to identify, select, groom and promote those with the 'right stuff'.

Selecting the right people is the greatest challenge for reasons that are, I suspect, common to most professions, be they in the political, military, diplomatic, civil service or corporate sectors. The qualities that you need for success at the tactical and operational levels are a necessary — but not a sufficient — gauge of those that you need for success at the strategic level. And the challenge is to identify those with the extra and different qualities needed for the highest levels.

What are these extra and different qualities, the ones that mark out those with the 'right stuff'? Given strategy's complexity, a very powerful intellect seems to be the baseline requirement. Certainly this is the consistent quality in great strategic leaders, strategists and strategic theorists past. Thereafter, it is more difficult to put your finger on it. Experience, knowledge and courage all have a part to play but there is also something more indefinable. The best way that I can describe it is that there are certain people who can 'see' strategic things that most cannot. This perhaps ties in with what Clausewitz called a *coup d'oeil*, attractively interpreted by Strachan as 'a sort of inner eye which vouchsafed the ability to judge strategic as well as tactical situations'.[12] Although we may term it strategic judgement, it remains, nevertheless, an indefinable quality. The best judges of those youngsters who might have it are those elders who have proved, through their actions, that they too have it.

Teams

Forming high quality strategy making teams is a quicker route to better strategy making than the individual selection and nurturing of strategic leaders and thinkers — because the balance of key qualities can be designed quickly into the team rather than nurtured slowly into the individual.

The makeup of such teams is so case dependent that there is not much more that can be said other than to make two observations based on personal experience. First, if the leader of the team is a recognized strategic thinker, then their chances of success are better.

Second, if the teams are made up of individuals who will implement the strategy and they are given creative space to think, they will be the best source of the ideas, judgements and decisions needed to populate a strategy and also the best placed to execute it having been in on the thinking from the outset. There is also, though, much to be said for using just one or two minds to draw the ideas together, if you like one or two pens to write the strategic script according to the strategic 'house style.'

Recipients

Although great leaders are always great strategists, great leaders are not two a penny. So it is routinely the case that the roles of leader and strategist are split. Nations need, therefore, to think through how their leaders — especially their political leaders — are, through training and experience, prepared for the task of directing strategy making and managing strategists.

Finally, how should we prepare those individuals who, although not executively involved in the strategy making, nevertheless deal with the product in some way? Politicians on foreign affairs and defence committees are a case in point. The short answer is 'education, education, education'. The world of war and strategy is not the place for uninformed and uneducated generalists, be they political, diplomatic, civil or military. For such people, a programme along the lines of a strategy module in an undergraduate Strategic or War Studies degree would have much to commend it — and it would seem to be a not unreasonable expenditure for those who, on occasion, may be called on to examine and occasionally sanction decisions that shape the fate of nations.

Conclusion

I cannot claim that philosophy, policy, processes and people are the only or even the most important areas where we could improve modern strategy making. But they do seem to me to be worthy of further investigation. The first and last shortfalls on the list, philosophy and people, should be the highest priority.

It will always be better if strategy makers have a higher foreign policy to provide high level direction and as a source of inspiration for their thinking. But devising this is easier said than done. And there will always be events in the future, not predicted in the policy analysis, that will require a from-first-principles strategy making approach. This is not to say that we should not try to devise grand strategy or foreign policy to deal with the great international security issues of our time. It will undoubtedly help us think though our current political contest when we are able to situate it within in a higher web of reason and rationality. Processes are similarly important, particularly when they imperceptibly influence strategy making and strategic behaviour in unhelpful ways. But shaping them takes time and effort, not least in overcoming the many vested interests of the different institutional groupings involved. And this is particularly the case when you are simultaneously conducting real world operations such as Afghanistan, engaged strategically in what we would term the 'contact battle.'

The easier wins are in philosophy and people. If I am right about the philosophy gap and the need to restock our intellectual arsenal, then I hope that this book will help us in regaining ground. If it motivates strategic leaders, strategists and strategic scholars to restock our body of theory and practical insight then much of its work will be done. But we also need to make sure that we identify, select, groom and promote the right people with the right stuff for the job. The right philosophy will be as nothing without them. Reflecting on the worsening Malayan crisis in late 1951, Field Marshal Montgomery famously wrote to the Colonial Minister:

> Dear Lyttelton,
> Malaya
> We must have a plan.
> Secondly we must have a man.
> When we have a plan and a man, we shall succeed: not otherwise.
> Yours sincerely,
> Montgomery (F.M.)

Although Lyttelton recalled, in his memoirs, 'I may, perhaps without undue conceit, say that this had occurred to me,'[13] Monty made an enduring point. Improvements in our philosophy of strategy making will give us the basis for working out a strategy (or plan in Monty's speak) but we need the right people to do the strategy creating and the right people to do the strategy executing if we are to be successful: not otherwise.

Conclusion

Theory cannot equip the mind with formulas for solving problems, nor can it mark the narrow path on which the sole solution is supposed to lie by planting a hedge of principles on either side. But it can give the mind insight into the great mass of phenomena and of their relationships, then leave it free to rise into the higher realms of action. There the mind can use its innate talents to capacity, combining them all so as to seize on what is right and true as though this were a single idea formed by their concentrated pressure — as though it were a response to the immediate challenge rather than a product of thought.

Carl von Clausewitz

Let me finish the story where I began, in Afghanistan. Returning from Kabul and, in January 2008, debriefing special advisors, officials and senior officers in No. 10 and Whitehall was a sobering experience. The content of my message was simple: there was no overarching strategy to guide the campaign; we needed one and this is what it could look like.

But my message fell on deaf ears and for two reasons. First, some felt I was wrong about the lack of strategy and pointed out the error of my ways by referring me to 'our strategy'. They were referring to, of course, a British strategy not a coalition strategy. To me the idea of a British strategy seemed then — and seems now — nonsensical. How was a British strategy, focused largely on directing a relatively small British deployment, in overall coalition terms, to just one of Afghanistan's thirty-four provinces going to make up for the lack of an overall campaign strategy? Second, I had not recognized that, because British forces were in Helmand Province, the minds of British politicians, senior officers, officials, opinion-formers and the press had become fixated there too. I had failed, in other words, to complete the first step in my Strategic Estimate and understand properly the peculiar political context to which I was returning. Having done my best to bring the key strategic message back, I watched the raging debates about the tactical issues such as equipment and the number of boots on the ground with much private frustration. But the positive outcome was a reinforcement in my mind of the need for new thinking on making strategy. This book is, in part, a consequence of that frustration and of that reinforcement.

As I write now, Afghanistan and Iraq are still playing out, arguably two individual campaigns of a more complex political contest where international terrorism, inspired by extremist Islam, is both a symptom and a tactic. Elsewhere, contemporary developments in North Korea, Iran, Pakistan, Georgia and Gaza give pause for thought. Layered over all this is an unprecedented economic crisis. Within this crisis, we see signs that our Western order, perhaps ultimately founded on affluence, may not be as secure as we had assumed. And ultimately the long-term iceberg out there for our Titanic of international politics looks to be global warming. The new international context looks volatile and history may yet have more mileage than Fukuyama predicted. All of this gives me reason to be cautious about our strategic future. We would surely do well to place a premium on our ability to create and, if necessary, execute superior strategy.

I have defined politico-military strategy as a rational course of action that uses state power to achieve a political object in the face of violent opposition. And I have outlined some of the key features present in superior strategy: a clear statement of political purpose, a coherent organizing concept, a sense of seizing the initiative, a capacity to bind key actors, and so on. But ultimately, when you seek out a piece of real strategy, to see what it looks, feels and smells like, you find something that is inherently organic in nature; something that lives. It is, to use my earlier phrase, 'the ideas, judgments and decisions of men and women, set out in a coherent and a communicable form which, in broad terms, answers the critical question: "How are we going to do this?"'

And when all is said and done, what seems to determine the quality of your strategy making and strategic performance is the quality of your people. Superior strategy making is all about clear strategic thinking and decisive strategic leadership. The key is to have people capable of both. In the medium-to-long term, the trick is thus to identify such people and work ruthlessly to get them into the right places. National leaders and politicians who fail to do this will have to accept the blame for future politico-military failures.

I think we can also do better in the short term. Here the responsibility for improvement lies in the hands of those who create and execute strategy now, be they politicians, diplomats, officials or military officers. The simple solution is self-education. Strategic leaders and strategists must work to understand strategy making in theory and they must work to apply rigour when strategy making in practice — for those vested with the power to commit military forces to armed conflict and war, this responsibility is not formal but is fundamental.

To help bring more understanding and rigour to our strategy making, I have tried here to bring back into contemporary consciousness and distil the thinking of distinguished theorists and practitioners past. I have also set out complementary ideas based on corporate theory, military doctrine, personal insight and arguments from first principles. But, whether or not I have enhanced our body of knowledge, strategy making will never be easy. And, with matters of high politics and war and with people's lives at stake, it feels right that it is not. But it also feels right to suggest that, when we choose to use armed force, our thinking to underpin operations should be as rigorous as humanly possible.

What then are the key lessons herein for strategy makers who wish to add rigour? They emerge naturally from the main structure of our analysis of strategy making in history, theory and practice.

Two lessons from the history of strategy sit above the individual insights. First, we must recognize the cumulative influence that historical ideas exert on our thinking today, often in ways more subliminal than conscious. As Bernard Brodie said, these ideas — be they on show in principles and axioms or hidden in doctrine and received wisdom — are 'part of a heritage of thought that even today dominates the great decisions of national defense.'[1] This leads us to the second lesson. Those who are — or aspire to be — strategy makers must know and understand this body of thought. Part II provides an introduction, but it is not a substitute for further study, at least not for those of conscience.

Two further lessons emerge from the theory of politico-military strategy making. First, if we choose to use state power, including armed force, to achieve a political object, then the rational way for us to do so is to create and execute a superior strategy. We are more likely to create superior strategy with a rigorous approach, for example using the frameworks and tools of Part III — but noting that these are aids, not substitutes, for hard thinking. This leads us to the second lesson, which draws on the Strategic Estimate. If we want to make superior strategy, we need to start our strategy making by answering two key questions: 'What is the political issue at contest?' and, 'What is the desired political object?' In other words, before we make a decision to fight, we must know what we will be fighting about and we must know what we want to achieve by fighting.

Two final lessons emerge in Part IV from the practice of strategy making. First, because of war's irrational nature, no matter how much rigour we use when we make strategy, events are unlikely to unfold as we envisage: 'No plan survives contact with the enemy.' Because of this, the very way we think will need to vary in different stages in our strategy making. A more prescriptive approach will be better as we create the strategy. A more reflective approach will be better as we execute the strategy. But these different ways of thinking — prescriptive Jominian and reflective Clausewitzian — are complementary, not alternatives. Second, sad to say, but processes matter. The principles I have proposed for a politico-military school of strategy making can help codify these processes. Through the act of codification, states and institutions can start to judge if their strategy making processes work and, if necessary, make changes. Improved processes will be no substitute for good people but, without improvement, the danger is that strategy making will remain a 'disorganized, undisciplined intellectual activity'.[2]

The bottom line lesson, probably more important than all others is that ultimately, it's all about people. To repeat Beaufre's view:

> In war the loser deserves to lose because his defeat must result from errors of thinking, made either before or during the conflict.[3]

I agree. Poor strategy is the result of errors of thinking. And people are the source of the thinking. So, if an operation or war is going badly, we need to look critically not only at our strategy but also at our senior people, political, diplomatic, civil and military and decide whether the source of the problem is broader than the strategy and, if necessary, be ruthless in making changes.

It will be interesting, in time, to see how history judges the strategies, the strategy making and the strategy makers of the modern campaigns in Afghanistan and Iraq. How will results measure up against our three tests of superior strategy: effectiveness, efficiency and durability of result? I suspect that, in the sober light of historical analysis, pluses and minuses will emerge. After all, strategy making is not easy, as historian Williamson Murray observes:

> Those involved, whether statesmen or military leaders, live in a world of incomplete information. ... circumstances often force them to work under the most intense pressure. When a crisis occurs they have little time for reflection.[1]

I know this to be true. Equally though, the school report of history may record areas where we 'could do better'. Certainly as a participant I would feel honour bound to examine a 'could do better' charge. But this book is not about salving a conscience. Rather it is an attempt to explore the question: if superior strategy is key to success in the great strategic endeavours of our time, *how* could we do better? As such the recent past should be of interest to us not for apportioning blame but rather as a source of insights — of strategic jigsaw pieces — to allow us to 'do better', to create and execute more effective strategy in the future. And we need to be prompt in learning these lessons because today's strategic leaders and strategists have work to do.

What we sometimes forget about strategy is that not only does it matter — but very often it matters now. When we get it wrong, we may fail to achieve critical political objectives. Precious and sometimes irreplaceable resources may be squandered. And too many will pay in blood. So I hope that scholars will forgive the flaws and roughness herein. Some of the theory feels raw and must be challenged. But for now my colleagues at the strategic level and their agents in the tactical field, are the ones who need our help, those people whose faces are marred by the dust and sweat and blood of the strategic arena.

Some say making strategy is easy. I simply do not agree. Nor does history. If it were easy, surely we would always be successful? Surely the campaigns in the Balkans, Somalia, Afghanistan and Iraq would have played out as their designers intended? Rather, as I said at the outset, strategy making is problem-solving of the most complex order because it deals with three of life's great imponderables, people, war and the future. But this does not mean that it is not susceptible to hard thinking. Indeed the historical record seems to shows that hard thinking by talented people is the cornerstone of strategic success. But, to better focus our hard thinking, we will need to turn strategy making into something other than Admiral Wylie's 'disorganized, undisciplined activity'. And if the theory presented in this book helps those creating and executing strategy do so in a more organized and disciplined way, my work will be done. For ultimately, as Bernard Brodie observed, 'a theory of strategy is a theory of action.'[5]

Further Reading

To keep things simple and focused, I have limited my recommended reading to just ten texts, six historical and four modern.

Historical

Carl von Clausewitz, *On War*, translated by Michael Howard, and Peter Paret (Princeton, 1976). The translation by Howard and Paret is the classic. It is worth noting, though, that there is an ongoing academic debate about their translation. An example is the key German word 'politik' and whether this might have been interpreted so as to suit a Western liberal idea of political control of the military. For an excellent analysis of this issue, see Jan Willem Honig's 'Clausewitz's On War: Problems of Text and Translation' in *Clausewitz in the 21st century*, edited by Hew Strachan and Andreas Herberg-Rothe (Oxford, 2007).

Anton Jomini, *A Summary of the Art of War*, translated by Captain Mendell and Lieutenant Craighill (1862) and introduced by Charles Messenger (London, 1992). Essential reading, given its impact on our strategic thinking, particularly via its influence on modern military doctrine. That said, I've struggled to find the best translation. Most modern texts draw on the 1862 version by Mendell and Craighill of the US Army; the best introduction seems to be Charles Messenger's in 1992.

Julian Corbett, *Some Principles of Maritime Strategy* (London, 1911, reprinted Annapolis, Md., 1988). Corbett's first six chapters still provide one of the very best analyses of Clausewitz's thinking. And on maritime strategy, the work remains the classic.

Bill Slim, *Defeat into Victory* (2nd Edition, London, 1956). The outstanding World War II narrative, the book is not about strategy *per se* but is nevertheless sprinkled throughout with diamond insights for the strategic thinker.

Bernard Brodie, *Strategy in the Missile Age* (Princeton, 1959). Perhaps the greatest strategic thinker of his era, his insights have an enduring relevance.

Bill Wylie, *Military Strategy: A General Theory of Power Control* (New Brunswick, 1967). Short and crisp, this is a key text. Wylie is, like me, keen that we are more ordered in the way that we create strategy but also focuses importantly on the art of control as we execute strategy.

André Beaufre, *An Introduction to Strategy*, translated by R.H. Barry (London, 1965). For me, the best book of the last century on the making of strategy.

Modern

Peter Paret, Editor, *Makers of Modern Strategy* (Oxford 1986). An update of the 1943 original, this is still the classic overview of strategy and would be top of my modern list.

Williamson Murray, Macgregor Knox, & Alvin Bernstein, Editors, *The Making of Strategy: Rulers, States and War* (Cambridge, 1994). Key insights on the challenges facing strategy makers throughout history and the nature of their responses.

Dick Yarger, *Strategy and the National Security Professional* (Westport, CT., 2008). The only significant modern book, other than this one, on the making of modern strategy. Although Professor Yarger and I approach our subject in different ways — I am interested in using the insights of history, whereas Yarger prefers to come at the matter solely from first principles — I am a great admirer of his work and the book is required reading for the strategy specialist.

Henry Mintzberg, Bruce Ahlstrand, & Joe Lampel, *Strategy Safari*, (London, 1998). For me, the best introduction to corporate strategy — light hearted but intelligent and insightful.

Readers with interests in particular areas of strategy will be able to chase these down via my endnotes but, for those who want a balanced overview, these ten books provide as good a start as any.

Endnotes

Introduction

1. Emphasis added. Carl von Clausewitz, *On War*, tr. Michael Howard & Peter Paret. (Princeton, 1976) p.579.
2. Harry R. Yarger, *Strategy and the National Security Professional*, (Westport, 2008).
3. J.C. Wylie, *Military Strategy: A General Theory of Power Control*, (London, 1966) p.v-vi,
4. Bernard Brodie, *Strategy in the Missile Age*, (Princeton, 1959) p.23.
5. Theodore Roosevelt, *Citizenship in a Republic*, Speech at the Sorbonne, Paris, April 23, 1910.

The Nature of War & the Role of Strategy

1. There is an argument to say that there is a fourth element, a national psychological posture, which is indicative of a changed popular mood. As the former US Army colonel, Harry G. Summers, Jr notes, '[The failure to declare war] was dangerous for the Army because in failing to mobilize the national will the United States lost what Clausewitz called the strength of the passions of a people mobilized for war'. However, I prefer to include the idea of posture within the more general idea of war as a political condition. Harry G. Summers, *On Strategy: A Critical Analysis of the Vietnam War*, (2nd edn. New York, 1995) p.28.
2. For a more detailed examination of this point, see Edward N Luttwak, *Strategy: The Logic of War and Peace*, (Harvard, 1987).
3. Robert F. Kennedy, *13 Days: The Cuban Missile Crisis*, (London, 1969) p.86.
4. John Coles, *Making Foreign Policy: A Certain Idea of Britain*, (London, 2000) p.9.
5. For an involved discussion on policy and strategy, see Edward N. Luttwak, *Strategy: The Logic of War and Peace*, (Harvard, 1987) p.114.
6. Basil Liddell Hart, *Strategy: The Indirect Approach*, (London, 1967) p.335.
7. MoD, *Joint Discussion Note 4/05: The Comprehensive Approach*, (2006). There is one danger with this term, which is the tendency to see the Comprehensive Approach as strategy in its own right. It is not. Rather, it is simply a way of saying that, when engaging in modern campaigns abroad, the likelihood is that a range of levers of power, hard and soft, will need to be used.
8. MoD, *Joint Warfare Publication 0-01: British Defence Doctrine*, (1996) p.18.
9. There is perhaps a question begged here, that of defining rationality, which I will not dwell on, but the complementary terms 'national interests' and 'national values' are key to the answer.

The Classical Epoch: 1750-1850

1. Hans Delbrück, *The Dawn of Modern Warfare*, tr. Walter J. Renfroe, Jr., (Westport, 1990) p.315.
2. For an in-depth exploration of this point, see Kyung-won Kim, *Revolution and International System*, (New York, 1970) p.94-95.
3. Kalevi J. Holsti, *Peace & War: Armed Conflicts and International Order 1648-1989*, (Cambridge, 1991) p.158.
4. *Principes Généraux de la Guerre*, completed in 1746, *Testament Politique* (1752), *Testament Militaire* (1768) and *Eléments de Castramétrie et de Tactique* (1771). R.R. Palmer, 'Frederick the Great, Guibert, Bülow: From Dynastic to National War,' in Peter Paret, ed., *Makers of Modern Strategy*, (Oxford, 1986) p.92.
5. R.R. Palmer, 'Frederick the Great, Guibert, Bülow: From Dynastic to National War,' in Peter Paret, ed., *Makers of Modern Strategy*, (Oxford, 1986) p.99.
6. Peter Paret, 'Napoleon and the Revolution in War,' in Peter Paret, ed., *Makers of Modern Strategy*, (Oxford, 1986) p.123.
7. 'All arms' is a military term used to describe the tactical combination of infantry, cavalry, artillery and support services.
8. Raoul Castex, *Strategic Theories*, tr. & ed. Eugenia C. Kiesling, (Annapolis, 1994) p.4.
9. Peter Paret, 'Napoleon and the Revolution in War,' in Peter Paret, ed., *Makers of Modern Strategy*, (Oxford, 1986) p.129-131,
10. Ibid. p.137.
11. John Shy, 'Jomini,' in Peter Paret, ed., *Makers of Modern Strategy*, (Oxford, 1986) p.144.
12. Marie von Clausewitz, in Carl von Clausewitz, *On War*, tr. Michael Howard & Peter Paret. (Princeton, 1976) p.66. There is no more moving pen picture of Clausewitz, the man, than in his widow's foreword.
13. Julian Corbett, *Some Principles of Maritime Strategy*, (London, 1911, repr. Annapolis, 1988) p.24.
14. Bernard Brodie, *Strategy in the Missile Age*, (Princeton, 1959) p.35.
15. John Shy, 'Jomini,' in Peter Paret, ed., *Makers of Modern Strategy*, (Oxford, 1986) p.146.
16. Ibid. p.169.
17. Ibid. p.177.
18. Harry G. Summers, *On Strategy: A Critical Analysis of the Vietnam War*, (2nd edn. New York, 1995).

The Industrial Transformation: 1850-1914

1. Raoul Castex, *Strategic Theories*, tr. & ed. Eugenia C. Kiesling, (Annapolis, 1994) p.14.
2. For the specialist, it is similarly interesting to speculate whether the new concept 'operational level of war', an analytic layer introduced to sit between tactics and strategy, was also a manifestation of theory and practice coming to grips with this new scope and complexity.
3. The naval case is elegantly explained in Andrew Gordon, *The Rules of the Game:*

Jutland and the British Naval Command, (London, 1996).

4. I am indebted to Major General Julian Thompson RM for this observation.

5. Kalevi J. Holsti, *Peace & War: Armed Conflicts and International Order 1648-1989*, (Cambridge, 1991) p.160-161.

6. Paul Kennedy, *Strategy & Diplomacy*, (London, 1983).

7. Kalevi J. Holsti, *Peace & War: Armed Conflicts and International Order 1648-1989*, (Cambridge, 1991) p.157-8.

8. Peter Maslowski, 'To the Edge of Greatness: The United States, 1783-1865,' in Williamson Murray, Macgregor Knox & Alvin Bernstein, eds., *The Making of Strategy: Rulers, States and War*, (Cambridge, 1994) p.236.

9. Eliot Cohen's lines are re-worded to draw out Lincoln's calculations in terminology appropriate for our strategy making perspective. Eliot A. Cohen, *Supreme Command: Soldiers, Statesmen and Leadership in Wartime*, (New York, 2002) p.30-32.

10. Russell F. Weigley, 'American Strategy from its Beginnings through the First World War,' in Peter Paret, ed., *Makers of Modern Strategy*, (Oxford, 1986) p.429.

11. Eliot A. Cohen, *Supreme Command: Soldiers, Statesmen and Leadership in Wartime*, (New York, 2002) p.50.

12. Emphasis added. Gunther E. Rothenberg, 'Moltke, Schilieffen and the Doctrine of Strategic Envelopment,' in Peter Paret, ed., *Makers of Modern Strategy*, (Oxford, 1986) p299.

13. Carl von Clausewitz, *On War*, tr. Michael Howard & Peter Paret. (Princeton, 1976) p.177-224.

14. Gunther E. Rothenberg, 'Moltke, Schilieffen and the Doctrine of Strategic Envelopment,' in Peter Paret, ed., *Makers of Modern Strategy*, (Oxford, 1986) p.289.

15. Ibid. p.301-2.

16. See, for example, Holger H. Herwig, 'Strategic Uncertainties of a Nation-State: Prussia-Germany, 1871-1918,' in Williamson Murray, Macgregor Knox & Alvin Bernstein, eds., *The Making of Strategy: Rulers, States and War*, (Cambridge, 1994) p.242-5.

17. Philip A. Crowl, 'Alfred Thayer Mahan: The Naval Historian,' in Peter Paret, ed., *Makers of Modern Strategy*, (Oxford, 1986) p.444.

18. *The Influence of Sea Power upon History, 1660-1783*, published in 1890 and its successor, *The Influence of Sea Power upon the French Revolution and Empire, 1793-1815*, published two years later in 1892.

19. Philip A. Crowl, 'Alfred Thayer Mahan: The Naval Historian,' in Peter Paret, ed., *Makers of Modern Strategy*, (Oxford, 1986) p.450-1.

20. Eric Grove, in Julian Corbett, *Some Principles of Maritime Strategy*, (London, 1911, repr. Annapolis, 1988) p.xi/xlv.

21. For my taste, the contemporary strategic scholar will still find few more concise and thoughtful overviews of Clausewitz, nor insight into Jomini, than the first six chapters of Corbett's great work. Julian Corbett, *Some Principles of Maritime Strategy*, (London, 1911, repr. Annapolis, 1988).

22. Julian Corbett, *Some Principles of Maritime Strategy*, (London, 1911, repr. Annapolis, 1988) Ch 3.

23. It is important to remember that manoeuvre, as discussed here, is to do with more than movement and encompasses a fluid and adaptable viewpoint that seeks to

dislocate and disrupt the enemy, but this does not undermine the logic of Corbett's case. Julian Corbett, *Some Principles of Maritime Strategy*, (London, 1911, repr. Annapolis, 1988) p.85.

24. As we shall see in Chapter 5, the interpretation of the term manoeuvre has changed over time, from something that was more geographic and physical, when Corbett was writing, to something that is now more psychological.

25. Julian Corbett, *Some Principles of Maritime Strategy*, (London, 1911, repr. Annapolis, 1988) p.86.

The Modern Epoch: 1914-1991

1. Two early examples were the homing torpedo and the radio-controlled anti-ship bomb; but both were essentially pilot projects toward the end of the War and neither was decisive.

2. Certainly those of us who flew from carriers in the Falklands War would always return to our 'friendly force' with some circumspection.

3. Bernard Brodie, *Strategy in the Missile Age*, (Princeton, 1959) p.64.

4. Bernard Brodie, *War & Politics*, (London, 1973) p.4.

5. Ibid. p.21.

6. Bernard Brodie, *Strategy in the Missile Age*, (Princeton, 1959) p.6, 37.

7. Gary Sheffield, *Forgotten Victory: The First World War: Myths and Realities*, (London, 2001) p.21-40.

8. Raoul Castex, *Strategic Theories*, tr. & ed. Eugenia C. Kiesling, (Annapolis, 1994) p.245.

9. Basil Liddell Hart, *Strategy: The Indirect Approach*, (London, 1967) p.219.

10. Ibid. p.339.

11. I use the terms blitzkrieg and doctrine here in the same way as James Corum: 'doctrine' is a 'simple and convenient way to describe the military tactics of the German army'; blitzkrieg is a popular and well-recognized word to describe the tactical doctrine that the German army created after World War I and around which its subsequent organization and training was built. James S. Corum, *The Roots of Blitzkrieg: Hans von Seeckt and German Military Reform*, (Kansas, 1992) p. ix-xvii.

12. James S. Corum, *The Roots of Blitzkrieg: Hans von Seeckt and German Military Reform*, (Kansas, 1992) p.199.

13. Michael Geyer, 'German Strategy in the Age of Machine Warfare, 1914-1935,' in Peter Paret, ed., *Makers of Modern Strategy*, (Oxford, 1986) p.585-6.

14. Basil Liddell Hart, *Strategy: The Indirect Approach*, (London, 1967) p.247.

15. James S. Corum, *Hans von Seeckht and German Military Reform: the Roots of Blitzkrieg*, Kansas, 1992. p.xiii.

16. Bernard Brodie, *Strategy in the Missile Age*, (Princeton, 1959) p.72.

17. David MacIsaac, 'Voices from the Central Blue: The Air Power Theorists,' in Peter Paret, ed., *Makers of Modern Strategy*, (Oxford, 1986) p.630.

18. Julian Corbett, *Some Principles of Maritime Strategy*, (London, 1911, repr. Annapolis, 1988) p.16.

19. Ibid. p.91.

20. Ibid.

21. Ibid. p.93.
22. The original versions were published between 1929 and 1935.
23. Raoul Castex, *Strategic Theories*, tr. & ed. Eugenia C. Kiesling, (Annapolis, 1994) p.207.
24. Ibid. p.209.
25. Ibid.
26. Maurice Matloff, 'Allied Strategy in Europe, 1939-1945,' in Peter Paret, ed., *Makers of Modern Strategy*, (Oxford, 1986) p.678.
27. Williamson Murray, 'The Collapse of the Empire: British Strategy, 1919-1945,' in Williamson Murray, Macgregor Knox & Alvin Bernstein, eds., *The Making of Strategy: Rulers, States and War*, (Cambridge, 1994) P.423.
28. Eliot A. Cohen, 'The Strategy of Innocence? The United States, 1920-1945,' in Williamson Murray, Macgregor Knox & Alvin Bernstein, eds., *The Making of Strategy: Rulers, States and War*, (Cambridge, 1994) p.434.
29. Williamson Murray, 'The Collapse of the Empire: British Strategy, 1919-1945,' in Williamson Murray, Macgregor Knox & Alvin Bernstein, eds., *The Making of Strategy: Rulers, States and War*, (Cambridge, 1994) p.400.
30. Eliot A. Cohen, 'The Strategy of Innocence? The United States, 1920-1945,' in Williamson Murray, Macgregor Knox & Alvin Bernstein, eds., *The Making of Strategy: Rulers, States and War*, (Cambridge, 1994) p.454.
31. Eliot A. Cohen, *Supreme Command: Soldiers, Statesmen and Leadership in Wartime*, (New York, 2002) p.115.
32. Eliot A. Cohen, 'The Strategy of Innocence? The United States, 1920-1945,' in Williamson Murray, Macgregor Knox & Alvin Bernstein, eds., *The Making of Strategy: Rulers, States and War*, (Cambridge, 1994) p.435.
33. Eliot A. Cohen, 'The Strategy of Innocence? The United States, 1920-1945,' in Williamson Murray, Macgregor Knox & Alvin Bernstein, eds., *The Making of Strategy: Rulers, States and War*, (Cambridge, 1994) p.464.
34. Eliot A. Cohen, 'The Strategy of Innocence? The United States, 1920-1945,' in Williamson Murray, Macgregor Knox & Alvin Bernstein, eds., *The Making of Strategy: Rulers, States and War*, (Cambridge, 1994) p.459.
35. John Baylis & John Garnett, eds., *Makers of Nuclear Strategy*, (London, 1991) p.1.
36. Colin S. Gray, *Strategic Studies & Public Policy*, (Kentucky, 1982) p.45.
37. Schelling goes on to note that 'the term is intended to focus on the interdependence of the adversaries' decisions and on their expectations of each other's behaviour. This is not the military usage.' Thomas C. Schelling, *The Strategy of Conflict*, (Cambridge, MA., 1960) p.1.
38. Although Schelling qualified this assumption — 'whether the resulting theory provides a good or poor insight into actual behaviour is, I repeat, a matter of subjective judgement' — the damage had been done. Thomas C. Schelling, *The Strategy of Conflict*, (Cambridge, MA., 1960) p.1.
39. Basil Liddell Hart, *Deterrent or Defence*, (London, 1960) p.66.
40. David Stone, *Wars of the Cold War*, (London, 2004) p.128.
41. Quoted in David Stone, *Wars of the Cold War*, (London, 2004) p.133.
42. Frank Kitson, *Bunch of Five*, (London, 1977) p.75.
43. James Corum fascinatingly contrasts the successful approach of British forces

in Malaya with their unsuccessful strategy in Cyprus. James S. Corum, *Training Indigenous Forces for Counter-Insurgency: A Tale of Two Insurgencies*, (US Army War College, 2006).

44. Indeed, the shortfalls in Thompson's subsequent application of counter-insurgency techniques to Vietnam is decisively exposed by Colonel Summers who suggests that, by Thompson's own definition, 'he was exactly wrong in seeing the war as "a classic revolutionary war". The guerrillas in Vietnam did not achieve decisive results on their own. Even at the very end there was no popular mass uprising to overthrow the Saigon government. ... it was a North Vietnamese Army corps, not "dialectical materialism" that ultimately conquered South Vietnam.' Harry G. Summers, *On Strategy: A Critical Analysis of the Vietnam War*, (2nd edn. New York, 1995) p.76, 85.

45. Bernard Brodie, *Strategy in the Missile Age*, (Princeton, 1959).

46. Ken Booth, Bernard Brodie, in John Baylis & John Garnett, eds., *Makers of Nuclear Strategy*, (London, 1991) p.44.

47. Bernard Brodie, *Strategy in the Missile Age*, (Princeton, 1959). Bernard Brodie, *War & Politics*, (London, 1973).

48. Bernard Brodie, *War & Politics*, (London, 1973) p.2.

49. Ken Booth, Bernard Brodie, in John Baylis & John Garnett, eds., *Makers of Nuclear Strategy*, (London, 1991).

50. George F. Kennan, quoted in Bernard Brodie, *War & Politics*, (London, 1973) p.159.

51. Bernard Brodie, *War & Politics*, (London, 1973) p.159.

52. John A. Nagl, *Learning to Eat Soup with a Knife: Counter Insurgency Lessons from Malaya and Vietnam*, (Chicago, 2005).

53. H.R. McMaster, *Dereliction of Duty: Lyndon Johnson, Robert McNamara, the Joint Chiefs of Staff and the Lies that Led to Vietnam*, (New York, 1997).

54. Harry G. Summers, *On strategy: a critical analysis of the Vietnam War*, (2nd Edn, New York, 1995) p.xiv.

55. Summer's argument for a more conventional alternative strategy has less merit. Ibid.

56. J.C. Wylie, *Military Strategy: A General Theory of Power Control*, (London, 1966).

57. Ibid. p.20.

58. Ibid. p.23-4.

59. Basil Liddell Hart, Forward in André Beaufre, *An Introduction to Strategy*, tr. Richard Barry, (London, 1963) p.10.

60. Beaufre employs the term 'dialectics' here in the third of its *Oxford English Dictionary* meanings: 'the existence or action of opposing social forces, concepts, etc' *Compact Oxford English Dictionary*, (rev edn, Oxford, 2003) p.300.

61. André Beaufre, *An Introduction to Strategy*, tr. Richard Barry, (London, 1963) p.22.

62. Ibid. p.133.

Modern Theory: Contemporary Thinkers, Military Doctrine & Corporate Theory

1. André Beaufre, *An Introduction to Strategy*, tr. Richard Barry, (London, 1963) p.20-21.

2. MoD, *Joint Warfare Publication 0-01: British Defence Doctrine*, (1996).

3. Ibid. pp1.4, A.2.

4. Offensive action and concentration of force.

5. MoD, *Joint Warfare Publication 0-01: British Defence Doctrine*, (1996) p.4.7.

6. MoD, *British Maritime Doctrine*, (BR1806 3rd edn., 2004) p.268.

7. MoD, *Joint Warfare Publication 0-01: British Defence Doctrine*, (1996) p.4.8.

8. MoD, *Design for Military Operations: British Military Doctrine*, (D/CGS/50/8, 1989). p.48.

9. MoD, *British Maritime Doctrine*, (BR1806 3rd edn., 2004) p.145.

10. Ibid. p.145.

11. Ibid. p.268.

12. US Department of the Army, *U.S. Army Field Manual No. 3-24/ Marine Corps Warfighting Publication No. 3-33.5: Counterinsurgency*, (2007).

13. Certainly the academics to whom I talked early in the conception of this book, such as Hew Strachan at Oxford in early 2006, were quite taken aback, but also open minded, to the suggestion that there might be significant shortfalls in our general theory of strategy.

14. The monograph's ideas are fleshed out at great length in Yarger's book, *Strategy and the National Security Professional*. Although I had largely completed my work before becoming aware of Harry Yarger's work, his thinking has been most useful in clarifying specific areas of my own. Harry R. Yarger, *Strategic Theory for the 21st century: The Little Book on Big Strategy*, (US Army War College, 2006). Harry R. Yarger, *Strategy and the National Security Professional*, (Westport, 2008).

15. Harry R. Yarger, *Strategic Theory for the 21st century: The Little Book on Big Strategy*, (US Army War College, 2006) p.1.

16. Ibid. p.2.

17. Ibid. p.3.

18. Ibid. p.6-14.

19. Ibid. p.13.

20. Henry Mintzberg, Bruce Ahlstrand, & Joseph Lampel, *Strategy Safari*, (London, 1998).

21. H. Igor Ansoff, *Corporate Strategy*, (New York, 1965) p.118. It is curious that Ansoff, writing in 1965, should posit games theory as the bridge, given that it was only just beginning to have an impact and then only on nuclear strategy, at this stage.

22. H. Igor Ansoff, *Corporate Strategy*, (New York, 1965) p.21.

23. US Department of the Army, *Field Manual No. 101-5: Staff Officers Field Manual, Staff Organization and Procedure*, (1954).

24. Edmund Philip Learned, C. Roland Christensen, Ken Andrews, Joseph L. Bower, Richard G. Hamermesh, & Michael E. Porter, *Business Policy: Text & Cases*, (5th edn., Homewood, 1982) p.93.

25. Henry Mintzberg, Bruce Ahlstrand, & Joseph Lampel, *Strategy Safari*, (London, 1998) p.3-18.

26. As well as offering planning and pattern as two fundamental descriptions of strategy, the authors also offer two further 'P's, position and perspective but these have little cross over with the politico-military world. Their fifth and final 'P' is ploy, a 'specific manoeuvre designed to outwit an opponent or competitor', which is something we in the politico-military world have been doing for a few millennia now.

27. Henry Mintzberg, Bruce Ahlstrand, & Joseph Lampel, *Strategy Safari*, (London, 1998) p.24.
28. Edmund Philip Learned, C. Roland Christensen, Ken Andrews, Joseph L. Bower, Richard G. Hamermesh, & Michael E. Porter, *Business Policy: Text & Cases*, (5th edn., Homewood, 1982).
29. Henry Mintzberg, Bruce Ahlstrand, & Joseph Lampel, *Strategy Safari*, (London, 1998) p.24.
30. David S. Fadok, John Boyd and John Warden: *Air Power's Quest for Strategic Paralysis*, (Alabama, 1995) p16.
31. Henry Mintzberg, Bruce Ahlstrand, & Joseph Lampel, *Strategy Safari*, (London, 1998) p.57.
32. Harry R. Yarger, *Strategic Theory for the 21st century: The Little Book on Big Strategy*, (US Army War College, 2006) p.47-48.
33. Henry Mintzberg, Bruce Ahlstrand, & Joseph Lampel, *Strategy Safari*, (London, 1998) p.234.
34. Ibid. p.235.
35. Charles E. Lindblom, 'The Science of 'Muddling Through' in *Public Administration Review*, 19/2, (1959).
36. Henry Mintzberg, Bruce Ahlstrand, & Joseph Lampel, *Strategy Safari*, (London, 1998) p.176.
37. Michael Geyer, 'German Strategy in the Age of Machine Warfare, 1914-1935,' in Peter Paret, ed., *Makers of Modern Strategy*, (Oxford, 1986) p.585-6.
38. Henry Mintzberg, Bruce Ahlstrand, & Joseph Lampel, *Strategy Safari*, (London, 1998) p.208-209.
39. Jack Welch, *Jack*, (London, 2001) p.xii.
40. Henry Mintzberg, Bruce Ahlstrand, & Joseph Lampel, *Strategy Safari*, (London, 1998) p.225.
41. Ibid.

Strategy's Context: The Information Transformation: 1991-Future

1. The ugly terms 'network centric warfare' (US) or 'network enabled capability' (UK) are used to describe sharing information in this way.
2. Francis Fukuyama, *The End of History and the Last Man*, (London, 1992).
3. Thinking in time becomes more complicated too, the complicating factor being to do with the political and strategic leverage that can be exerted through early actions in time. It is rather like investment. A little strategic expenditure made early can have a lot more impact than a lot made late. By way of example, in 1976 the British Government, under James Callaghan, in response to concerns about Argentine intentions in the Falklands, deployed a small task force to the South Atlantic. In the event, the perceived concern passed but the deployment of the force was never exposed to the Argentine Government — one wonders whether, if it had, it might have changed calculations in Buenos Aires in 1982.
4. Steven Jermy, 'Back to an Offshore Future: Past and Present Lessons for Britain's Future Defence Policy,' in Alessio Patalano ed., *Maritime Strategy and National Security in Japan and Britain*, (London, 2010).

5. Note, for example, Baroness Eliza Manningham-Buller's judgement, at the UK's Chilcott inquiry, that the West's military actions abroad increased the threat of domestic terrorism in UK. <http://www.iraqinquiry.org.uk/transcripts/oralevidence-bydate/100720.aspx>.
6. I am indebted in these thoughts to discussions with my brother, Lt Cdr Richard Jermy RN, an Arabist and veteran of both the Iraq and Afghanistan campaigns.
7. Joseph Stiglitz & Linda Bilmes, 'Three Trillion Dollar War,' *The Times*, (23 February 2008).
8. James Lovelock, *The Vanishing Face of Gaia: The Final Warning*, (London, 2010).
9. Mark Lynas, *Six Degrees: Our Future on a Hotter Planet*, (London, 2007) p.159.
10. For a migration focused overview, see Oli Brown, 'Migration and Climate Change,' Paper 31, International Institute of Migration, (Geneva, 2008), at <http://www.migrationdrc.org/publications/resource_guides/Migration_and_Climate_Change/MRS-31.pdf>.
11. Rupert Smith, *The Utility of Force*, (London, 2005).
12. Francis Fukuyama, *The End of History and the Last Man*, (London, 1992).
13. Colin S. Gray, *Another Bloody Century*, (London, 2005) p.24.

Making Strategy: Thinking about Thinking

1. Indeed, in trying to organize this particular chapter, one was thinking about thinking about thinking, something of a challenge for the naval aviator's brain!
2. Kenichi Ohmae, *The Mind of the Strategist*, (New York, 1973).
3. Henry Mintzberg, Bruce Ahlstrand, & Joseph Lampel, *Strategy Safari*, (London, 1998) p.150.
4. Kenichi Ohmae, *The Mind of the Strategist*, (New York, 1973) p.13.
5. Hew Strachan, *Carl von Clausewitz's On War: A Biography*, (London, 2007) p.127.
6. Andrew Roberts, *Masters and Commanders: How Roosevelt, Churchill, Marshall and Alanbrooke Won the War in the West*, (London, 2008) p.340-1.
7. *The Rommel Papers*, tr. Paul Findley, ed. Basil Liddell Hart, (New York, 1953) p.521-3.
8. Shelford Bidwell, *The Chindit War: Stilwell, Wingate and the Campaign in Burma*, 1944, (New York, 1980) p.464.
9. Eliot A. Cohen, 'The Strategy of Innocence? The United States, 1920-1945,' in Williamson Murray, Macgregor Knox & Alvin Bernstein, eds., *The Making of Strategy: Rulers, States and War*, (Cambridge, 1994) p.463.
10. Quoted in John Coles, *Making Foreign Policy: A Certain Idea of Britain*, (London, 2000) p.49.
11. Eliot A. Cohen, *Supreme Command: Soldiers, Statesmen and Leadership in Wartime*, (New York, 2002) p.108.
12. MoD, *Joint Warfare Publication 0-01: British Defence Doctrine*, (1996) p.4.2.
13. Alex Danchev & Dan Todman, eds., *War Diaries 1939-1945: Field Marshal Lord Alanbrooke*, (London, 2001) p.405.
14. Andrew Roberts, *Masters and Commanders: How Roosevelt, Churchill, Marshall and Alanbrooke Won the War in the West*, (London, 2008) p.120.
15. Bill Slim, *Defeat into Victory*, (2nd edn, London, 1956) p.209.

16. And the best of, in corporate strategy theory, the leadership-entrepreneurial and planning schools.

17. The precise number of EXCOM members varied over the crisis, with some members attending on an ad hoc basis.

18. Robert F. Kennedy, *13 Days: The Cuban Missile Crisis*, (London, 1969) p.35, 46-47, 49.

19. *Principes Généraux de la Guerre*, completed in 1746, *Testament Politique* (1752), *Testament Militaire* (1768) and *Eléments de Castramétrie et de Tactique* (1771). R.R. Palmer, 'Frederick the Great, Guibert, Bülow: From Dynastic to National War,' in Peter Paret, ed., *Makers of Modern Strategy*, (Oxford, 1986) p.92.

20. Bill Slim, *Defeat into Victory*, (2nd edn, London, 1956) p.213.

21. Thomas B. Buell, *The Quiet Warrior: A Biography of Admiral Raymond A. Spruance*, (Annapolis, 1987) p.213.

22. Bill Slim, *Defeat into Victory*, (2nd edn, London, 1956) p.213.

Making Strategy: Thinking about War

1. André Beaufre, *An Introduction to Strategy*, tr. Richard Barry, (London, 1963).

2. Raoul Castex, *Strategic Theories*, tr. & ed. Eugenia C. Kiesling, (Annapolis, 1994) p.206.

3. Raoul Castex, *Strategic Theories*, tr. & ed. Eugenia C. Kiesling, (Annapolis, 1994) p.207.

4. Harry G. Summers, *On Strategy: A Critical Analysis of the Vietnam War*, (2nd edn. New York, 1995) p.1.

5. Carl von Clausewitz, *On War*, tr. Michael Howard & Peter Paret. (Princeton, 1976) p.88.

6. See, for example, Professor Gray's seventeen dimensions of strategy: people, society, culture, politics, ethics; economics & logistics organisation, military administration, information & intelligence; strategic theory & doctrine; technology; military operations, command, geography, friction, the adversary. Colin S. Gray, *Modern Strategy*, (Oxford, 1999) p.23-44.

7. Carl von Clausewitz, *On War*, tr. Michael Howard & Peter Paret. (Princeton, 1976) p.88.

8. André Beaufre, *An Introduction to Strategy*, tr. Richard Barry, (London, 1963).

9. Raoul Castex, *Strategic Theories*, tr. & ed. Eugenia C. Kiesling, (Annapolis, 1994) p.20.

10. Carl von Clausewitz, *On War*, tr. Michael Howard & Peter Paret. (Princeton, 1976) p.357, 358, 524.

11. Harry G. Summers, *On Strategy: A Critical Analysis of the Vietnam War*, (2nd edn. New York, 1995) p.116.

12. R.R. Palmer, 'Frederick the Great, Guibert, Bülow: From Dynastic to National War,' in Peter Paret, ed., *Makers of Modern Strategy*, (Oxford, 1986) p.111.

13. MoD, *British Maritime Doctrine*, (BR1806 3rd edn., 2004) p.270.

14. Ibid. p.240.

15. Bill Slim, *Defeat into Victory*, (2nd edn, London, 1956) p.296.

16. MoD, *Design for Military Operations: British Military Doctrine*, (D/CGS/50/8, 1989).

17. Colin S. Gray, *Modern Strategy*, (Oxford, 1999) p.177.
18. Wylie graciously suggests Dr Herbert Rosinski as another possible source. J.C. Wylie, *Military Strategy: A General Theory of Power Control*, (London, 1966) p.24-26.
19. Basil Liddell Hart, *Strategy: The Indirect Approach*, (London, 1967) p. 25.
20. Robert Lyman, *Slim, Master of War: Burma and the Birth of Modern Warfare*, (London, 2005) p.2.
21. Bill Slim, *Defeat into Victory*, (2nd edn, London, 1956) p.535-551.

Strategy for Action: Frameworks for Thinking

1. Bill Slim, *Defeat into Victory*, (2nd edn, London, 1956) p.208.
2. Indeed with a collection of smaller ideas, the key role of the strategist appears to be to order the smaller ideas — working out which is dominant, which are supporting, which prioritise, which connect and which structure — and thus make them coherent.
3. A strategy may, as Matloff suggests of the Allies during World War II, be the sum of the common denominators — but the point surely is that, to mix mathematical metaphors, because of the common agreement to it, the strategy's whole is greater than the sum of the common denominator parts. Maurice Matloff, 'Allied Strategy in Europe, 1939-1945,' in Peter Paret, ed., *Makers of Modern Strategy*, (Oxford, 1986) p.678.
4. Michael A. Gress & Lester W. Grau, *The Soviet-Afghan War: How a Superpower Fought and Lost*, (Kansas, 2002) p.xxi-xxiii.
5. Supplemental Foreign Assistance Fiscal Year 1966 — Vietnam; Hearings Before the Committee on Foreign Relations, United States Senate, 89th Congress, 2nd Session, on S.2793, p. 331 ff. quoted in Bernard Brodie, *War & Politics*, (London, 1973) p.158-9.
6. Kenichi Ohmae, *The Mind of the Strategist*, (New York, 1973) p.17.
7. Bill Slim, *Defeat into Victory*, (2nd edn, London, 1956) p.118-9.
8. Harry G. Summers, *On Strategy: A Critical Analysis of the Vietnam War*, (2nd edn. New York, 1995) p.105, referring to Douglas Kinnard, *The War Managers*, (New Hampshire, 1975) p.25.
9. Bernard Brodie, *War & Politics*, (London, 1973).
10. Bill Slim, *Defeat into Victory*, (2nd edn, London, 1956) p, 210.
11. Ibid.
12. One of the failings that one sees in weaker military commanders is the adoption of a leadership technique which they perhaps admire in another but which fails when they adopt it for themselves because it is out of the grain of their character. Their people see them as trying to be something they are not. So it is, I suspect, with strategy formulation. A process that suits a Slim may not suit a Napoleon; one that suits a Churchill may not suit a Roosevelt and so on.
13. Bill Slim, *Defeat into Victory*, (2nd edn, London, 1956) p.210.
14. Ibid. p.211.
15. There is, of course, a charge here that Slim is talking about planning not strategy making, to which the response is that, based on the definitions adopted throughout the book, this element of Slim's approach falls clearly within the strategy making area.

Bill Slim, *Defeat into Victory*, (2nd edn, London, 1956). p.210.

16.   Harry R. Yarger, *Strategic Theory for the 21st century: The Little Book on Big Strategy*, (US Army War College, 2006) p.47-48.

17.   'Mission Command: A style of command that seeks to convey understanding to subordinates about the intentions of the higher commander and their place within his plan, in order to enable them to carry out missions with the maximum freedom of action and appropriate resources.' MoD, *British Maritime Doctrine*, (BR1806 3rd edn., 2004) p.275.

18.   Harry G. Summers, *On Strategy: A Critical Analysis of the Vietnam War*, (2nd edn. New York, 1995) p.105,155.

19.   Ibid. p.105, 134.

Strategy Making & Institutions: A Politico-Military School

1.   Titular possession being 9/10ths of the law!

2.   Henry Mintzberg, Bruce Ahlstrand, & Joseph Lampel, *Strategy Safari*, (London, 1998) p.29.

3.   Ibid. p.208.

4.   There will, no doubt, be those in the strategic studies and military doctrine communities who will continue to develop and peddle, in the spirit of Liddell Hart and Jomini, generic solutions. The way, perhaps, to think about the work done by these communities is that they are purveyors, but not sole sources, of theoretical paint to the strategic painters who must compose the strategic picture.

5.   The role of Principal Staff Officer is equivalent to Executive Assistant.

6.   Herbert A. Simon, *Administrative Behavior*, (New York, 1957) p.238.

7.   Bill Slim, *Defeat into Victory*, (2nd edn, London, 1956) p.393.

8.   Ibid. p.211.

9.   MoD, *Joint Warfare Publication 0-01: British Defence Doctrine*, (1996) p.A-2.

10.   Although the politico-military school is focused on politico-military matters, my military intuition tells me there is open ground 'out there' for its application to the corporate realm but, if so, this is a task for later and probably for others.

11.   J.C. Wylie, *Military Strategy: A General Theory of Power Control*, (London, 1966) p.v-vi.

Strategy Making in Coalition: Internal & International

1.   Although the term 'nation-building' is more in vogue, it is not clear to me that external actors have much of a useful part to play in building nations. I thus prefer the term 'state-building'.

2.   'Three Block War' — the simultaneous overlap of conflict, peace-keeping and humanitarian relief in a single location. Charles C Krulak, 'The Strategic Corporal: Leadership in the Three Block War,' *Marines Magazine*, (January 1999).

3.   Interestingly, although I have been rather critical of the lack of recent literature on strategy, the position with the literature on diplomacy is even worse with George Kennan's work of the 1950s and 1960s still one of the best referential analyses and that of Sir John Coles as the most important recent UK equivalent.

4. Quoted in John Coles, *Making Foreign Policy: A Certain Idea of Britain*, (London, 2000) p.49.
5. <http://web.worldbank.org/WBSITE/EXTERNAL/TOPICS/EXTPOVERTY/EX TPRS/0,,menuPK:384207~pagePK:149018~piPK:149093~theSitePK:384201,00. html>.
6. The same curious assumption of no-conflict underpinned the Afghanistan Multi-National Drug Control Strategy.
7. Raoul Castex, *Strategic Theories*, tr. & ed. Eugenia C. Kiesling, (Annapolis, 1994) p.217.
8. Carl von Clausewitz, *On War*, tr. Michael Howard & Peter Paret. (Princeton, 1976) p.88.
9. Andrew Roberts, *Masters and Commanders: How Roosevelt, Churchill, Marshall and Alanbrooke Won the War in the West*, (London, 2008) p.574.
10. Jock Covey, Michael J. Dziedzic, & Leonard R. Hawley, eds., *The Quest for the Viable Peace*, (Washington, DC., 2005) p.16.

Strategy Making in Time: Contests & Culminations

1. Carl von Clausewitz, *On War*, tr. Michael Howard & Peter Paret. (Princeton, 1976) p.249.
2. Ibid. p.566, 570.
3. Quoted in John Cloake, *Templer, Tiger of Malaya: the Life of Field Marshal Sir Gerald Templer*, (London, 1985) p.201.
4. I recall visiting Kabul in early 2005, with the UK Chief of Defence Staff, to be told by a British general that Afghanistan was, in terms of security incidents, 'no worse than a bad day in Northern Ireland.'
5. <http://www.whitehouse.gov/the-press-office/whatsquos new strategy afghanistan-and-pakistan>.
6. Bernard Brodie, *War & Politics*, (London, 1973).
7. In Britain, when capitalized, the term 'Commando' is used to describe a Royal Marines' military unit of equivalent size and make up to an Army battalion.
8. By all accounts, the first of the mobile cookery's soldiers to be handed a rifle exclaimed, 'What do you want me to do with this, batter it?'

Strategy Making Improved: Philosophy, Policy, Process & People

1. Hew Strachan, 'The Lost Meaning of Strategy,' in *Survival*, 47/3, (2005).
2. Colin S. Gray, *Modern Strategy*, (Oxford, 1999) p.115.
3. Bernard Brodie, *War & Politics*, (London, 1973) Ch 10. Harry G. Summers, *On Strategy: A Critical Analysis of the Vietnam War*, (2nd edn. New York, 1995) p.2.
4. Bernard Brodie, *Strategy in the Missile Age*, (Princeton, 1959). Brodie's other key work, *War and Politics*, comes in at a reprint snip of £55 from Macmillan.
5. John Baylis, James Wirtz, Colin S. Gray & Eliot Cohen, *Strategy in the Contemporary World*, (2nd edn, Oxford, 2007).
6. Raoul Castex, *Strategic Theories*, tr. & ed. Eugenia C. Kiesling, (Annapolis, 1994) p.252-3.

7. Ibid.
8. George F. Kennan, *Realities of American Foreign Policy*, (Princeton, 1954) p.5-11.
9. Raoul Castex, *Strategic Theories*, tr. & ed. Eugenia C. Kiesling, (Annapolis, 1994) p.21.
10. Basil Liddell Hart, *Strategy: The Indirect Approach*, (London, 1967) p.142.
11. Henry Mintzberg, Bruce Ahlstrand, & Joseph Lampel, *Strategy Safari*, (London, 1998) p.172.
12. Hew Strachan, *Carl von Clausewitz's On War: A Biography*, (London, 2007) p.127.
13. Quoted in John Cloake, *Templer, Tiger of Malaya: the Life of Field Marshal Sir Gerald Templer*, (London, 1985) p.201.

Conclusion

1. Bernard Brodie, *Strategy in the Missile Age*, (Princeton, 1959) p.23.
2. J.C. Wylie, *Military Strategy: A General Theory of Power Control*, (London, 1966) p.v-vi.
3. André Beaufre, *An Introduction to Strategy*, tr. Richard Barry, (London, 1963) p.133.
4. Williamson Murray & Mark Grimsley, Introduction to Williamson Murray, Macgregor Knox & Alvin Bernstein, eds., *The Making of Strategy: Rulers, States and War*, (Cambridge, 1994) p.22.
5. John Baylis & John Garnett, eds., *Makers of Nuclear Strategy*, (London, 1991) p.38.

Index

9/11 134, 138, 139, 149, 257

14th Army 22, 161, 190

18th Century 35

19th Century 14, 35, 49, 52, 53, 54, 60

20th Century 2, 4, 32, 70, 78, 81, 108, 172, 235, 242, 247, 278

21st Century 2, 32

Afghanistan ix, xiii, 1, 2, 3, 8, 9, 15, 20, 24, 72, 73, 97, 100, 104, 107, 134, 137, 139, 140, 141, 142, 143, 144, 147, 150, 172, 176, 193, 199, 200, 202, 205, 229, 230, 231, 236, 241, 242, 245, 246, 247, 248, 250, 251, 252, 257, 266, 268, 270, 273, 279, 286, 292, 294, 295, 299, 300

Afghan National Development Strategy 244, 245

Afghan National Security Forces 270

Afghan War (2001 - present) 143

Ahlstrand, Bruce 101, 111, 113, 114, 116, 117, 118, 119, 120, 121, 123, 124, 128, 129, 153, 224, 237, 303

aircraft 51, 68, 69, 79, 129, 134, 135, 136, 148, 154, 261

aircraft carriers 68, 129, 148, 261

air forces 61, 65, 68, 69, 70, 97, 134, 136, 148, 186, 188

airmen xiii, 20, 245

air power 75, 79, 80, 83, 118

Alanbrooke, FM Viscount 68, 83, 121, 156, 157, 158, 159, 160, 164, 229, 252, 282

Algeria 96

all arms 30, 39

al-Qaeda 141, 142, 143, 270

America. *See* **United States of America**

American Civil War 49, 51, 55, 57, 64, 169, 289

American Enterprise Institute 264

Ansoff, H. Igor 111, 112

AQ. *See* al-Qaeda

Arabian Gulf 140

Arab-Israeli Wars 89, 170

ARA General Belgrano 261

ARCADIA Conference 85

area campaign 51, 70

Argentina 174, 257, 259, 260, 261

    Argentine Air Force 261

    Argentine Navy 261

army   32, 33, 35, 36, 39, 40, 45,
     49, 50, 51, 52, 53, 55, 56,
     59, 64, 68, 69, 74, 79, 80,
     97, 121, 136, 137, 142,
     147, 148, 160, 188, 210,
     244, 268, 289
artillery   30, 38, 39, 50, 51, 68,
     69
Atlantic, battle of. *See* Battle of
     the Atlantic
attritional warfare   33, 53, 70,
     105, 182, 183, 186, 189
Austerlitz, battle of   57
Austria   54
Axis Powers (World War II)   72,
     84, 85, 97, 266
Bagnall, FM Sir Nigel   xiii
Balkan Conflict (1990s)   16,
     134, 140, 245, 300
Barker, Capt Nick, RN   259
Basra, Iraq   205
Battle of Britain   76, 184, 186
Battle of the Atlantic   76, 96,
     184, 186
Bay of Pigs   271, 272
Beaufre, Général d'Armée
     André   4, 73, 89, 95, 96,
     100, 151, 167, 168, 179,
     180, 278, 279, 298, 302
Beirut, Lebanon   269
Belgrano   261
Berlin, Germany   32, 231, 273
   Berlin Wall   32
Bismarck, Otto von   55, 59, 74,
     229
blue-on-blue   69, 136

bomber (aircraft)   68, 69, 135
Bonaparte, Napoleon I. *See* Na-
     poleon I
Booth, Ken   93
Borodino, battle of   41
Boyd, Colonel John,
     USAF   118, 278
Briggs, Lt Gen Sir Harold Raw-
     don   89, 90, 264
Brimstone (WWII Opera-
     tion)   156
Britain   3, 19, 20, 42, 53, 54, 55,
     56, 60, 61, 71, 72, 74, 75,
     76, 79, 83, 84, 85, 86, 87,
     89, 96, 103, 122, 139, 146,
     156, 157, 159, 160, 161,
     180, 184, 186, 187, 197,
     202, 205, 209, 230, 232,
     239, 242, 244, 252, 257,
     259, 260, 261, 262, 264,
     270, 281, 284, 294, 295
   British Army   xiii, 75, 83, 106
   British Empire   84, 242
Brodie, Bernard   7, 29, 42, 72,
     73, 74, 79, 89, 91, 92, 93,
     95, 100, 151, 271, 278,
     279, 297, 300, 302
Brooke, Alan Francis. *See* Alan-
     brooke, FM Viscount
Budiansky, Steven   xiv
Bülow, Baron Dietrich Heinrich
     von   39
Burma   22, 83, 89, 160, 161,
     167, 189, 195, 203, 232
Bush, George H. W.   268, 269
Bush, George W.   205, 265

C130 Hercules   1
Cambridge University   ix, 61, 75
campaign design   16, 21
campaign objectives   22
campaign strategy   23, 24, 90, 295
Castex, VAdm Raoul   51, 75, 81, 82, 151, 169, 180, 247, 278, 283, 284, 285, 288
cavalry   30
Chicago, USA   91
Chief of the General Staff (British Army)   xiii
Chief of the General Staff (German Army)   77
Chief of the General Staff (Prussian Army)   58
Chief of the Imperial General Staff (British Army)   164
China   30, 89, 140, 149, 199
Christensen, Roland   112
Churchill, Sir Winston   68, 73, 83, 84, 85, 86, 90, 121, 156, 158, 163, 164, 213, 229, 252, 282
Classical Epoch   7, 29–47, 31, 32, 34, 36, 37, 39, 41, 45, 46, 47, 49, 50, 51, 55, 70, 168, 169, 170
Clausewitz, Carl von   xiii, 1, 4, 13, 30, 35, 37, 40, 41, 42, 43, 44, 46, 47, 49, 54, 57, 58, 60, 61, 62, 63, 65, 68, 74, 87, 88, 89, 92, 93, 94, 95, 102, 104, 110, 111, 112, 150, 151, 155, 163, 173, 174, 178, 179, 181, 192, 217, 219, 248, 252, 256, 266, 267, 273, 290, 294, 298, 301
Clausewitz, Marie von   41
Clemenceau, Georges   71
climate change   xi, 141, 144, 145, 146, 148, 295
coalition   2, 4, 8, 36, 40, 64, 74, 86, 98, 121, 122, 226, 236, 238, 239–255, 263, 269, 270, 279, 287, 288, 294, 295
coalition-optimized strategy   249, 251
cognitive school   116, 289
Cohen, Eliot A.   55, 56, 85, 157, 158
Cold War   xiii, 24, 31, 69, 73, 87, 88, 89, 89–97, 120, 129, 134, 137, 143, 150, 170, 184, 245, 252, 266, 273, 280, 281
Combined Chiefs of Staff   85, 86
command   3, 21, 23, 33, 39, 40, 59, 65, 69, 70, 75, 77, 78, 80, 83, 97, 99, 106, 114, 115, 123, 135, 136, 148, 156, 161, 164, 165, 193, 196, 203, 209, 218, 219, 234, 235, 244, 251, 252, 287
Commander's Estimate   192, 197–198, 218
communications   31, 33, 49, 50, 52, 110, 136, 171, 186,

245

Comprehensive Approach 20

computers 31, 69, 133, 134, 136

conceptual space 116, 214, 218

Confederacy (US Civil War) 55, 56

configuration school 116, 126, 224, 225

Congress (US) 94

conscription 35, 36, 39, 55

containment strategy 24, 87, 93, 94, 143, 281

contingency plans 2

Corbett, Sir Julian 42, 55, 60, 61, 62, 63, 64, 65, 80, 92, 151, 278, 301

corporate strategy xi, 25, 101, 111–130, 193, 202, 210, 218, 224–226, 241, 280, 281, 289, 296, 303

Corpus Christi College, Cambridge 75

Corum, James 78

counter-insurgency 3, 91, 94, 120, 141, 142, 143, 147, 149, 163, 177, 186, 189, 190, 193, 205, 229, 242, 265, 270, 279

counter-revolutionary warfare 87

counter-terrorism 141, 147, 149

Crimean War 57

Cuban Missile Crisis 17, 160, 161, 207, 232

cultural school 116

Dartmouth College 92

Darwin, Charles 38, 45, 53, 54, 96

D-Day 160, 187

decision making xiii, 8, 34, 40, 44, 101, 106, 112, 136, 152, 165, 210, 231, 257, 258, 262, 268, 286, 289

decisive point 43, 69, 160

declaration of war 15

Defence and Overseas Policy Committee xiv

defence budget xiv

Delbrück, Hans 30, 74

deliberate strategy 114, 193, 210, 211, 257, 272

democracy 6, 31, 54, 85, 137, 143, 160, 226, 237, 278

Denmark 54

design school 116, 117, 118, 119, 120, 225, 226

destroyer (ship) 68

development agencies 246

diplomacy 35, 39, 175, 245, 247, 284

diplomats 3, 5, 18, 20, 36, 37, 82, 93, 98, 107, 157, 200, 243, 244, 245, 284, 285, 296

dislocation 76, 78, 187, 247

disruption 76, 78

doctrine 4, 8, 23, 41, 44, 46, 58, 59, 77, 78, 83, 100, 101, 101–108, 112, 114, 123, 126, 127, 128, 129, 152, 159, 163, 165, 180, 182, 183, 184, 189, 192,

197, 212, 214, 218, 227,
229, 235, 244, 265, 270,
279, 280, 296, 297, 301
Douhet, Gen Giulio 75, 79
Drake, Sir Francis 61
Druze 72
economists 88, 245
Egypt 273
emergent strategy 114, 116,
124, 193, 211, 212
HMS Endurance 259
English 4, 60, 75
English Channel 77, 84, 160
entrepreneurial school 116,
225
environmental school 116
Europe 32, 34, 35, 36, 37, 48,
54, 57, 64, 66, 71, 74, 84,
85, 155, 156, 184, 237,
251
European Union (EU) 139
Falklands War 1, 4, 8, 174, 257,
259, 261
Fascism 31, 67, 97
Field Manual 107, 112, 311
fighter (aircraft) 68, 135
First Sea Lord 259
First World War. *See* **World War
I**
**Fisher, Adm of the Fleet Baron
John 'Jackie'** xiv
Flag Officer Sea Training 155
**Fleet Air Arm (Royal
Navy)** 261
**Fleet Headquarters, Northwood
(Royal Navy)** 260
fleets 33, 45, 50, 51, 52, 64. *See*
also navy
Florida, USA 237
force development 25
formation schools 116,
121–126
formulation schools 116–120
fortifications 51
Fort Leavenworth 264
Fourteenth Army 22, 161, 190
France 4, 33, 34, 35, 36, 39, 40,
41, 44, 54, 55, 71, 72, 73,
75, 77, 78, 89, 95, 96, 108,
160, 163, 176, 183, 185,
187, 229, 283
French Army xi, 40, 89, 108
French High Command 78
French Revolution 33, 34, 35,
36
**Frederick II 'The Great' of Prus-
sia** 30, 37, 38, 40, 45, 51,
110, 163, 230
Freedman, Sir Lawrence 108
freedom of action 51, 60, 70,
80, 87, 104, 106, 262
friction 42, 46, 110, 127, 179,
215, 217, 273
frigate 68
Fukuyama, Francis 137, 149,
295
Fuller, Maj Gen J.F.C. 83, 183
Gaddis, John Lewis 128
Gaia theory 144
Galtieri, Gen Leopoldo 260
Gangaw Valley, Burma 233
de Gaulle, Charles 77
Gaza 295
General Electric 124

generalship 4

General Staff (German) 77, 223

General Staff (Prussian) 58, 59, 64

General Staff (Soviet) 199, 201, 271

Georgia 295

Germany xiii, xiv, 22, 30, 55, 62, 69, 71, 74, 75, 76, 77, 78, 82, 83, 84, 85, 105, 121, 122, 157, 160, 174, 183, 185, 186, 187, 223, 250, 301

German Army 78, 83, 85, 160, 187

'Germany-first' Strategy 22

Geyer, Michael 77, 123

globalization 138, 146

global positioning systems (GPS) 31, 133

global warming xi, 141, 144, 145, 146, 148, 295

Global War on Terror 182

grand strategy 23, 24, 40, 70, 75, 87, 93, 94, 129, 143, 144, 157, 223, 224, 244, 283, 284, 292

Grant, General of the Army Ulysses S. (US Army) 55, 57

Gray, Colin 88, 95, 108, 133, 149, 184, 185, 278, 279

Great Britain. See Britain

Great Society 94

Great War. See World War I

Grove, Eric 61

Guderian, Generaloberst Heinz Wilhelm 77, 83, 183

guerrilla 90, 182, 199

Guibert, Gen Jacques Antoine Hippolyte, Comte de 39, 183

Gulf War (1991) 268

Gulf War (2003) 144, 150, 269

Gurney, Sir Henry 90

Hannibal 128

Harvard Business School 112, 116

Helmand Province, Afghanistan 270, 295

Herat, Afghanistan 250

Hercules (aircraft) 1

Hiroshima, Japan 67, 73, 87

historical school 26, 41, 217

Hitler, Adolf 17, 72, 223

HMS Endurance 259

HMS Invincible 1

Holocaust 82

House of Commons 260

Houses of Parliament 259

Howard, Sir Michael 108

humanitarian intervention 138

Hussein, Saddam 268, 269

Imphal-Kohima, battle of 184

India 141, 149

Indian proverb 150

indigenous security forces 105, 143, 147

indirect approach xiv, 76, 84, 108, 122, 180, 186, 187

Indochina 96

Indo-Pakistani Wars 89, 170

Industrial Revolution 31, 48

Industrial Transformation 7, 31, 40, 48, 49, 49–66, 51, 52, 53, 54, 55, 57, 63, 64, 66, 72, 169, 170, 230

infantry 15, 30, 50, 51

information management 31, 133, 200

Information Revolution 31, 133, 134

Information Transformation 7, 31, 32, 108, 111, 133–150, 171, 229

initiative 52, 53, 59, 106, 125, 182, 196, 209, 296

instability 16

instrumental 14, 15, 16, 17, 19, 26, 36, 44, 45, 64, 93

insurgency 3, 89, 90, 91, 94, 107, 120, 141, 142, 143, 149, 163, 177, 184, 186, 188, 189, 190, 193, 229, 242, 250, 265, 270, 279, 280

intelligence 40, 69, 94, 135, 136, 192, 209

intended strategy 114, 115, 211, 212

International Criminal Court 15

International Monetary Fund 245

international politics 14, 67, 134, 146, 150, 168, 295

International Security Assistance Force (ISAF) 3

inter-war years xiv, 72, 97, 154

HMS Invincible 1

Iran 89, 295

Iran-Iraq War 89

Iraq xiii, 2, 20, 24, 89, 100, 134, 137, 140, 141, 142, 143, 144, 147, 150, 172, 205, 229, 230, 231, 241, 242, 245, 246, 248, 252, 257, 264, 265, 266, 268, 269, 270, 295, 299, 300

Iraqi Armed Forces 264

Iraq War. See Gulf War

Irrawaddy River, battle of 233

Islam 141–144, 146, 147, 148, 295

Italy 3, 75, 79, 250

Jackson, Lt Gen Thomas Jonathon 'Stonewall' CSA 56

Japan 2, 51, 62, 63, 82, 85, 154, 174, 178, 179, 186, 209, 233

Japanese Army 85, 233

Japanese High Command 178

Japanese Navy 85

Jena-Auerstedt, battle of 41, 43, 57, 63

jihadists 142, 143

Johnson, Lyndon B. 94, 95, 120

Joint Chiefs of Staff 94, 170, 268

Jomini, Baron Antoine-Henri 30, 37, 41, 43, 44, 45, 46, 47, 57, 58, 60, 69, 76, 83, 94, 102, 103, 104, 105, 151, 160, 180, 217, 219, 298, 301

jungle warfare 89

Jutland, battle of 50, 52

Kabul, Afghanistan 1, 3, 294, 317

Kaiser Wilhelm II 74

Kandahar, Afghanistan 1, 270

Keane, Gen John 'Jack' US Army 264

Kennan, George F. 93, 201, 285

Kennedy, John F. 17, 160, 161, 271, 272

Kennedy, Robert F. 161

Khrushchev, Nikita 17

Kimura, Gen Heitarō 233

King, Fleet Admiral Ernest J. USN 121

Kinnard, Brig Gen Douglas US Army 204

Kohima, battle of 184

Korean War 89, 118

Kosovo 8, 150, 253

Kriegsakademie, (Prussian War Academy) 41

Kuwait 268, 269

Lampel, Joseph 101, 111, 113, 114, 116, 117, 118, 119, 120, 121, 123, 124, 128, 129, 153, 224, 237, 303

lawyers 245

Leach, Adm of the Fleet Sir Henry, RN 259

leaders 2, 5, 6, 13, 14, 21, 32, 35, 36, 37, 38, 42, 45, 53, 64, 65, 72, 74, 81, 83, 85, 86, 89, 92, 98, 99, 109, 124, 142, 147, 152, 153, 155, 156, 158, 162, 163, 165, 178, 189, 191, 196, 215, 219, 224, 227, 229, 230, 231, 235, 239, 242, 252, 257, 271, 277, 278, 282, 286, 287, 289, 290, 291, 292, 296, 299

League of Nations 71

learning school 78, 116, 122, 123, 124, 125, 126, 128, 214, 218, 225, 226, 235

Lee, Gen Robert E. CSA 56

legal institution 15

lessons identified 125, 235

lessons learned 125, 235

liberal democracy 67, 72

Liddell Hart, Sir B. H. xiv, 19, 75, 76, 77, 83, 89, 96, 105, 108, 180, 183, 186, 189, 278, 279, 288, 289

Lincoln, Abraham 55, 56, 57, 64, 169, 229

Lindblom, Charles E. 122

lines of communication 70

Lloyd George, David 71

logic 1, 16, 17, 21, 23, 80, 89, 100, 109, 150, 179, 180, 184, 187, 197, 198, 202, 211, 256, 286

logistics 70, 135, 148, 250, 273

London, England 60, 231, 264, 273

Lovelock, James xi, 144, 145, 146

Ludendorff, Generalquartiermeister Erich Friedrich Wilhelm 75, 76

Luttwak, Edward 108, 109,
    187, 217, 278
Lynas, Michael 145
Lyttelton, Sir Oliver 91, 229,
    232, 264, 293
McArthur, General of the Army
    Douglas US Army 121
MacIsaac, David 79
McMaster, Brigadier General
    H. R. US Army xi, 94,
    95, 265
Mahan, RAdm Alfred Thayer
    USN 55, 60, 61
Malaya 89, 90, 91, 94, 229,
    232, 242, 248, 264, 267,
    293
  Malayan Communist Party 89
Mandalay, Burma 233
manoeuvre 62, 63, 66, 75, 94,
    105, 106, 180, 182, 183,
    184, 185, 189, 190, 203
Mao Tse Tung 90, 229
marine 1, 20, 186, 245
Marshall, General of the Army
    George C. 68, 73, 156,
    159, 160, 229, 252
mass 43, 136
mass production 31, 50, 51
Mazar-e-Sharif, Afghani-
    stan 270
MBA 116
McNamara, Robert S. 94, 95,
    120, 162, 281
measuring campaign pro-
    gress 22
media 4
Mediterranean 84, 122, 187,

273–274
mentoring 253
Metropolitan Police 264
Meuse (River) 77
Midway, battle of 129, 154,
    163
military operations 6, 102, 119,
    189, 245, 284
military strategy. See politico-
    military strategy
miniaturization 31, 133
Ministry of Defence (UK) 209
Mintzberg, Harry 101, 111,
    113, 114, 115, 116, 117,
    118, 119, 120, 121, 123,
    124, 128, 129, 153, 193,
    210, 212, 213, 224, 237
  Mintzberg's Diagram 114, 212,
    213
mission-optimized strate-
    gy 249, 250, 251, 252
Modern Epoch 7, 31, 49, 63,
    66, 67, 68, 70, 71, 73, 95,
    96, 97, 98, 99, 134, 135,
    147, 170, 171
Moltke the Elder, General-
    feldmarschall Helmuth
    von 48, 55, 57, 58, 59,
    64, 74, 78, 110, 114, 115,
    118, 151, 163, 211, 213,
    217, 229, 233
Morgenstern, Oskar 112
Mujahedeen 199
Murray, Williamson 83, 84,
    299
Muslim. See Islam
Mussolini, Benito 17

Nagasaki, Japan   67, 73, 87

Nagl, Lt Col John US Army   94, 95

Napoleon I   36, 37, 39, 40, 41, 43, 44, 45, 46, 51, 56, 58, 59, 60, 105

Napoleonic   31, 33, 35, 36, 37, 39, 40, 41, 44, 45, 49, 62, 63, 66, 137, 182

  Napoleonic Wars   35, 36, 39, 41, 49

national interest   138, 139, 140, 141, 176, 201, 241

national security   2, 92, 138, 139, 142, 172, 176, 201, 205

National Security Council (NSC)   xiv

national survival   2, 70, 138, 139, 146, 172

nation-building   141, 142, 143, 316

NATO   1, 3, 102, 103, 106, 139, 141, 176, 184, 199, 236, 237, 247, 248, 250, 251, 253, 270, 279, 287

nature of war   7, 31, 36, 42, 44, 47, 65, 168, 193

naval picket   33

Naval War College, Rhode Island (USA)   129, 154

navigation   35

navy   32, 33, 35, 49, 53, 68, 69, 70, 79, 80, 97, 121, 134, 136, 148, 186, 188. See also Royal Navy; See also United States Navy

Neumann, John von   111

Ney, Marshal Michel   43

Nobel Prize for Literature   163

Normandy, France   122, 187

North America   49. See also United States of America

Northern Alliance (Afghanistan)   270

North German Plain   xiii

North Korea   295

North Sea   50

North Vietnam   172, 181, 182, 219, 220

  North Vietnamese Army   181, 182

  North Vietnam's high command   219

Northwood, Fleet Headquarters (Royal Navy)   260

nuclear strategy   68, 73, 87–89, 92, 99

nuclear war   87

nuclear weapons   32, 67, 82, 87, 170, 280

Obama, Barack   270

Odierno, Gen Raymond US Army   265

offensive action   43, 51

Ohmae, Kenichi   151, 152, 153, 165, 202

OODA loop   118

operational analysis   124

operational plans   21, 22

Operation Brimstone   156

operations   1, 2, 3, 4, 6, 7, 8, 19, 21, 22, 33, 39, 48, 65, 70,

77, 81, 102, 103, 105, 107,
119, 123, 126, 138, 139,
140, 147, 148, 150, 165,
169, 171, 172, 184, 189,
195, 205, 216, 224, 230,
235, 238, 242, 243, 245,
246, 249, 254, 257, 261,
263, 265, 272, 284, 287,
288, 292, 297

opponent   13, 16, 19, 20, 34,
42, 46, 58, 62, 70, 80, 99,
109, 127, 128, 137, 140,
171, 177, 178, 179, 180,
186, 187, 188, 193, 194,
195, 208, 217, 218, 220,
235, 262, 271, 273

Osgood, Robert   94
Oxford University   3
Pacific campaign   96
Pacific strategy   121
Pakistan   89, 295
Pakokku, Burma   233
paradox   16, 108, 205
Paris, France   231, 273
Pashtun (Afghan ethnic
group)   1, 250, 270
peace-keeping   15
Pearl Harbour, attack on   2
Pentagon (US Department of
Defense)   281
Petraeus, Gen David US
Army   163, 264
Philippines   121
planning school   116, 118, 119,
120
point battles   34, 51, 70
police   245, 264

policy   14, 16, 18, 19, 20, 24,
25, 35, 37, 42, 45, 49, 53,
54, 71, 74, 75, 81, 82, 86,
87, 92, 93, 98, 109, 122,
128, 139, 140, 147, 148,
158, 168, 169, 170, 175,
178, 190, 195, 204, 206,
209, 246, 247, 269, 277,
281, 283, 284, 285, 286,
288, 292

policy, definition   18
political calculation   17
political condition   14, 15, 16,
17, 25, 72, 173, 174, 179,
216, 217
political contest   17, 165, 167,
175, 195, 196, 200, 259,
292, 295
political decisions   6
political objectives   14, 23, 64,
73, 84, 134, 138, 139, 225,
236, 249, 269, 284, 299
political problem   17
political rules   16, 20, 25
political science school   26, 41,
217
political scientists   7, 32, 88
politicians   3, 5
politico-military strategy   3, 20,
23, 24, 25, 61, 65, 78, 88,
90, 91, 92, 99, 101, 102,
107, 108, 111, 112, 113,
114, 116, 125, 126, 129,
150, 153, 154, 165, 167,
172, 180, 190, 198, 209,
210, 212, 213, 224, 225,
226, 238, 256, 280, 295,

297
Porter, Michael 280
Portugal 55
positioning school 116, 119, 120
post-Cold War 2, 6
Potsdam, Germany 252
Poverty Reduction Strategy Paper (PRSP) 244
Powell, Gen Colin US Army 268, 269
power school 116, 121, 122, 226, 241
precision weapons 149
Prime Minister (UK) 86, 230, 259, 260
Princeton University 91, 163
principles of war 43, 95, 99, 103, 189
private sector 4
processes 8, 119, 124, 152, 153, 165, 224, 226, 235, 237, 238, 262, 277, 286, 287, 288, 289, 292, 298
PRSP (Poverty Reduction Strategy Paper) 245
Prussia 30, 38, 39, 41, 49, 51, 54, 55, 57, 58, 59, 61, 64, 92
Prussian Army 38, 41, 58, 59
RAF. See Royal Air Force
Rail 50
RAND Corporation 92
realized strategy 114, 116, 193, 213
recognized political picture 200

reconnaissance 33, 68, 69, 136, 199, 282
Regional Command (East) 3
Regional Command (West) 3
religion 199
Renaissance 30
revolutionary war 90, 229
Roberts, Andrew 156, 223, 252
Roman Army 128
Romania 250
Rommel, Generalfeldmarschall Erwin German Army 77, 183
Roosevelt, Franklin D. 2, 68, 84, 86, 121, 229, 252
Roosevelt, Theodore 9
Royal Air Force xiv, 161, 206
Royal College of Defence Studies ix, xi, xiii, 279, 282
Royal Marine 273
Royal Naval College, Greenwich 61
Royal Navy ix, xiv, 61, 139, 155, 261
Rumsfeld, Donald 265
Russia 43, 141, 149, 174, 199, 201
Russian Campaign (1812) 43
Russo-Japanese War 51
Saddam Hussein 268, 269
sailor xiii, 5, 20, 55, 75, 95, 245
San Carlos, Falkland Islands 261
Sardinia, Italy 156
Scharnhorst, Lt Gen Gerhard von 41

Schelling, Thomas 88, 89, 94, 120
sea control 60, 61, 80
Sea Harrier (aircraft) 261
Second World War. *See* World War II
Sedan, battle of 63
Seeckt, Generaloberst Johannes Friedrich 'Hans' von 75, 77, 78, 83
Senate Foreign Relations Committee 93, 201
Seven Years War 37
Sheffield, Gary 74, 75
Sherman, General of the Army William 57
Sicily, Italy 156
Sierra Leone 139
Silesia 37
Simon, Herbert 231
slavery 56
Slim, FM Viscount William "Bill" 1, 22, 83, 156, 160, 161, 162, 163, 164, 167, 184, 189, 195, 196, 203, 206, 207, 209, 210, 212, 213, 232, 233, 234, 282, 302
Smith, Gen Rupert 147, 282
socialism 31, 67, 87, 97
soldier xiii, 1, 4, 20, 30, 37, 39, 41, 44, 47, 55, 57, 64, 71, 73, 75, 95, 96, 101, 157, 174, 189, 210, 245
Somalia 140, 300
Somme, battle of the 76
South Atlantic 261

South Vietnam 182, 201, 219, 220
South Vietnamese Government 17
Soviet-Afghan War 271
Soviet socialism 87
Soviet Union 17, 72, 87, 97, 137, 184
Spain 3, 43, 55, 241, 250
Spanish Campaign (1808) 43
Special Forces 1
spectrum of conflict 14, 102
Spruance, Adm Raymond USN 129, 154, 163, 164
state-building 242, 243, 254
St Helena 40
Strachan, Hew xi, 278, 290, 301
strategic bombing xiv
strategic calculations 14, 17, 92, 200
strategic communications 33
strategic concept 6, 56, 157, 160, 213, 244, 284
strategic decisions xiii, 9, 86
Strategic Defence and Security Review xiii
Strategic Estimate 192, 198–210, 218, 248, 252, 263, 268, 295
strategic leader 5, 6, 13, 17, 37, 38, 42, 86, 109, 114, 152, 153, 155, 156, 158, 162, 163, 165, 189, 191, 200, 219, 227, 230, 243, 252, 259, 263, 271, 272, 277, 278, 286, 289, 290, 292,

299
strategic mobility   50
strategic nuclear forces   15
strategic planning   21, 22, 41,
    118, 119, 196, 207
strategic studies   68, 87, 88,
    100, 282
strategic theory   4, 7, 91
strategic thinkers   13, 26, 42,
    71, 83, 102, 110, 164, 264,
    265
strategist   xiv, 5, 6, 14, 30, 32,
    35, 38, 55, 61, 76, 78, 92,
    109, 110, 113, 116, 121,
    128, 129, 152, 153, 154,
    162, 208, 213, 229, 230,
    257, 263, 277, 280, 286,
    289, 290, 291, 292, 296,
    299
strategy, definition   19, 23
strategy formulation
    schools   116
strategy making schools   111,
    116, 224, 225
strategy, role of   7, 14, 19–23,
    51, 122, 193
submarine   51, 68, 74, 186
Suez Crisis   96, 199, 200, 273
Summers Jr., Col Harry G. US
    Army   46, 94, 95, 171,
    172, 181, 182, 204, 219,
    279
Sunni Triangle, Iraq   264
Sun Tzu   30
Supreme Allied Commander
    Europe (SACEUR)   237
surge (Iraq)   265, 270

surprise   42, 54, 60, 77, 156,
    162, 163, 179, 195, 196
Swift, Jonathon   212
Switzerland   30, 43
SWOT analysis   117
tactical (level of war)   xiii, 21,
    24, 34, 38, 39, 50, 52, 70,
    71, 78, 102, 105, 106, 108,
    110, 111, 125, 136, 137,
    142, 155, 156, 163, 181,
    182, 187, 193, 197, 210,
    219, 220, 256, 263, 265,
    290, 295, 299
tactical mobility   38, 50
Tal Afar, Iraq   265
Taliban   143, 250, 270, 280
Templer, FM Sir Gerald   89, 90,
    91, 229, 232, 264, 267,
    268
territory   35, 38, 51, 54, 70, 80,
    93, 201, 205, 248, 251,
    252, 287
terrorism   138, 141, 142, 143,
    146, 148, 149, 188, 295
Tet Offensive   182, 219, 257
Thatcher, Baroness Marga-
    ret   259, 260, 268
theory   xiv, 4, 5, 7, 8, 13, 14, 25,
    32, 35, 37, 41, 42, 47, 49,
    57, 63, 66, 73, 78, 79, 80,
    82, 87, 88, 89, 94, 95, 99,
    100, 101, 102, 103, 105,
    107, 108, 109, 110, 111,
    112, 116, 118, 120, 126,
    127, 131, 144, 150, 151,
    193, 215, 218, 219, 223,
    229, 249, 253, 266, 277,

278, 279, 280, 281, 282,
284, 288, 292, 294, 296,
297, 299, 300, 302
Thirty Years War 34
Thompson, Maj Gen Julian,
RM xiii
Thompson, Sir Robert 91
Three Block Wars 242
torpedo boats 68
Total Exclusion Zone 1
totalitarian 67, 82, 84, 85, 97
Trafalgar, battle of 34, 50, 60
Trenchard, MRAF Viscount
Hugh xiv
trenches 51
Trinity College, Cambridge 61
Triple Entente 74
Turkey 57
Twin Towers 138
Ulm, battle of 43
UN. See United Nations
Union (US Civil War) 56, 57
United Kingdom. See Britain
United Nations 194, 250, 251,
253, 268, 279
United States of America xi, 3,
5, 7, 17, 24, 42, 49, 51, 55,
57, 60, 63, 64, 71, 72, 73,
74, 79, 83, 84, 85, 86, 87,
89, 93, 94, 95, 96, 101,
107, 109, 112, 121, 122,
129, 135, 137, 140, 141,
142, 144, 147, 157, 158,
159, 160, 163, 169, 170,
172, 176, 180, 182, 186,
187, 199, 213, 219, 220,
231, 236, 237, 239, 242,

248, 252, 257, 264, 265,
268, 269, 270, 271, 272,
285, 286, 289, 301
United States Air Force 92
United States Army xi, 94, 107,
112, 160, 204, 301
United States Navy 60, 89, 92,
135
US Central Command 237
unrealized strategy 114, 115,
211
Uruzgan, Afghanistan 270
US Civil War. See American Civil
War
USSR. See Soviet Union
Varro, Gaius 128
Viet Cong 182, 201, 220
Vietnam 17, 46, 73, 79, 89, 91,
93, 94, 95, 97, 109, 118,
120, 126, 172, 176, 181,
182, 199, 200, 201, 204,
219, 220, 229, 235, 242,
248, 257, 269, 271, 273
war, definition of 17
War of Bavarian Succession 37
Washington, USA 85, 142, 231,
252, 273
Waterloo, battle of 34, 36
weapons 32, 33, 49, 50, 51, 67,
68, 69, 82, 87, 97, 135,
136, 149, 169, 170, 280
Wehrmacht. See German Army
Welch, Jack 124
Weltpolitik 74
Western liberal democracy 31
West Point (United States Military Academy) 60

Whitehall, London   91, 232,
    259, 264, 294
Wilhelm II, German Emper-
    or   74
Wilson, Thomas Woodrow   71,
    84
World Bank   245, 251
World War I   xiv, 31, 49, 51, 52,
    53, 55, 63, 64, 66, 67, 68,
    71, 72, 73, 74, 75, 76, 77,
    83, 84, 87, 97, 105, 108,
    126, 169, 229
World War II   22, 24, 68, 69,
    71, 72, 73, 77, 78, 79, 82,
    84, 85, 87, 89, 97, 99, 105,
    111, 112, 121, 125, 129,

135, 144, 157, 160, 164,
    187, 239, 252, 254, 266,
    268, 270, 280, 302
Wylie, Rear Admiral J.C.   5, 6,
    89, 95, 96, 151, 185, 238,
    277, 278, 279, 300, 302
XIX Panzer Corps   77
Yale University   91
Yarger, Harry R.   4, 101, 108,
    109, 110, 111, 119, 126,
    128, 129, 212, 278, 279,
    302, 303
Young, Sir Arthur   264
Zabul, Afghanistan   270